voices
of
BROOKLYN

voices
of
BROOKLYN
an anthology

edited by
sol yurick

sponsored by
brooklyn public library

American Library Association
Chicago 1973

Library of Congress Cataloging in Publication Data

Main entry under title:

Voices of Brooklyn, an anthology.

  1. American literature—New York (City) 2. American
literature—20th century. I. Yurick, Sol, 1925– ed.
PS549.N5V6   810′.8′032   73-6791
ISBN 0-8389-0140-9

Printed in the United States of America

Contents

Transitions

Violence

Blackness

Power

Drugs

Preface

by Dorothy Nyren

Communication with its community has been a major goal of the Brooklyn Public Library during the past few years. Much of what we have been trying to do in this direction was described in *Community Service: Innovations in Outreach at the Brooklyn Public Library* (Chicago: American Library Assn., 1970).

Another step towards neighborhood involvement was taken in 1969 when we received a grant from the National Endowment for the Humanities to undertake the Voices of Brooklyn project, a two-year program which ran from September 1970 until May 1971. The purposes of Voices of Brooklyn were to acquaint the diverse peoples of Brooklyn with the variety of humanistic traditions that exist in the borough, to demonstrate the library's interest in and desire to assist all the peoples of the city, and to act as a channel of communication from Brooklyn to beyond Brooklyn.

The entire project consisted of two parts, the public presentation phase and the anthology phase. The aim of the public presentation phase was to show the common needs and desires of mankind, how their expression differs from culture to culture, and the beauty of the variety of these differences. The presentation phase was made up of two series of five programs each, each of the programs repeated in three locations, making a total of thirty presentations. Each series consisted of programs in the following cultural areas: songs, poetry, movies, music, dance, and folklore. The first series consisted of contrasts and interrelationships among Jewish, Irish, Scandinavian, Italian, and old New York cultures. The second series investigated African, Spanish-American, Haitian, and American Negro cultures. The typical format of each program was the presentation of an appropriate aspect of each of the cultures under consideration tied together by interpretive comment.

The auditoriums used for the performances seat 100 to 150 people each. The audience was made up chiefly of local non-academically oriented general public. Many of the people attracted to the library presentations were people who cannot afford expensive commercial productions and would be unlikely to be interested in a strictly lecture approach to the humanities.

The European programs were:

1. A Festival of Poetry and Song. At all three presentations Norman Rosten read from *Under the Boardwalk,* the Oosting family sang English and Appalachian ballads, and Jerome Rothenberg and Cyrelle Forman presented a mixed media event, entitled *Poland 1931.* In addition various poets read at each presentation.

2. An International Dance Festival. At each presentation the S'dot Israeli Dancers, the Scandinavian Folk Dance Ensemble, and the Hirten Irish Dancers performed. In addition, at each presentation either an Armenian, Italian, or American Indian group danced.

3. A Night at the Movies. "Nobody Goes There," "The Visit," "Goodnight, Socrates," and "Sighet Sighet," films in which immigrants and children of immigrants to the New World reflect on their European heritage and its relationship to their present lives.

4. An International Music Festival. The Pennywhistlers entertained with traditional folk songs from the Balkans and Eastern Europe, Joe Heany with Gaelic ballads; Cyrelle Forman with songs in Yiddish, Israeli, Arabic, and Greek; and the Norwegian Singing Society.

5. Ellis Island Elegy. A collage of drama, song, dance, and folklore celebrating Irish, Italian, Jewish, Scandinavian, and Middle Eastern contributions to America presented by the Riverside Theatre Workshop.

Host and interpreter at each of the fifteen European presentations was Professor David Brandstein of Bard College, a folklore expert. In addition, Professor Stan Solomon of Cooper Union led discussions at the film showings.

The African programs were:

1. An African Poetic Night with Music from Africa and the Caribbean. Dramatic scenes and poetry presented by Jane and Scott Kennedy with music by Jay Roze, Bobby Sykes, and Malki.

2. An African Musical Night. Spirituals, gospel, jazz, soul, African, Latin, and Calypso music.

3. A Night at the Movies. "Family of Ghana," "Que Puerto Rico?" "The First World Festival," "The Rhythm of Africa," and "Voices of the Drum" plus slides and music.

4. An African Night of Dance. Pearl Primus, Percival Borde, and Doris Green's Afro-American Dance Troupe.

5. An African People Theater Experience. Scenes from plays by Langston Hughes and LeRoi Jones, African drumming and music of the islands, and a Haitian Folkloric Group led by Wanda Weiner.

Host and interpreter for each of the fifteen African programs was Professor Scott Kennedy of the drama department of Brooklyn College.

Approximately 3,000 persons attended Voices of Brooklyn presentations; many were people who might not have entered a library facility if not attracted by special programming.

We learned that intercultural experiences are most easily conveyed in nonverbal terms. Audiences empathized with music and dance from cultures other than their own much more easily than with explanations of cultures.

Voices of Brooklyn generated much favorable publicity for the library and enabled us to get in friendly contact with a number of community groups with which pleasant relationships developed. For example, Voices of the Children, a writers group, began holding its meetings at one of our units and held a party there when a collection of its work was published by Holt. The Haitian Artist Association Abroad staged an art exhibit which was very well attended. The New York State Council of the Arts became interested in our efforts and contributed money towards ethnic poetry readings.

Brooklyn College's television department made a documentary tape on Voices of Brooklyn, which was shown on education channels in New York during January 1971 and at the ALA convention in Dallas in June 1971.

During the public presentation phase of Voices of Brooklyn we began soliciting contributions for a Voices of Brooklyn anthology. What we were seeking was city-oriented writing by nonprofessionals.

Sol Yurick, author of *The Bag, Warriors,* and *Fertig,* was chosen to edit the anthology. His empathy with and concern for beginning writers has been an important factor in attracting manuscripts to the project and in winnowing out the most interesting and characteristic statements.

Much that we have gathered here is about Brooklyn, much is about the world outside Brooklyn. What brings it together is the fact that all the writing was done in Brooklyn. Common attitudes and stances toward reality and myth can be found here, as well as the particular coloration that individual experience and varied ethnic backgrounds give these common concerns.

We are very grateful to the National Endowment for the Humanities whose funds made possible the Voices of Brooklyn series of programs and the beginning stages of assembling this anthology. We are proud that the American Library Association is issuing our anthology under its auspices.

We hope that Voices will continue in Brooklyn, changing its form, perhaps, to a series of workshops and meetings for writers, the library adding to the role of protector and purveyor of the literature of the past the newer function of welcoming, sheltering, and encouraging the literature of the future.

Introduction

by Sol Yurick

Right after World War II, when I was going to college, I used to take the elevated train home. Every evening I would pass a window where I would see a young man seated in front of a typewriter. I used to wonder about him; since he worked at it every night for years, he could only be writing a novel. And I would become impatient for the train to get me home. I would rush in and begin to work on my own book instead of doing my homework, feeling both competitive agitation and a curious comradeship with that writer. I wonder what became of him: Did he finish the novel? Did he publish it? Did he become famous? Or what?

One of our contributors got out of the army after the Second World War (he carried *Ulysses* with him in the beachhead at Anzio) and decided to be a writer. He's been writing unsuccessfully for twenty-six years. With his stories he sent a long autobiographical letter about his frustrations. Some would think it a crank letter, but I recognized from my own experience and the experience of others I know that the letter is true. He's written in all the forms and been encouraged just enough to go on. Maybe it was someone like him, if not he himself, I used to pass on the train every night.

Recently, the Brooklyn Public Library in conjunction with the National Endowment for the Humanities, which put up the money, decided to produce an anthology to be called *Voices of Brooklyn*. They asked me to edit the anthology and I agreed to do so on one condition: that only people who hadn't been published would be eligible. This is the anthology. There may be some published writers here who slipped by, but no one who writes for a living.

That stipulation grew partly out of my own experience. I spent years trying to get published; wrote poetry, three and a half novels, a play or two, and finally succeeded in getting my first story published mostly because I knew Aaron Asher who was then an editor of *The Noble Savage*. I thought that would open the gates. But then followed years when I tried to get my first novel published (actually the four and a half-th).

Frustration in some sense educated (and embittered) me. To protect myself, my sanity, my ego ("What do you do?" "I'm a writer." "Oh, anything published?" "No, but . . ." And the eyes sort of shift and you know what they're thinking and you feel defeat and failure—and maybe resentment and want to talk about all the *encouraging* rejections you've gotten.), I began to study the publishing industry, to mount a sociology of publishing to show myself that something was wrong with *them,* not me. I was sure that there were a lot of writers around who are talented and who, for a variety of reasons that have nothing to do with talent, aren't going to get a chance. Unless a different structure for creative expression existed. I had a theory that, aside from talent, it is luck, chance, connections, a system of channelling, competition, price structuring, demands of the market, exclusionary enclaves of mutual assistance, hipness and fads, systems of education that winnowed out most writers, that determined who would get published. This confusion helps kill the imagination by shaping it along certain paths. In short, there's a sociology of literary taste (not God-given) which leads to trying to write for a mind-narrowing market: and that applies to "high" literature as well as the low.

There are a lot of things working against the new, the obscure writer: the decline of fiction, the rise of what we call fact, but which is mostly fiction anyway. The rise of the new technology with its easy McLuhanoid attitudes which tell us that the printed word is dead and exhort us to groove on the electronic media, media which are simply not going to be *creatively* available to the multitude. The investments are too high. Rising prices and the competition of different forms for attention, and the unit cost of the production and marketing of an image work against the writer. The cost of educating (training) a literate (which is to say non-passive) person is much higher than the cost of training a TV media consumer (which is to say a person acted-upon). In spite of all of this, why do people still want to write? Well, the word and the voice are the only things that are left to them and the only way in which some things can be said.

Many published writers, as well as editors and critics, keep telling me that if a person is *really talented,* he is going to make it sooner or later. Of course, we don't know of all the people who wanted to write, and did; of the thousands, no, *hundreds of thousands* of novels and poems and short stories in paper cartons and trunks and garages and garbage cans. Who can tell how many had flashes of greatness which when nurtured, would have become truly great? On the other hand, why should we nurture a Harold Robbins or a Jacqueline Susann? But we do. And why should incredible compulsive determination be part of the writer's equipment? But it has to be. If one studies the *politics* and sociology of how Hemingway or Joyce made it, there's more to it than mere greatness. If there had been no early encouragement, to say nothing of self-salesmanship, what then? Would *Ulysses*, or *Finnegans Wake* have even been written?

There are those who announce proudly that they write for themselves. I say that's a lie. Talent grows on feedback, even if you have to round up a small mutual assistance group and persuade them (which is what I mean by politics) of your genius and, more, get the true followers to persuade others of your genius and, if possible, get the followers to set up little magazines and so forth. But there are dangers. Determination can lead to overspecialization—like the saber-tooth tigers who cannot close their mouths or whose teeth grow into their lower jaws: Hemingway's virtue became a narrow, even a cancerous overgrowth. There have been cases in which determination and genius are happily wed, birthing the long delivery from obscurity, but what I'm talking about is what happens to *most* people who want to and do write. It's a waste and spillage of sensitivity and a drain on our *real* Gross National Product. Some countries consider their writers national treasures: we do not.

On the other hand, I was cautious too: I remember, as they say, the lessons of the thirties when the drive to Zeus-out a Minerviad of "Proletarian" genius had such deplorable results. What, after all, if genius and near genius can make its way in a free competitive society? What if this anthology was to be a repository of untalented amateurs? It didn't turn out that way.

The project had more than five hundred submissions. Maybe five thousand pages in all; I wish I could print them all. Not that everything was great; some entries are, as far as I'm concerned, very bad: but set in a context, in an overall view, there are a lot of good voices, voices that can mature into greatness if given the chance.

What stunned me is the amount and degree of first-rate ability there is. Some of it is quite rough (though I'm not sure what that means anymore), some of it is polished, and a lot of it is equal to what is already published and praised. As for the crudeness, my observation is this: being in print, in a book, makes a surprising amount of crudeness simply disappear—especially when there's some critic around who can make a virtue out of a badly handled obscurity. We worship the artifact; published books confer excellence: if it's in a book, how bad can it be? We are trained to be suspicious of packets of mimeograph paper torn loose from the staple or the typed page passed around. The handwritten page is out of it.

There were those who thought the anthology was to be about Brooklyn—a kind of running celebration, but most of the material was not about Brooklyn. It was about life and feeling. It just happened to be written in Brooklyn. Brooklyn—it used to be a bad comedian's joke when his own material was flagging. You said "Brooklyn" and the audience dissolved. But the concerns of the writers here are the concerns of writers all over. The voices of Brooklyn are the voices of America. In fact, most of the material which was in praise of Brooklyn turned out to be bad. I wish it hadn't been so.

Blacks, Irish, Puerto Ricans, Filipinos, Italians, Jews—people from the whole ethnic gamut have written. In some cases the material has a special ethnic flavor. But in many cases there has been a cultural leveling and that is something new. Something is being lost in America which is why you can't laugh at the word "Brooklyn." Brooklynites have been at home in Taos and Haight-Ashbury and Nebraskans walk the streets of Crown Heights and go down to Sheepshead Bay for seafood—and a lot of them speak the same language in the same sounds. Blacks whose families have come from the deepest South speak with what we used to call a New York accent, the famous Brooklyn accent, and Irish youth dress in styles immediately recognizable in Portland, Oregon. They range from the straights who adhere to old values to the freaks who live in a liberated part-space Utopia. I would have thought that for these people linearity, the written word, was dead. Who said so?

Why do people still want to write? Maybe because they just have to. Animals mark their territory with a pungent individual spray. The young court immortality by magic-markering their spoor on the immortal tile walls of the subway stations. Poets leave tracks first on paper and then in people's memories. Writing, speaking in rhythms, maybe are the few tools left to people in which they can express the world, their own world and the world of their special grouping, the world you're not going to find in the media. The odd event which not only moves us but through which we can express ourselves. The thing the writer just *knows* that some audience *has* to know about too. Rhythm, image, metaphor are just attention-getting devices. A feeling, an incident, an emotion, each of these remains undigested, troublesome, till we partially lay it to rest and understand it by speaking or writing of it.

It can also change the world. For example: I could take ten words and fourteen changes of tone (and leave off the laugh machine) and show you the world of Archie Bunker or "I Love Lucy" the way it really is. Every writer, and every person who is not a writer but sensitive, knows the media never show you things straight. Things straight (not dull) is what creative writing is about. It is a moral act. The rest is hype.

When the material began to arrive I realized that I had not only to struggle with what I had hitherto thought constituted good literature but with my own attitudes (born from reading all the great books and the books of writers who had also read all the great books and the attitudes of editors and critics who had read all the great books and anthologies too) which had been developed, instilled, programmed into my subconscious, attitudes which I thought I had gotten rid of. I was still possessed by college reading lists. I'm talking about *emotional* resistance. But one sure sign of excellence I knew: the felt twinge of competition; why hadn't *I* written that?

What constitutes excellence? (Which is almost the same in this particular case as asking how did I choose what I did and how did I reject what I rejected.) What are the ways in which one expresses passion and sees the world? Material I might have passed off as banal once had to be looked at as if I were discovering the world in a new exciting way. Which is to say that for a variety of reasons I had stopped looking at the world in this way. I had to feel back to what had moved me a long time ago and why it had moved me and why I wanted to talk about or write books about things that other people took for granted which were meaningful and symbolic for me. I also had to think about the way things worked against one another, the balance of the anthology, the *gestalt* of it, for in some ways two, three, four, five writers worked together on a viewpoint without even having met. On these pages these voices confront one another and perhaps for a moment are reconciled, fused. Now what if the college anthologies included in their material the new instead of the tried and the tired? Some of *these* writers, maybe.

Now we are all hooked on the notion of the solitary and splendid individual in America. You may say that such a method violated the integrity, the vision, the special creative singular God-given ability of the artist. People have peculiar notions of what a writer is and how he works—notions that writers and poets have assisted in perpetuating for profit—that he is heroic and singular and has a never-to-be-duplicated vision, a unique creativity, alone, romantic, tortured, of and against a hostile and philistine universe. In some sense that's true. Writer-survival teaches bitterness and arrogance, but also that such attitudes pay off. The fact of the matter is that most writers work in groups and enclaves and cliques and not only share tastes but exchange material, criticize one another, try things out on one another, defer to one another, draw back timidly from a daring imaginative flight when the criticism grows too hot. This common behavior is not only for the beginning writer but for the arrived, enshrined, and heroic writer. (There are exceptions. They are not necessarily the greatest.) Also the writer's imaginations are informed by the standard canon of Western literature. The active collaborators of living writers are in the anthologies. Writers' imaginations are both shaped and amplified (though some may make small violations of this canon) by tradition. Their differences, their singularities are less than people imagine. Read Hemingway, Dashiell Hammett, and Gertrude Stein together. After all, Pound and Eliot, Joyce and

Dujardin and Svevo, Wordsworth and Coleridge were collaborators, as were Joyce, Nash, and Shakespeare who never even met.

Certain patterns emerged in the original submissions, certain ongoing and universal concerns. There were many songs and stories of lament: lament for love not given and love not received, lament for the inability to connect only; dead fathers and dead mothers and dead friends (and dead chances) to whom one only wanted to address oneself, to say something warm while there was still the chance. Strange how often the sense of specific loss and anguish arranges itself into traditional forms which, while narrowing and distorting, give power to the emotion. There are some poems by those who have only learned to transmit their passions in certain very stylized ways (and these are not the old either, but the young in their bells, grass, and hash-heads with expanded consciousness): they have no sense of the concrete and so can't transmit themselves. They have internalized all the abstract forms they read, learned high, poetic language in its antique, established meanings, used words like "tis" and "oft," channelled out intensely personal reality, suffered passions learned from long outmoded poetry collections.

One of the refurbishers of our language has been street talk, the language of the ghettos, slang, patois. Some of the more imaginative revolutionaries have given us a new vitality. The language of the social sciences while coming up with new formations strikes me as mostly funny: Can the social scientists really be serious? The woman's movement, by casting a new light on women creates new content for literature and reveals old ongoing feelings that people didn't use to write about. Can any writer write about woman the way he did before?

It is the art of interconnection, of metaphor, of analogue, of ritual which makes art and apprehends reality. A good part of this practice takes place in the language of everyday life. It's this kind of thing that is locked into the slang word. Heroin is called "smack" and that's what the rush of the drug does. But it's not only this intersection of folk detail in a group-unconscious treasury which transforms the simple words into something else. What the difference is I don't know, but it's something that can be worked for consciously. And how many established writers have lusted for that ability to be able, with simple words and in a short space, to evoke an involuted space haunted with demons, to create an aura, a beautiful, complex attitude warp; how many then discover they have wrenched their heads open onto paper only to find there the approved contents of the *Folk-Motif Index*?

There are firemen and policemen in this compendium, and there are too the prey of policemen and their natural enemies, those we call criminals: each of them has had a poetic moment. They have one thing in common: they have written in secret, for to be a writer in this society is to be somehow effeminate. I could go on. This introduction may sound almost maudlin, a paean to democracy—the whore with the heart of gold and the novel-writing taxi driver, democratic vistas and everyone a poet and everyone's got the chance to make it. Am I maudlin? No, I'm cynical and full of rage. I know what it takes to be a writer, and that doesn't always have to do with talent because most poetic and novelistic traits, most feelings for beauty, are going to be stifled unless something's done about it.

Why, I wonder, do we extol those writers who have done a lot of things? We all know those book jackets. We equate a variety of experience with a depth of experience. But most writers will tell you that they begrudge the circumstances that make them work; time spent working is time spent being tired and having your brain dulled. Why do many writers do a lot of things? Because they have to.

Flaubert, I think it was, said that in his or her youth everyone is a poet. And therefore so many people need to, do write, want to, all over the country: The voices of Brooklyn are the voices of America. Story telling, expression, speaking poetry, rhythmic utterance is a need —a need to speak and a need to hear. The lucky ones (let's not even talk about those rare ones who sustain their lives by writing alone; poets are out of it entirely) publish their first book and feel actually grateful, servile towards an industry that has given them a chance at the immortality sweepstakes.

But most writers end up defeated. They don't write anymore or if they publish a few poems, even a novel, they find out they can't make a living out of it. Neglected and unpaid, if they have talent, they end up in the entertainment and media industries as reporters and copy-writers, as screen writers, as letters-of-regret writers for the insurance companies, as teachers, critics, and even as editors. I never met an editor who didn't want to be a writer—though there must be some of them. Editors dream of a time when they will make enough money to get away and write that great book, that great American novel. And if they ever do, their minds have become crippled. Maybe that's why the vision of the writer who sold out haunts us—and haunts the writer himself.

And now, we are presented with a time of crisis, a time of economic fluctuation when the funding that in one way or another supports the artistic vision is being eroded. Funds are being withdrawn from the libraries, and the universities are phasing out their humanities programs and becoming more and more vocational/technological schools of a limited order. Imaginative space is closing down now. Wire and air-wave networks diminish our perceptions. Satellite reality and a central committee of gag writers, the rising cost of production, paper, printing, and educational systems bleach out the memory of yesterday's quiet murders (and those that are not so quiet) across the airshaft, leach out the rapes taking place behind the windows of the Hopper houses all in a row just across the Sunday Street, turn it into a consciousness network which must turn everyday life into "Mission Impossible" or a situation comedy. More and more we discard *our* dreams, anxieties, and fantasies and accept those brought to us by products and media networks. Publishers become more timid. Libraries close down or shorten their hours or cannot buy new books, while rising transportation costs keep us home and curtail our consciousness. The desperation of hungry populations driven out into the streets besieges the imagination where, behind the double-locked doors, afraid or unable to venture out, it atrophies, while cost-accountants accumulate our dreams and convert them into bullets.

Yet people persist in wanting to write imaginatively. Why? Joe Flaherty, Pete Hamill, Jimmy Breslin—all known to Brooklyn lore, all reporters who have made it—want to venture into this high risk area. Men with established reputations in other fields think of writing that novel in which, under a variety of masks and guises, they will tell it the way they can't tell it in daily life. I have met straight corporation lawyers in bars who say that they wish they could freak, declaim, and roar like Allen Ginsberg. Poetic thoughts pop into their heads at odd times and are suppressed to become dreams and fantasies and longings. Already we have seen a time in the sixties when hundreds of technicians have left their jobs and gone out to live in communes and to paint and write. There seemed to be something romantic about it, like vows of poverty. You take vows of poverty because no one is going to pay you for doing the thing you have to do: it's as simple as that without the illusions. The illusions are what we make up to keep us going longer than any sensible man would go.

What should we do then, those who want to write and realize the odds against them? Already some people are setting up new and alternate publishing houses, breaking their traditional ties with the New York houses. There will be more ventures. Clubs, meeting places should be arranged and writers should set them up themselves. And, most important, unless we learn that printed books with all the magic of the imprimaturs of publishing houses of repute can contain trash junkier than the material that appears in a mimeographed leaflet, we will get nowhere at all. Unless we listen to one another's writings with respect and love and criticise with the aim of helping, not merely tearing down and surviving at any cost, we will go nowhere. People who write are fortunate: they don't need much money. Poems and stories can be handed around. People can be read to. Clubs or groups can exchange their writings. Libraries can help by encouraging use of their facilities. The possibilities are endless if only we will forget the magical entities and artifacts that come from the established publishing media. Twenty people with a mimeograph machine, patience and determination can produce a lot of work.

And maybe that's what *Voices of Brooklyn* can help show in some way: how many people there are around who can write and who should. And we've only scratched the surface. What lies beneath must awaken itself.

The Cardboard Drum:
A Study in Brooklyn Sound and Silence

by Madeline Lee

We were on the street corner looking for what had been advertised as a parade. Christmas Eve, 1969. Third Moratorium. Clear-as-a-bell night air, chilling, unwelcome cold nagging at the comfortably fleshed bones that had so lately sat cuddled in a Herman Miller chair, clutching a drink whose warm, iridescent glow invited us, as if it were a prank, to go outside and find that goddam parade, what the hell, we've had it with carol singers, and this is where it's at. Dig?

Now the streets were deserted and why hadn't we brought the news clipping or whatever it was that had turned us on. Oh lovely peace. Oh holy night. Nothing, nothing at all.

"So. Another one of your bright ideas, for Christ's sake. Are you sure this is the night?" ("And a star appeared in the west that would be to them a guide . . .") An ugly, empty silence wrapped us in its gloom. "Stop talking for a minute, will you?"

"Who's talking?"

Sorrowful, sorrowful sound stumbled down the chasm of the streets of Brooklyn, a tiny hint, a little hope. A noise, nothing more, a curious, undefinable noise, not very loud. We walked toward Third Street, to those proud and lofty houses with brownstone facades like makeup lending impossible grandeur to old and withered women, looked over sententiously by leaning, leafy boughs, lit smugly from their curtained windows by golden light. Figures starkly dressed moved together in the darkness, furtively, accosting our innocence. Maybe fifteen.

The signs said bravely, "Follow the sound of the beating drum." Someone held aloft a cardboard packing carton, big enough to hold a refrigerator. It was arduous, unholy work. Another young man beat at it with an improvised club, frenzied with dismay, embarrassed by the clumsy sound. The figures moved on, lumbering into a shuffling gait, joyless in that dark night. There was no one we knew. This was a ragged band of ruffians, chastened for the night's procession, blue jeans and ragged shirts where once, perhaps, altar boy's lace had hung. They were not much older than boys, none of them, only some of them were girls. A solemn-faced policeman dutifully led the way, and two more closed in at the end, shuffling along with us, eyes averted. There were no signs, not even a candle. Such a pitiful group could only be for peace.

Someone my age with a beard, a neighbor, a novelist.

"Welcome aboard."

"What happened to the drum?"

"You were at the meeting?"

"What meeting?"

"Hennessey came. Jenkins. Shapiro. Some 'Women Strike,' you know, the same people. There was a lot of talking. So much talking, so many ideas, we never really did appoint committees." A doleful pause. "Or even delegate jobs."

"Like the drum."

Four kids ahead of us held aloft the refrigerator carton. A kid in tight blue jeans and an army jacket with the American flag sewed on the sleeve struck random blows.

"Yeah. The guy who was supposed to get the drum waited one day too late, and today he went down to the place to pick it up. The place had closed early."

"Too bad. A drum would have been good. Or even some signs."

"Even some signs!" Eloquent exasperation.

We walked along Eighth Avenue. Christmas trees shone in happy windows and here and there a curtain was carefully parted and a face peered out into the night at our grotesque parade, our sacrilege.

On Seventh Avenue someone in a passing car divined our intent. He made a V-sign with his fingers, grinning broadly. We made it back at him. Some desultory drinkers stared at us from Corrigan's Bar.

One of the boys was inordinately tall, maybe seven feet. He had a beautiful face like a madonna, with softly waving black hair to his shoulders, parted in the middle. He swore gently and kept passing around a small bottle of wine. He stopped frequently to bestow on his small companion a kiss. She was a girl, I could see that now, and she walked with her arms around his hips; her head just fitted underneath his armpit.

Someone decided we needed more order; walk single file, beat the drum with a strong, regular beat, never mind that it sounded lugubrious. The "drum"—half coffin, half toy—led us grimly up Union Street to Grand Army Plaza. A family had joined us, a young mother in a mini-skirt and boots, and three dancing children. Someone kicked over a garbage can and the raucous sound of steel and concrete grated over us like acid. A kid kicked the can in his turn and his father snarled "Don't do that!"

They were yelling "Peace Now! Peace Now!" and beating a hollow accompaniment. An itinerant company, gambling for their lives, jesters in the game of fortune, we straggled over the barren desert of our hopes. A few more people joined us, lending an altogether unwarranted sense of respectability. We were criminals, walking in despair across the Siberian wastes of our time, cursing at the fates that spawned us, that dangled us over the abyss, frustrated, impotent.

When we got to Grand Army Plaza the policemen held up traffic and we filed docilely over to the lighted Christmas tree in the center of the arch. Headlights of waiting cars glared impersonally at the sorry group. One boy carried cymbals and jangled medieval notes to our funeral march. Jagged pieces of hope on a wintry landscape; itinerant actors in a passion play, pilgrims in Jerusalem, we assembled without a murmur, mindlessly, before the lighted Christmas tree, demonic automobiles careening around us like an inferno.

The fragile geometry of the scene broke apart as three squad cars pulled up behind the arch and half a dozen uniformed policemen tumbled out and stood watch impassively.

"What do we do now?" we asked the novelist.

"Sing," he said with perfect aplomb.

Two of the children began "Last night I had the strangest dream I ever ha-a-a-d before," and several voices chimed in all in different keys. The policemen moved in closer.

Someone else began, "We shall overco-o-ome," and we looked around abashedly; there was not one black person among us, so we ended that one, too.

The tree towered over us, its orange, red, and yellow lights casting a merry glow on our cold faces. We decided to disperse. The police captain bowed from the waist.

"And a Merry Christmas to you!" he bellowed, indulgent, amused.

Reminiscences

Weekend Visit from Creedmore

by Francesca De Masi

to A.P.

home for three days;
black coffee
chipped with the scent of anisette,
my porch aunt
sits with her pinned hip
on the wicker chair
sipping the night so slowly,
that hospital, iron bar
locked air is forgotten

in harmony
shaken off the polluted night.

my porch aunt.
English coffee. French slurps,
Italian America
35 years at Creedmore
sucking some peace
off the rotten humid night
better than a child.

gone on Monday,
she leaves no broken pieces.
but I cry,
breaking off bits of my pity.
thin water.

but on the porch,
the scent of the night that's gone
is left with a grace,
a clinging thick and slow:

her anisette.

(and someone
    licking leftovers
        of contentment).

3

Union Street Changing

by Pamela Wardwell

Every evening in the summer the man next door sits on his stoop drinking beer and watching his three sons. He is grizzled, usually drunk, and he will not allow the boys to go out of the tiny, enclosed yard or touch the fences or the steps of the stoop. As we sit in our living-room, the front window open wide to catch the breeze that always climbs the hill from the bay, we hear him: "Stay away from that fence, you son of a bitch," "Get down from there, you little bastard." Our two-year-old son sits on the window sill and happily imitates him, yelling gruffly and wordlessly.

His name is Duffy. His sons are pitifully small and underdeveloped, with large, pale heads on spindly bodies. They talk rapidly and unintelligibly if I pause near them or smile and ask how they are. The littlest, four years old, cannot make himself understood even to his brothers. It is the favorite scandal of the neighborhood wives that their mother, a good twenty years younger than her husband, is mentally retarded and an alcoholic. She rarely leaves her apartment— when I see her hanging out clothes in the littered back yard she smiles shyly, but will not speak.

Our block lies halfway up the hill that rises from the factories and housing projects of the Gowanus Canal to Prospect Park. Recently the late Victorian brownstone and limestone row houses near the park have been "discovered" and renovated by young, enthusiastic, middle-class families who love the city and are determined to stay in it. They call themselves "brownstoners." The real-estate prices have soared, salvable rooming houses are eagerly sought, and at every meeting and party there's an underlying refrain, "The neighborhood's changing, the neighborhood's changing."

As you move down the hill from the park the houses grow smaller, and narrower, and more dilapidated. Four blocks down, our block, the elegant, tree-lined sidewalks have become shadeless, filled with yelling, running children and blowing newspaper. On summer evenings everyone seems to be in the street, sitting on stoops, leaning out of windows, walking up and down. Children seem to have no bed hour here and race through the dark, along the sidewalks and back and forth across the street, bringing blasts of loud, angry honking from startled motorists. Tiny, weeping children follow their parents slowly toward home. We, too, sit on our stoop, enjoying the activity and the evening cool, but our child is sleeping soundly in his crib upstairs. We are the pioneers, the first "brownstoners" on our block, and we, too, repeat constantly, "The neighborhood's changing, the neighborhood's changing." We say it hopefully, ritualistically; it is a protective incantation.

My parents drive in from the suburbs one Sunday for lunch. Duffy is on his stoop as usual, drinking and cursing his children. My mother, clearly alarmed, says only, "Who is that very peculiar man?"; my father ignores the situation, heading into the kitchen to make us all preprandial martinis. Later, over dessert, he reminds us of the many fine homes available in their town and promises to help us "swing it" if need be.

I sit outside on our stoop, enjoying the baking sun, and my son plays through the iron fence with the two little girls who live in the old brownstone apartment house down the block. They are sweet children. Annie, the older sister, is about five, Linny perhaps three; they have pretty, delicate faces, always dirty, round, blue eyes, uncombed straw-blond hair, and are usually dressed in ill-assorted checks and plaids. Annie tells me long stories, sitting beside me on the steps, or shows me the treasures she carries with her in a tiny plastic pocketbook. Linny stands by with a grubby thumb in her mouth and indicates her wants (a gum ball, her shoe tied) with urgent, wordless noises. Today they are alone on the sidewalk and my son, who is not allowed to play beyond our fence, is trying to climb the bars.

I hear him ask, "Where's your Mommy?" and Annie reply, "We don't have a Mommy. Don't you know our Mommy died?"

My heart sinks. Where I come from, the safe suburbs, children's mothers don't die. Now many things fall into place. So the tall woman I often see walking with them up or down the block, almost always with rows of pink curlers in her hair, is not their mother. I had often wondered why they were so unkempt while she was carefully dressed. So that's why Annie always pulls my arm and tells me, "That's my father," whenever he comes into sight. And that's why he looks so tired and sad. The girls do not look sad, playing on the sidewalk outside the fence, but I am very sorry.

In our back yard, cemented over except for a meager band of earth around the edge, is a gate leading into the next yard. The people who sold the house to us were good friends with the couple next door, and soon we became friends too. They and their twenty-three-year-old daughter live in three rooms on the ground floor and rent the three apartments that constitute the rest of their house. They seem to be in their late forties. The husband, Jerry, works as a longshoreman; small, with stooped shoulders and a heavy paunch, he has something the shape of a descending teardrop. Dark circles under his eyes and a soft, deep, gravelly voice add to his general air of weariness. In the early evening I often see him trudging up the hill toward his house, head bent and hands plunged in the pockets of his battered leather jacket.

Maria, his wife, also seems worn, but tireless. Always carefully dressed and made-up, she knows most of the people on the block and is forever helping someone—finding a new apartment, cooking for a family while the mother is in the hospital, babysitting for a casual friend. She spends much of her time cooking and sewing clothes for her daughter.

The daughter, Denise, is, perhaps, surprising. Beautiful, educated, exquisitely dressed, she steps from their front gate like a fairy-tale princess, leaving behind all darkness and frustration. And yet she has just broken her engagement to a young man from a wealthy family because, she tells me, "He could never know what it's like to grow up in three rooms on Union Street."

In the evenings I often hear Maria calling to the Spanish woman who lives in the apartment above hers, "Lydee, Denise is working late in the city. *Tu quiera?* You want some macaroni?" Soon she is offering us pizza, macaroni with meatballs, eggplant Parmigiana, across the back fence. At first we accept this delicious food with some hesitation, not sure how we can return such favors, but she seems to give purely from overflowing generosity and soon we have learned to take the warm, foil-wrapped dishes she hands over the wire fence.

Soon, too, I begin to use the gate in the fence and find myself in her immaculate kitchen, drinking tea in the early afternoon while my son snoops around her apartment or her well-tended, flourishing garden.

Maria has lived in this neighborhood all her life and in this dark, ground floor apartment since she was married twenty-five years ago. A large formica table dominates the kitchen, which is always scrubbed shiny and brightly lit by a double fluorescent halo on the ceiling. Beyond an open arch is the dark living-room divided by a long bureau jutting into the room; on one side the couch and TV, on the other, jammed into a corner, Jerry and Maria's double bed. An accordion door closes the next arch, beyond which is Denise's small bedroom with its single window giving onto the street.

Maria tells me about the neighborhood in the old days. When she was a child her family lived several blocks from here and Union Street was considered very elegant. She remembers her mother taking her and her three sisters for walks; when they reached Union Street the

6

mother would put her finger to her lips and caution the children to be quiet. "Shh, the signoras are napping." I imagine the Sunday-afternoon street lined with silent houses, the hard-working, respectful mother slowly climbing the shade-dappled hill followed by a string of wide-eyed, whispering little girls. They are all in white. I think it is May and heavy, wooden shutters already bar the windows of some of the houses; the families have closed them for the summer season and left for the Cape, the Catskills, Saratoga.

"Maybe someday it will be nice like that again," I say.

"Oh, no, darling." Maria smiles. "It will never come back to that. It's come down too far." She tells me how "the old people," our Italian neighbors, are giving up, selling their houses and moving out to Bay Ridge and Flatbush, the suburbs of Brooklyn. Some of them have lived on this block for thirty years, watched the houses depreciate, the trees die, the gutters fill with garbage; watched strange races and strange languages move in and finally, angrily, packed up and left.

"But their kids are the worst trouble-makers of all," I say, thinking of the gang of nine-year-old boys that ranges up and down the block from early morning 'til long after dark each night, ringing doorbells and running, knocking over garbage cans, breaking soda bottles on the sidewalk, and playing interminable games of handball on our stoop. By contrast the Vasquez children across the street are quiet and well-behaved—it is Vinny and Tony and Little Michael who bother me. When I leave my house in the afternoon to go shopping and find five or six of them sitting on my stoop I am uncertain of how to approach them. What are they planning? Why are they giggling? What kind of mess will I find when I return from the store?

"Come on, boys, off the stoop," I say. They come down reluctantly— "Aw, come on," "We weren't doin' nothing"—and I know they will be back as soon as I turn the corner. I try to be nice, partly because I like kids and partly because I am afraid of the trouble they can cause me if I antagonize them.

"Why don't you boys go up to the park to play? It's only a couple of blocks and it's a beautiful day."

Vinny answers me, a gutter cherub with a mass of curly dark hair and limpid brown eyes. "We aren't allowed to go off the block."

"Why not," I say, amazed. These are kids who run wild at all hours of the day and night and constantly risk death dashing into the street after lost balls. Surely they could get to the park and back unharmed.

"Well, when our mothers come home from work they want to know where we are. Besides, there are rough kids up in the park."

What can I say? I sympathize with these children who are often locked out of their own homes until their mothers return in the evening and who can find very little to do except break things. Their

7

parents' discouragement has rubbed off on them. I remember when a house across the street was abandoned; the next day they climbed in at a window and spent a week breaking all the glass, opening man-sized holes through the walls, and pulling down and demolishing the carved marble fireplaces. One day when I was passing and they were sitting on the broad window sill, dangling their feet against the brown-stone like conquering Visigoths, I asked them, "How come you guys broke up this nice, old house?"

"This junky place?" says Tony. "Who cares? Nothing around here is any good anyway."

"Yeah," echos Vinny, "no one wants this junk."

Soon, I suppose, their parents will give up and follow the others to Bay Ridge. I'll be only half sorry to see them go.

"What's happening about Duffy?" I ask Maria. She has told me that the man who owns the house, a neighbor up the street, is trying to sell it rather than continue with Duffy as his tenant.

"Good news, darling, didn't I tell you? The house is sold. And they're delivering it vacant, so Duffy has to go. It won't be long now."

I ask who is moving in, but Maria doesn't know. A young couple, she thinks. So the neighborhood really is changing! I rush home to call my husband and tell him the good news.

A few weeks later we see Duffy's furniture being carried out and piled into a rackety-looking pick-up truck. Finally the truck pulls away from the curb and lurches off down the street. Duffy follows slowly, leading his wife and children toward the bus stop on the corner. Where are they going? I wonder. Will they be happier somewhere else? Or are they just being pushed from place to place, bringing their misery with them? Oh, well, never mind, I tell myself; the neighborhood's changing!

Brooklyn/Luzon 1945

by Alan Morentz

on Dumont Ave.
my mother swooned
to Basie
as she rocked me
to sleep.

what song
did my father hum
on that Philippine highway
the day a mortar shell
carried him
to eternity?

Invisible Forces Determine Our Destiny

by Terence Malley

The pure products of America go crazy.
William Carlos Williams

Where have they gone?

that woman locked long years
in a cellar on a quiet side street,
in her dark cellar,
her dark hair so long
it crusted in strings
down her back;
and, a block away,
another,
a shrew, ancient,
who painted her front door black,
who cried, "Repent, you jewboys!"
as we sidled to mass.

So many.
So many
I lost track
of my mother's stories.

Where have the old men gone,
the ones she called
"shelled-shocked from The War"?
(Their heads lolled
from side to side,
their cracked hands
fluttered like wounded birds.)
You don't see them anymore,
not in Brooklyn.

I'll bet even the Village Eccentric
(twitching in the heart of America)
is gone.

They've all been
       (quietly)
eliminated
in the name of Better Living
OR (just possibly)
they've been promoted.
(Just possibly)
the Village Screwball now
somehow runs the town.
The ranting atheist
raves from his pulpit;
blackrobed figures
flap through courthouse square;
that strange army
shout speeches on TV,
hold long press conferences.

Midnight Reading

by Sherry J. Jacobs

Trying to forget
how I gulped the wine
as he scoffed his brandy
and beer
and beer.
Laughing at his joke
trying to ease the embarrassment
of whiskey words.
The crowd waited for jewels,
some other man.

A huge red belly
lapping up the floor
and his shamed eyes
could not speak.

He was lost in Missoula.
They all loved him
                    out West.
Speaking of rivers and Indians
a woman wrapped in bitterness.
His loss
when time should be turning
                        to happiness.
Four books written
three published
all dedicated.
Ears to hear
          his pacing,
yet no comfort.
Each city
each mountain
is still.
They all loved him out West.

So the Wind

by Allen Brafman

        so the wind.
    and there's no thing
    keeps me warm
    my jacket
    from fort dix
i contracted frost bite
there on a machine-gun range
the snow there
in new jersey
    my jacket
    has no liner
    i climb into
    my jacket
    huddles
    at street corners
    waiting traffic to stop threatening
    everybody
    no warm enough
    to stop
    walking
    the belly of the wind
    no home
    to be seen

Domestic Life in Crown Heights

by Wendy Lopate

I could sleep so easily, but this morning I can't. The blabbermouth West Indian man, I sense a certain snideness through the wrinkles in his face, all smile wrinkles. When you smile that much I guess you have to be snide. Anyway, he's coming to tile the bathroom. What does one do when some strange, snide person is tiling one's bathroom, or what does one pretend to do? I should have stayed at my mother's and I wouldn't have run into the two of them there in the lobby grinning unbelievably grinny grins, the snide West Indian and Mr. Hill the super who loves everybody. Ho ho ho. Boy, am I nasty.

I couldn't understand what they said to me, so I smiled and apologized for not leaving the keys. It was so much for me to do, to stay out of my daze, *I misunderstood this morning. I thought you weren't coming until next week but that's the painter. I'm awfully sorry to hang you up.* Sorry I got up this morning, it's been a smashing day so far. And then of course they think you didn't leave the keys because you don't trust them. Ridiculous. They can ship the whole apartment to Haiti if it makes them happy. And still he hasn't rung the damn bell. I keep hearing the elevator door. Wish he would come so I can cope with him, cope cope cope.

My mother has completely lost her marbles, rapping and rapping. I couldn't even see her clearly, she was all blurry through the haze of discomfort, detours, and whatever else I took out the door with me to visit her this morning; but she went on like a dripping faucet with me straining my eyes and ears trying to get even the vaguest inkling of what all her lukewarm water was about. Couldn't do it. Had my shoelaces tied so tight there wasn't even any room for them to stretch and there was this pool of water between us turning to ice. I kept having images of fingers popping near my head, *Snap out of it, Wake up, this isn't one of your dreams. Christ, this is real. Isn't it a gas?*

I've never felt that I was a part of my mother's photograph collection even though I'm in some of them. Never really felt I was a part of her life or that she would be a part of mine. Maybe that's good. It is Thursday and October, and I stopped by to see if everything was all right. He had another mild attack as they called it this morning, pains in his chest, an inability to breathe. She is very upset. Her friend the psychiatrist has prescribed both some ups and downs for her. They both sit on the counter. She has gone out to visit him and to the grocery. I feel as though I shouldn't touch anything, as though I shouldn't be here, the feeling like when I was younger and living with her and pulling out her dresser drawers one by one. I always liked the jewelry drawer best, almost a fear feeling. I was looking through her address book before, to find my name, my full name, not just my first name. . . . People are so weird. What the hell does she think I want from her? I'll keep my distance.

When I woke up this morning at ten having turned off the alarm and gone back to sleep I opened my eyes to sun coming in through the shutters and some record or other and didn't look at the clock for at least five minutes and just lay there wondering whether it was too late to get up to go to work. Wasn't very upset when I found out it was too late. I find it so easy to overcome that nagging feeling of guilt messing around in the back of my head.

Last night I felt tired and wanted to sleep, too, I didn't want to argue any more. I wanted it all to disappear. I had cleaned the house and taken a bath purging myself of the resentment and annoyance with him. Then I lay on my back, becoming tense. He had already jumped up once, gone into the kitchen to eat some cake, and as usual he drank the milk straight from the carton. I watched him and it annoyed me in the same way that it always did. I've never told him that I don't like it. There doesn't seem to be any reason why it should irritate me in the way that it does. He came back to bed and lit a cigarette, making a very loud hiss as he blew out each puff rather like a disgusted *whew!*, only drowned out.

I waited for him to speak. I knew he would if I turned out the light and tried to sleep. I would begin to relax and it would catch me unawares like a blowout when you are daydreaming in the street. He would come up behind me and say *"Boo!"* and I would twitch and my eyes would jerk open and I would have to catch the echo of the actual words in my head in order to understand them and not have to say What? I preferred to wait.

If I had thought that anything I'd said was hostile or nasty, I would apologize. As it is, the only thing left to me is not to say anything because everything is interpreted in a way that always surprises me.

It was louder than I expected and I wondered if he had prepared it all and how long he had been thinking about it, if he had chosen those words quickly but cautiously in the same way I would have.

"It seems to me that a lot of the things you say are easy to misinterpret, and I don't think that your not saying anything now will solve anything. Perhaps you should think a little before you do say things."

I waited a moment. I apologized because apparently I was wrong. He made me repeat it and then he sat back and waited. I was angry again, and began to read. He tossed around a little and then said,

"You're never going to get up tomorrow."

"Yes I will. I got up yesterday and today."

He rolled over again and finally said, "Well, will you *please* turn the light out? I can't sleep."

I thought of all the times he has slept with the light and the television on and I got up and left the room, feeling a strange satisfaction in having driven him to something as ridiculous as that. Even though he always surprises me when he does stupid things, I like it in a way, because at that point he becomes a little boy and I am no longer intimidated or frightened by his anger.

It got me, though, even though I thought I was prepared for it. It seemed to zoom around my pitiful little detours and there it was, Christ almighty—hurt.

Now I wanted to cry, I knew I shouldn't feel this way. I thought I was in the driver's seat and then suddenly now my ears were ringing, for hours it seemed, and I couldn't hear or see or feel anything except a vague echo of an ache sweeping over me and making me tired and woozy. There, I had described it, why didn't it go away, why didn't I go away, why didn't both of us go away? Seemed as though there was nothing else I should have to do now, as if I had bundled up a whole week and stuffed it into that moment, or maybe it was two. It was awful. I was sick to my stomach.

When I woke up this morning I was awake, really, and I was thinking, which doesn't happen often. Feel like I'm losing control when I'm just thinking away like that. Generally I just receive impressions, soft perceptions that I suddenly discover only after having thoroughly absorbed all the little symbols which seep into my semi-self and lead to some conclusive perception. These perceptions then have to pass through my filter or censor and that's the thing that decides whether or not I can handle whatever it is. And then suddenly, pop, there it is like magic, *Yes, that lady sitting across from me on this bus IS wearing shocking pink shoes and a fuchsia and green plaid coat and chewing gum like a cow.* This system doesn't always work this well. Sometimes my filter gets clogged. At those times nothing enters my head for days on end or at least until the plumber gets there. On about the third day of oblivion I usually scald my hand while cooking, fall down a flight of stairs, or just generally get the idea that there's something wrong.

Today I find myself speaking the English language, something to be used only as a last resort. I used to wonder why people misunderstood

16

me. It's simply that I don't speak the language very well, never felt there was much use for it. Language for fun and profit and all that shit, too. I feel like I'll die this morning if I don't sleep. It still hurts.

The little man is in the bathroom tearing down the plaster and whistling and humming alternately. I suppose he is uncomfortable as me. I wonder if any housewife has tried to seduce him. I really just want to sleep. There must be someplace I can sleep. Very drafty in here. There are things I could do, wash dishes, make beds, make tea. My stomach hurts.

The couch next to the radiator in the living room seems to be the only safe place right now. The little man's cigar—violently ill, I have vomited twice. Why did I make that up? It's frightening. It has simply given me a splitting headache and made me nauseated and I'm freezing my tail because all the windows are open. Why is everything so complicated?

Nine Year Old Maja

by Lawrence Garvey

nine year old maja
short black hair curled
tight to caribe skin
street spanish floods from
your woolworth pink lips
you burn latin darkness
in my direction
stretch thin brown arms
high above your head
ride slowly away
on a green bicycle

Plum Beach

by Richard Levy

As Itchie turned the heater up to full blast, the smell of Nathan's french fries and lobster rolls spread rapidly throughout the car. The temperature outside hovered near zero.

With every pot hole we hit, the hotdogs tried desperately to make a comeback. I shoved another Tums into my brace-filled mouth. As our big Hudson rolled past the Sheepshead Bay exit, Mendy said something about Lundy's Seafood Restaurant. It was met by a barrage of groans. Artie coughed like he was dying as he took a long, last drag on his Lucky. A solid sheet of ice covered the Belt Parkway. It was always like this after a February rain.

Allan Freed's familiar voice was barely audible on the radio—somebody had broken off Itchie's antenna. (The Italian kids used the bottom half of car antennas for the barrels of their zip guns.) "Earth Angel," "Soldier Boy" and "Long Tall Sally" had trouble competing with Artie and Seymour, as they told of their conquests of the past week. They were the so-called lovers of our clique. If they were such great ass-men, what were they doing squashed into the back of Itchie's father's car on a Saturday night? Not that I was any Valentino . . . I was still carrying around in my wallet the first rubber I had ever bought. It made such a bulge I was embarrassed to take my wallet out in mixed company.

Itchie hit his brakes suddenly, and we skidded past the Plum Beach sign. The silhouettes of the '50 Fords and the '56 Mercs in the parking lot were now coming into view. Their windows were fogged and their exhausts belched. Artie rolled down his window; Eli who was riding shot-gun did likewise. The freezing salt air nearly threw us into shock. As we slowly glided past the parking lot, Artie and Eli yelled out, "Give me back mine daughter!" "What are you doing to mine daughter?" We laughed hysterically. In a few minutes we were past Plum Beach. Itchie now floored the accelerator throwing the old beat up Hudson into a tailspin. A chorus of obscenities rang out as he tried frantically to wrestle the car back onto the frozen highway.

19

As if the poor guys freezing their asses off back there in the parking lot didn't have enough troubles.

At least once every evening a patrol car would come barreling into the parking lot, their bright spotlights spraying the unsuspecting cars. The wailing siren handing out instant heart attacks. You see, it was against the law to park at Plum Beach after midnight. Before midnight you can do whatever you want. As the guilt-ridden cars fled, they revealed a bleak parking lot surrounded by a scraggly, pock-marked beach. There wasn't a plum in sight.

Most guys seldom even got their girl to Plum Beach in the first place. After all, a girl didn't want to get a bad reputation. One of my favorite lines was, "I think my rear-left tire is flat, before we get a blow-out we'd better pull over and check it out." This said just as we passed the Ocean Parkway, the one before Plum Beach. A few other favorites were, "I'm getting sleepy (yawn), let's pull over for a few moments," or "I have to make an important phone call . . . it'll just take a second . . . I'll pull over in this place . . . there's a telephone booth here." (It had been out of order since my older brother used to park here in the late forties.) Boy, just once I would have loved to have said, "We're going to park, and I'm going to rip your panties off." Very often though, when the moment of truth came, I chickened out and sadly sped past the damn place, rationalizing that I wouldn't have gotten anything anyway. And even if we did park, there were still hassles. The parking lot was always very, very icy and there was nothing worse than getting stuck on the ice with a frigid girl.

All the girls wore these hard, pointy brassieres. They had hooks in the back that seemed welded together (by the girls' fathers, no doubt). And the metal-ribbed girdles they wore were always camouflaged by at least two crinolines. How anyone ever got laid, I'll never know.

You'd finally work up enough nerve to try something and she'd accuse you of being "Jack the Ripper." So, calmly as possible you'd throw your car into reverse, taking out your frustration on the gas pedal. Before you'd know it, you were digging yourself into the icy parking lot like a gopher. The tires would whine, and whine, and whine. It was awful to have to get out of the car at two o'clock in the morning at Plum Beach and try to get a push from a nearby car. Staring into the parked cars for some sign of life must have made me look like some sort of pervert, especially to the couples in the back seats: (How do you ask a girl to get into the back seat? I was thankful to get a girl into the front seat.)

I always used to envy Artie and Seymour whenever they'd start rubbing it in about how well they made out: "I got inside on the top, and outside on the bottom." I'd clasp my hands over my ears tightly, and I'd think about the last time I hit two sewers in a game of stick-ball.

20

Robert Smith

by Steven Michael Bellayr

sometimes he'd smell of the sweat of wet horses
he was a jockey
slim and blond
like the flicker of a candle

he spoke of strange things
dealing dirty blackjack in Vegas on oval tables
of the night he saw Frank Sinatra slide across a diamond casino floor
and his teeth bounced like pennies beneath a roulette table
of seeing a giant banshee swallow a bridge
when he crossed America on a tab of acid
and he had to cross the bridge
because the demon's eyes might be real
and trace him back to Manhattan

he died the night I was with Michelle
she answered the phone
I felt my cock dripping to the red carpet

he spun sixty feet
wrapped in the August air
like a living top in a silk racing jacket

I went to the funeral
a stranger at a minuet of ebony statues
who wailed in silhouettes about a sealed coffin

I clutched a ten inch joint
rolled in paper of raspberry orange
and peppermint green
banana yellow
and cinnamon blue in a single four colored jay
he made for me when we were stoned out and balled our chicks
over fruit cakes and jasmine tea
in a borrowed apartment
and watched John Wayne circle wagons on the late late night show

I smoke the joint in an empty bus
rumbling down Coney Island Avenue

between the lights of used car lots
and recalled the time we rode the trotter together
around the track at Johnson's Park
bouncing to the clap of the mare's hoofs
as she kicked sod on us without looking back

at Johnson's Park they named a race after Robert Smith

I wrote this poem

the 8th of October 1970

Notes on the Wind

by Stanley Taikeff

Memories are hunting horns
Whose notes die on the wind.

Apollinaire

In the cemetery that March morning
you stood under freezing rain
the rabbi spit between words
sighed curled a finger to his lips
mumbled a prayer
then hurried off into black clouds

You saw the hole fill up
with worms and mud
each to the other wedded

As they lowered the box
you saw your father as he never was
laughing a big round face
full of mirth
with yellow teeth
feigning happiness and grace

The tar slicked down with oil
was really the midnight gutter
after a shower in the morning
exhaust fumes and punchball
brought you out again the girls
watched leaning against parked cars
swapping wallet photos secrets gum
adolescent queens in pink rubber breasts
giggling while Solly the
undisputed two sewer king got up
in the ninth and punched air
cracking shoulder joint and bone

At night after fudgicals you
gathered on a stoop talking batting averages
the girls in sheer cotton blouses
passed like perfume through the air
scented with summer's dew making
you want to eat every inch
of their soft spongy skin

Sitting in darkness full of
leathery leaves you touched and kissed
Phyllis (the nitwit) a girl of twelve
who brought a sudden flush of heat
searing cement blocks at your feet

There is a silent sadness in stoops

Generations have beat them dumb
with baseballs pinkballs every
conceivable ball thrown kicked
tossed punched slapped rebounding
chipping cutting sheets of plaster
slivers of stone fragile glass

Sat upon spat upon shat upon
they remain silent a bench
for weary travelers

And what secrets lay buried in
their caverned bones
kisses floating Chagall-like
over hardened cement faces
wind hissing violently through
pores of ageless bedrock
black ants finding whole cities
and kingdoms within illimitable concrete
tears of children
crying with scraped elbow and knee
of teenage lovers and embittered widows
have seeped unnoticed into this
gray marble staining innumerable
forgotten lives
there is a silent sadness in stoops

In *shul* you saw an old Jew
wrapped in the corner
lids trembling like wind blown petals
after the *Kaddish*
you went up the aisle to the door
looking back you saw
the old Jew pasted to the hardwood bench
as if some violent storm had lashed him there
with his eyes locked and staring
with a fly winging near his spittle
you'd think him one of Soutine's fish
in *tallith* and skullcap

On Saturday afternoons there were
bike races through the park and on
to Coney Island on gleaming chrome horses
named Rudge Dunelt Schwinn you raced
headlong pumping pedals fiercely
until aching ankles and sore shoulders
brought you trembling to the boardwalk
there you stripped to swim trunks and skin
plunged recklessly into the cold ocean
emerged with seaweed and bubbles
knotting fingers and throat

Mounted up again
you coasted to Nathans
filled your belly belched like
army men passed the Steeplechase
the roller coaster and all the
desperate men and women sailing
on the merry-go-round reaching
high for heaven youth and
the little gold ring
homeward you pass through
Brueghel country behold the
toothless wonders the sagging flesh
parade up Surf Avenue
a fashion show of fugitives creeping
like insects to lonely rooms filled
with mementoes and memories
behold weary hags blistered with
yellow lizard skin and purple veins

dragging torn beach chairs
and unmarried daughters back home
the girls you see in red suits
licking hot cotton candy with pink wet tongues
these same mermaids who squirmed and kicked
in the water against your hairless chest
are tomorrow's mothers
bitchy pin-curled
sad

Like the pounding surf
you pump on toward home
blood ringing singing like the
ocean's roar in your head
skin raked with coals
and when you reach the door
the desire to go back
and curl up in a wave forever
drinking white foam and brine
electric jellyfish nipping
the salty taste of brunette hair
in your teeth burns like the
white sun and the lazy swarm
of gnats in your eyes

One night you left the Temple
heart filled with terror and shame
ran twenty blocks the ancient mourning
song of the Hebrews chanting plaintively
in the trees
the room you enter is dark
damp the walls dripping summer moisture
and desire in the middle of the floor
with only the point of a flashlight on her
eyes lies demented Phyllis
a girl of thirteen quite grown
in nothing but panties the color
of the moon
you bend down close breathe in the hush
of pungent flesh watch the sudden rise
of young breasts and the virgin lush
playing under blue veiled shadows
for one whole minute an eternity

spanning the stars and beyond
you observe her
then leap touching groping in the dark
pressing caressing with fumbling hands
her naked flesh
this is no Helen no Diana
no queen of the night but a
grinning brain damaged child
giving generously of everything
soft and rich
like flowers to glutted bees

On those muggy August nights
they sat on stools and canvas chairs
like bloated chickens sucked watermelon
peaches and juicy pears
lined up in rows stern judges of the block
they sat jury judge executioner all
raising angry brows passing malicious quips
complained of arthritis bursitis corns
swollen ankles rheumatoid joints
squawked cackled or else murmured
with misery a history of plagues
the young ones sitting not quite so near
in house coats slippers late escapees
of kitchen and kids yawned with boredom
while the perfume from their teased hair
hung thick like cream in the gray air
one old one with a snapping mouth
a sandpaper heart and one green tooth
curled over lower lip pulls
suddenly at her hair foams at the mouth
twitches with violent spasms
shakes her fist then falls quietly back
when no one is looking
she turns her face into a lace
handkerchief which she pulls from her sock
and cries
a sudden shower sends them back inside
to noisy brats
empty walls

One day you go back
as lawyer teacher bum
which is to say poet

you are there in the walls
in the scratched initials
carved among alien symbols
and new minted obscenities

you are there in the rusty radiator
where smoking gloves caked with snow
sat and steamed on that fiery stove

you are there on the roof
the day Phyllis screamed for life
her fall a siren
calling sparrows to her feet

outside the house
you pass the place where
the wretched ladies shook
their last gray hairs
and watch as young men guzzle beer
to the tune of pitched pennies

you cross the street
find the familiar stoop
and spend the minutes dreaming
of frozen eskimo pies dark rooms
rosy cheeks shy girls and fireworks
on the Fourth

"Hey, what do you want here?"

the man's voice is old
and mangy like the skinny
dog at his feet

"Just a memory or two"

"No memories here
go away"

as you cross the street the
visions melt like the sun
dipping behind crooked buildings

night comes in heavy and desolate
pulling with it dreams and despair

like distant fireflies
in a silent wilderness
a billion stars blaze
in your eyes then burn out

and dawn

Tampa—June 2, 1898

by Henry Korn

Tampa—June 2, 1898. Hot and fetid Tampa by the bay. The Rough Riders are sweltering in their woolen winter uniforms. The cheap blue dye stains through to the skin. They came by train from San Antonio, they and their three mascots; a mountain lion from Arizona, an eagle from New Mexico and an ugly but very wise little dog from New York.

TR commandeers the rust transport "Yucatan." He puts his weight upon the rail in the style of a man with a sense of himself. TR, Soldier, Statesman, Author and Naturalist (ugly but very wise little dog from New York) who stares at the sky and speaks of that which is necessary.

It is impossible to walk anywhere, fore or aft, without stepping over the bodies of sleeping men. The rations are insufficient because the meat is bad. No salt. Stringy and tasteless. No ice. And the water is no good, also.

The ships weigh anchor and lurch forward pumping grey smoke into the tropical sky. The bands play, the flags fly and the riggings are black with shouting sailors.

Some days later. Close under the bluffs that rise from the beach are the busted, hungry iron mines of squalid Daiquiri. The surf is high and the long boats cannot close to more than 200 yards of the beach.

The Rough Riders plunge through the waves and stay the night on Cuban soil.

They fry their pork and boil their coffee. They rise with a whoop and strike the Spanish lines at daybreak. A Cuban hillside is alive with the likes of Bucky O'Neill, iron-willed Arizona sheriff, Allyn Capron, crack rifle shot and wolf-hunter, Ben Curry, New Mexico gunfighter of skill and fame and Jess Ballard, Texas Ranger who engineered the break up of the feared "Black Jack Gang."

Then there were the rich boys, fraternity men and college athletes. Tough Ike, Sheeny Solomon and Metropolitan Bill. Cowboys and rich-boys; America's dead-level best.

"I knew I couldn't be far wrong," TR reported remarking half-way up the hill, "if I went forward."

> My Grandpa proudly reads the news,
> Shakes hands with strangers in the street.

Two months later. The Rough Riders land on a sandy beach at the eastern end of Long Island.

> The rich send fruit, roast turkeys and gold.
> In many a tent beautiful women sit and read to sick soldiers
>   through long
> September afternoons.

One day Sergeant Wright takes down the colors and Sergeant Guitilias strikes the standard.
The men shake hands and say goodbye.

> Grandpa sadly reads the news while on his way to work.
> Grandpa died when my Father was his child.
> It has been the cause of such amazing sadness.

> There are no newsreels to remember him by,
>   no souvenirs of whistle stops or agreeable rankings of "near
>   great."

> There is only this dinner plate bearing the likeness of TR himself
>   that my Father buys at auction.

Address to Fifth Avenue

by I. Arguelles

chic and cool people of paradise
I address you
you who wake in mercury mirrors
you whose finance is the worm of history
you whose bone is the daily bread of the poor
you of the radiant fifth avenue
you of the vast chemical education
you of the leisurely voyages to pompeii
you the childless founders of the moon
I address you in this manifesto of salt
I address you with chains of artificial language
you of the easy platinum poetry
you of the air-conditioned hospitals
you of the banyan and yogi telegram
you whose gilded navel supports the buddha
you whose philosophy is so well indexed
I address you with a hundred mouths
you whose dance is the effortless show
you of the sugar-domed cities
you whose marine life is catalogued in silk
you whose libraries contain all truth
you of the forged money suits
you of the intellectual manna wars
I address you with my burning rose
you whose sands simulate the heavens
you with your fossil treatises of politics
you with your symposiums of spanish thought
I address you with my mercurial hands
you of the holy geranium and stool
I exhort you to turn your faces
the final mud is here
a man has become his overcoat
hats assume the function of heads
gloves grope across the careening controls
pants suffer the crucifixion of the lord
shirts ascend in heraclitean flame
no one answers the calls of saint-john-the-telephone
a radio ignites the volcanic residue
earth turns like a crazed saltimbanque

reeking of patchouli and sandalwood
a guru dies twisted his foot on his back
a poet is burnt like a dog in lime
by the worshippers of saint jesus the broker
a child born with college intelligence fixes clocks
all time is rendered nil by his magnetic thumb
look you who have spent lives in ermine death
look you who have lived in speeding metal
look you who have timed games of chance
while believing in the double life of grace
look you who have created the literature of pity
the everlasting moment is here
the everlasting moment is truly here
oh listen to the presence of stone and ice
oh place your finger in the geometry of light
oh unburden your hasps of crawling meat
and forget forget simply forget

If I Give You a Calendar

by L. Neukrug

Did you ever hear a children's song?
So cotton-candy light.
So weightless and clear as glass.
I sang one song when I was young.
When I was a child I sang a song of joy.
No fear or pain.
Pure joy.

If I give you a calendar
Can you show me when I forgot the words?

Family

C'mon You

by Joan Wertheim

"C'mon you," she screamed to the messy kid playing in front of the A & P on Atlantic Avenue. He made believe he didn't hear his mother and climbed into another box of his carton train.

"God damn that kid," she muttered. Her two grocery bundles were heavy. A week's worth of those Welfare food stamps for two lousy bundles, she thought. Yeah, her friend Gloria was right. Last night at the protest meeting, Gloria told them all, "Shit, Whitey's just afraid we's all gonna feed our babies with Pabst Blue 'stead of Pablum."

"Clifford, you better get over here." She tried again, this time louder and threatening. Now a half block away from the supermarket, she stopped to wait for him. The bundles were making her arms ache and she put them down. She remembered the other shopping days, days when she held the little babe close, his warm head pressing into her breasts. Fred used to say, "Honey, you take the baby, I'll get all the bags." The baby, the bags, and her man. Now all she had was this pest in a box.

"Come here, love. Give mama some sugar." Arms outstretched, she'd envelop the toddler racing toward her. "Honey, you sure look right with a babe in your arms," her man would laugh and hug the two of them. "We gotta make us another one soon." He'd grab at her playfully. *"Real* soon, Dell."

"Hush up, nigger, you shush up," she'd giggle, the little one sleepily curling up in her lap. She'd gently lift the baby into the crib.

Lawd, could that man love . . . . "Fred, he's crying, I gotta go feed him."

"No, you stay here, hon, don't move, I'll be right back." He'd go get the bottle, heat it up, and everything. He'd even burp him good. She'd hold that man real tight when he came back to bed. Damn it, if you could only keep things you hold real tight . . .

The kid peeked through a hole in the side to watch her pick up the bundles and trudge back down the street towards the A & P. He started getting a little nervous, his thumb was moving real fast now, in and out of his mouth, his eyes never leaving the watchpost hole.

Last time he didn't have a train for protection. She was ready to start for home but he was busy making a watchtower with empty egg cartons. When she finally cornered him, hiding in the alley at the side of the store, he got it but good. One hand grabbed him, the other an egg carton. She clobbered him with the carton, it broke, and she finished the beating with her hand.

"Clifford, I'm telling you for the last time, you better get yourself outta that box. You hear me child?" She was coming to the closed box now, clutching the bags, one in each arm. The kid just watched, he knew he was in for it. She bent down to place the bags on the pavement so that she'd have her arms free. As she lowered the bags, a carton of eggs and a ketchup bottle balancing precariously on the top of one bag slipped out. "Those clerks never pack the bags good," Fred'd always say. Some eggs spilled out onto the pavement, the broken ketchup bottle splattered over the kid's caboose car and onto her stockings.

The kid saw it all. Instinctively he crouched down deeper into the box and wrapped himself into the emergency air-raid position they taught him at school—left arm wrapped around the back of his neck, right arm shielding the eyes, the head bent toward the stomach.

"Lawd, Lawd, look at what I done," she muttered to herself. "That boy's making my nerves bad." She wearily retrieved the few unbroken eggs and repacked them. Then she kicked the glass chunks toward the gutter.

Now, for the boy. Inside the carton, the kid was chanting softly, very softly, "Ha ha you can't get me 'cause I'm in my own train." But hearing her pulling up the cardboard flaps, he stiffened. The chant became a wordless whimper.

She got the box open now. There crouched inside was the kid, knees and head bent close together. She watched him quickly jerk his arm to cover his exposed rear end. He looks just like a trapped jack rabbit, she thought.

"Clifford, come home with me now. Come home with mama." The reply was louder whimpering. She saw his little body heave with each sniffle.

"Get up on your two feet, son." She reached into the box and lifted him out and onto his feet so that he faced her. She saw him automatically raise his arms to his face for a shield. The self-pitying whimper changed to convulsive sobbing. That always got her more angry, but he forgot. She bent forward, and placed his shaking arms back down at his sides.

38

She waited, her head shaking slowly. She studied her whimpering son, the son of a soldier. She wished he'd run from her, just once. He always just stood there, whimpering and waiting. But he never did look at his mama either.

His little body heaved with a last sob. Now she spoke. "Come to me, Clifford," she commanded quietly, stretching out her arms toward him. Her strange calmness puzzled him. He looked up warily. "Come to mama, child," she urged. He was staring at her now, confused. "Don't you be afraid." Whimpering, he inched toward her beckoning arms, and wrapped his around her waist. Burrowing his wet face into her belly, the kid pleaded, "Don't beat me mama, please don't hit me mama."

"No, child, no. Mama won't hit you." She held him tight.

Her heavy arms rocked him back and forth against her belly. Clutching each other, her head bent over his, mama and the kid cried in front of the A & P.

The Visit

by John Lynch

"To tell you the truth, I've had a drop or two . . . excuse me son, but on my way here I passed a bar and because of the heat I had to have a couple of cool beers . . . it's hot out there in the sun, my boy."

Jim Kelly looked at his father mop the sweat from his forehead with a handkerchief. He noticed his father's young face tasting the first touches of age. His temples were greying and wrinkles were making their marks around his forehead and eyes.

"I've only come in for a minute, Jim," he continued, looking at his son's brooding eyes that rested heavily upon him, "but on a highly important matter . . ." he began fidgeting ". . . you see son . . . excuse me I'm disturbing you but . . ."

Not for a moment did Jim try to ease the embarrassment and anxiety of his father. Passively he sat there, his eyes dark, melancholy and steady in their gaze, his black wavy hair falling over his forehead.

". . . do you have ten dollars you could lend me son? Just a loan till Tuesday you understand . . . you see it's your mother's birthday today and I don't have any money . . . maybe I can get her some perfume or something . . . you know . . . she always likes those kind of things."

Jim took out his wallet and handed his father the money without a word. With obvious relief in his voice his father relaxed, stuffing the money into his pocket.

"Well, it's been a long time son since we've seen each other. How are you? You're looking alright. Are you getting along OK? I wanted to come to see you sooner but I never could find the time . . . oh it's no use . . . you know I'm lying Jim. I've been out of work now for quite a while . . . just hanging around Fahey's Bar talking to all the guys. There's not much work on the docks now."

There was a moment of silence; then Jim's father, with a pained expression, sighed deeply.

"Aren't you going to offer me a beer or something, son?"

Jim went to the refrigerator in the other room and took out two cans of beer. He opened them and gave one to his father. At the sight of the beer, Jim's father became animated.

"Yesterday they had the races on TV at Fahey's . . . Bill and Stingo were there. Ed came in for the bets and I couldn't resist it . . . Black Dancer had to win, so I put five dollars on the nose. Bill and Stingo started ribbin' the hell out of me . . . damn it that race was exciting . . . Black Dancer made his move at the stretch. What a drive! Fifth . . . fourth . . . third . . . second . . . then nose to nose with Sea Gull—the favorite. They crossed the wire. If he had only begun his drive just a few seconds sooner . . . twelve to one odds, son. Nothing to be sneezed at. Why, I would have been a millionaire. I've been watching that horse for months now. I tell you, he was due . . . ah, if I had to give up the ponies Jim . . . I'd go nuts . . . I couldn't live . . . do you understand me, son?"

Again silence fell in the room. Jim's father didn't like silence.

"Aren't you going to ask me about your mother, son?"

It was a drowsy Sunday afternoon and the light from outside made the lonely, bare room look glaringly dirty. Jim's father fidgeted and his voice carried a beginning note of anger.

"Don't worry, I know what you're thinking. You're thinking that she's not really your mother, only a stepmother. But she's been taking care of you since you were eight years old. Surely, Mary has some claim as a mother. Don't look at me like that. Now I know that other people blame me for your mother's death, but surely you don't. Do you son? No, of course not—she died when she gave birth to you."

Jim's father took a long drink of beer from his can—then before taking another swallow, "If you want to blame someone for her death, it has to be yourself."

A car's horn became stuck and the noise grated both men's nerves. Finally it stopped. Jim's father worked his face into a sneer.

"What's this I hear about your high and mighty ways? Stingo says that you feel that you're too good to live with your own family now just because you have a clerk's job in the city. I just don't understand you. Other children live at home with their family, but you, you're different. You think you're too good, don't you? You're too good to live with your brothers and sisters. And are you too proud to see your own family once in a while? What's the matter with us anyway son— we're your own flesh and blood—are we no better than sewer water in the gutter? . . . But don't worry, I know what you're doing up here. I was young too son, don't forget that. I wasn't born yesterday. Although Mrs. Murphy said that she doesn't allow any girls in your room, I know what goes on up here. You think that you can fool your father, do you? You have to get up pretty early to do that. I've seen you talking to some young girls in the street. You can't fool me son. But I'm not so old yet, Jim. If you want to have a party up here one time . . . just four

41

of us you understand . . . sometimes these young girls want an experienced man . . . but never mind we'll talk about that later."

Jim's father finished off the rest of his beer. He banged the empty can on the table.

"God damn it . . . you're my son, aren't you, Jim? My own flesh and blood. Then for heavens sake, act like a son, and come on over to the house tonight . . . eat some dinner with the family. Everyone will be happy to see you, Mary will be happy to see you."

Jim's face darkened for a moment. Hesitation and indecision burned in his heart.

"Come on," his father took him by the arm raising him, "let's go to Fahey's first, the boys will be glad to see you and then we can go to the house. You aren't ashamed to be seen with your father now, are you? Let's go."

They had been about an hour or two at the bar. Jim's father had bought the house a couple of rounds and was playing the part of the prodigal son's father. How many times the phrase, "this is my long lost son returning to the fold in whom I am well pleased" turned up, Jim couldn't count. Needless to say the ten dollars that was borrowed from Jim soon disappeared. As soon as this happened old friends vanished and Jim's father pressed his son to come home and join him for a fine home-cooked dinner.

Soon they were out on the street. They walked up the block a few houses and soon entered a red-brick apartment house. The smell of garlic, cabbage and dirty garbage met them in the hallway. The hallway was dark and the wood and carpet were in an advanced state of decay. A door was open at the end of the hallway.

"Mary, look who I drug up!"

A woman in her early thirties entered the living room.

"Oh, him . . . what's he want, a free meal?"

"I met him at Fahey's and he said he wanted to see everyone again— his beloved family. Where are the kids?"

"They're out as usual when it's time to have dinner. I see you've been to Fahey's again."

"A man has to have some kind of pleasure in the mean world. Don't be so hard on us, Mary."

Mary left the living room. The sound of her shout sent a chill through Jim's bones.

"Suzan, Tommy, come here now. It's time for dinner."

"And here is my pride and joy," he says pointing to a baby in a high chair, "young Kathleen . . . only a year old but smart as the devil," he winked and whispered in his son's ear, "your mother still got what it takes."

42

Mary returned.

"And what are the likes of you two fussin' about in here? Stay away from Kathleen now. I can see that both of you are up to your old tricks again, huh? Where did you get the money to go drinking, Charles Kelly? Did you fluce your own son?"

"Is that the way to talk when Jim comes home now, Mary? Here I met him in the bar now and he said simply that he missed home and the family . . . here you go making up all kinds of stories on his visit."

"Well, who told him to come here anyway? It was bad enough when he was living here all the time—just hanging around doing nothing all day. Now that he's got a job he's too good to live here and give some of his earnings for food and rent to help the family . . . no . . . he gives it to Mrs. Murphy, he's too good for us now."

"Listen Mary, the poor boy is homesick; he wants a good meal, a good substantial home-cooked meal. Now, what's the sin in that? Come on son, let's have a drink before the meal."

Noises and shouts entered the living room as Suzan, a twelve-year-old shining, blond-headed girl, and Tommy, a ten-year-old scrawny boy with straight brown hair, raced into the kitchen.

"I beat you," cried Suzan to Tommy.

Then seeing Jim, she ran up to him and flung her arms around him.

"Any presents, Jimmy?"

Both were disappointed when he nodded no.

"Why not?" asked Tommy.

Suzan pushed him. Tommy got his revenge.

"Suzan has a boy friend, Suzan has a boy friend. Suzan let Johnny kiss her on the stairs before. She thought that I wasn't looking. But I saw."

Mary immediately went up to Suzan and slapped her in the face.

"Don't let me hear of anything like that again young lady. Didn't I just give you a little talk last week, you know what can happen."

"Oh, leave the poor girl alone, Mary. You were young before we married."

Mary almost screamed.

"Keep out of this, both of you! What do you know or care about this family anyway? First it's a kiss, then she allows him to put his hand up her dress . . . what do you care about it anyway? You're only her father . . . and you, you're only her older brother."

She started out of the kitchen, passed her shocked and red-faced daughter, then she returned immediately and with accusing eyes looked at Jim.

"Why do you come in like this and cause all kinds of disturbances? Why don't you go back to your Mrs. Murphy?"

"Come on, Jim, maybe we had better go. Mary's a little upset now. It's that time of the month you know."

They both walked to the hallway. Jim could hear Suzan crying.

"Listen, Jim, maybe you could lend me five dollars till next week. After all, it is your mother's birthday and I had to buy some booze with that other ten dollars at Fahey's. We couldn't show them that we were paupers, could we?"

Jim reached into his pocket and gave his father the five dollars.

"Come over to Fahey's sometime, Jim—I'm over there all the time. One of these days my horse will come in and we'll celebrate, huh?"

He pressed his son's hand warmly.

"It was good to see you again, son."

Jim walked out into the darkening street alone.

"Push!" the Midwife Screamed

by Anne Grant West

"Push!" the midwife screamed.
I pushed with all my stomach muscles taut,
My breath stopped halfway up my throat.
I pushed until I thought my brains would split.

And when the child had grown
to ask how he was born,
his father laughed
and told him of a stork.

Everytime I See an Old Man

by Rosalyn Jackmin

Everytime I see an old man with your look,
I stop and remember
Your desperate time
When you lived between other lives:
A father visiting,
A man in the park, looking,
A man in the clinic, waiting
At my wedding, smiling through wet eyes,
old on the train, stumbling and falling,
sitting in my house and crying,
The man at the nursing home, dying.
I try to forget
When you began to hate
And cry, and turned
Your face to the wall.

The Manhood of Neilly Sullivan

by Joan Conlin

Neilly Sullivan swished his tongue around his mouth, sucked up saliva and spat. He knew that it was illegal to spit in the subways, but he didn't care. A few days in jail would be better than getting the infantile. His friend Jackie Maloney had died of the infantile the summer before, and Neilly still had nightmares in which he saw his friend's small, thin body, clad in the white of his First Holy Communion suit, stretched out in a big mahogany casket. They had said that Jackie had been completely paralyzed before he died and that it was better that God took him. Neilly didn't think it was better. Even now, in November, he pondered bitterly why it had been Jackie who had contracted infantile paralysis. How did he get it? With that thought, Neilly swished out his mouth with his tongue and spat again. He wasn't going to get the infantile. Perhaps, Jackie had been sucking on the iron bar of the exit of the Independent Subway, just as he had been doing. Heaven knows, many a hot summer afternoon they had sought refuge in the cool dark of the Carroll Street Station of the subway. They would stick their feet in between the rungs of the exit gate, wrap their skinny arms around the middle bars and rest their chins on a bar higher up on the rung. It was a monkey-like squat, but no one who had travelled New York's subway system would find it odd or unusual. Squatting thus, they would watch the afternoon trains, as Neilly was doing now. When the trains began to enter the station, without the usual lapse of five or ten minutes, they knew it was five o'clock and time to be starting home. Once in a while, if they were exceptionally lucky, they would catch a glimpse of Neilly's father, Big Mike Sullivan, who was a conductor on the Eighth Avenue Line. He would wave and both boys would practically fall from their perches to release their arms in time to wave back. No one could mistake the stance of Big Mike. He would stride confidently between the trains like a red haired Colossus in a navy blue uniform. And now, Jackie was dead and Big Mike was dead. Neilly remembered the hot September day that he followed his father's casket down the aisle of St. Agnes' Church. He remembered strange snatches like the fact that he was wearing his school uniform

47

and that his new shoes squeaked. He remembered the black novice veil on his sister Kathleen's head; the veil that said she was protected from the world. He wondered if now that she was a nun it hurt as much to know that her father had been killed in an accident. Once again, the words came back to him, "It was better that God took him. The train went right over him . . . such a large family . . . insurance and . . . compensation . . . ," and Neilly hated the words. He didn't hate God, but he hated the words and the memories.

Neilly felt the hot tears burn his cold cheeks and he pulled his chin up from the iron, once more realizing that he had been sucking it. Oh well, maybe it was better to get the infantile and die, he reasoned. With his friend Jackie gone and his father gone and his oldest sister, Kate, in the convent, and Mike, Jr. and Frank fighting Hitler in Europe and young Brian waiting to be called up for military service, there wasn't much of a Sullivan family left. No, he didn't mean that and he hoped that God didn't know he had thought it, although Sister Ursula insisted that God knew everything. No, there was still his mother, Rose Flaherty Sullivan, and his oldest brother, Pete, who had been exempt from the draft because he had a club foot and worked on a newspaper, and then there was Agnes. Neilly sighed, "I guess there'll always be an Agnes," he thought.

Agnes was the apple of his mother's eye. "I named her for the patron saint of my parish church and she's always been a joy to me," his mother had told all the mourners at his father's wake. On the other hand, Neilly, only three years younger than Agnes, had always felt that he was a thorn in his mother's side. Once in temper, his mother had said, "Every rose has its thorn and, Neilly, I guess you're mine." She probably had not meant it, but it stuck in Neilly's mind, so that even now his heart leapt in shame and fright when he saw the crowd getting off the train and knew that it must be the beginning of the rush hour. His mother would be angry if he were late for supper and supper was early now that there was no need to wait for his father. Neilly jumped from the bars, just ahead of the onrushing crowd pushing from the train and scampered up the stairs of the station. The cold wind nipped at his neck and slipped up the sleeves of his plaid mackinaw. He moved agilely in and out through the crowds on the darkening streets, past Mulvaney's Saloon, Steiner's Delicatessen—he didn't even have to look up to know he was passing Steiner's—past Cuneo's Fruit and Vegetable Store, past the Boston Fish Market—he wondered why they had called it Boston when it was in Brooklyn—past Mueller's Bakery and around the corner to a row of brownstones. In the middle of the block, just halfway between the bakery and St. Agnes' rectory, Neilly popped in the gate to the basement of his home.

Even as he entered the house, he was aware of the smells he loved, camphored closets, Kirkman soap, homemade bread and Irish stew. They welcomed as well as warmed him and his spirits rose as he passed through the narrow dark hallway to the back of the house and the large white kitchen.

"Oh, there you are, Neilly!" his mother greeted him.

Neilly eyed her hoping that he was not going to be chastised for being late, or, even worse, interrogated about his fascination for the Independent Subway System. But as his father often put it, "Rosie was blooming," and Neilly knew that something had pleased her. He wanted to ask, but resisted. He knew better than to deprive her of the appropriate moment of celebration. Usually it came with an odd mixture of ceremony and casualness, as she finished apportioning the dinner and sat queen-like at the foot of the table. No one, not even Pete, the eldest son, had assumed Big Mike's place at the head of the table, and Neilly watched his mother, as she looked from side to side at the faces of Agnes, Pete and himself. He thought that his mother looked like a great star of the movies who was about ready to address herself to her loyal but dwindling audience.

"Well," she said, "I'm very happy to announce that Agnes is to play the part of the Blessed Virgin in the Christmas pageant. Isn't that grand?"

"Nice going, Agnes," Pete smiled across at his freckled-face sister with the dark brown braids. He chuckled inwardly at what Raphael would have thought of such a Madonna. Any one of the several Italian girls in Agnes' seventh grade class would have been more ideal, but he sensed that the nuns had chosen Agnes more out of consideration of his widowed mother, than for his sister's appealing image.

"Isn't that grand, Neilly?" Rose reiterated. "Don't be jealous of your own flesh and blood. Share your sister's joy."

"Oh, yeah, that's great, Aggie," Neilly mumbled, as he smouldered inwardly. Agnes had used his mother's moment of concentration to stick out her tongue at Neilly. Neilly apparently remained oblivious, but silently plotted his revenge. "Swell, Aggie," he said, deliberately emphasizing the nickname that his sister hated.

"Well, let's hope that some day it will be your turn, Neilly, and you'll play the part of Saint Joseph," Rose Sullivan speculated hopefully but without much real confidence.

Pete sensing Neilly's discomfort responded, "Ah, no Neilly, wait for the Passion Play at Easter and be Judas. It has much better lines. After all, Joseph was a silent man." He winked at Neilly and the boy smiled back a smile of comradeship as well as gratitude.

"No, don't be puttin' crazy ideas into the boy's head. He has enough of them as it is and I still have Brian to contend with."

With this remark Neilly watched his mother's face shadow with

49

seriousness. He knew that she worried about Brian being drafted, but that she worried even more about the new friends he had made while working on the Brooklyn docks.

"Why is Brian always late for supper?" asked Agnes.

Neilly wondered why Agnes' questions always seemed to come out like whimpering rebuffs.

"Your brother works hard. He's helping load supplies to the men overseas and he's very important to the war effort. He can't help it if he's late once in a while. Besides, we should be glad he was deferred for these past few months after . . . after . . . after everything."

Rose Sullivan's voice broke off, but her eyes were dry and her face remained controlled.

"She's tough," thought Neilly, "My mother's a tough old gal."

Luckily Pete looked up and said, "Ma, that's Brian now. He's coming."

"Good," was all Rose answered, but she looked up with cheerful defiance as her handsome eighteen-year-old Brian swung into the kitchen.

"Hi, Rose, old girl!" he greeted his mother with a brashness that showed no disrespect. He swung his right arm around her shoulders and kissed her on the left cheek.

Rose stiffened and made no attempt at affection, but Neilly noted the traces of amusement around the corners of her lips and her eyes shone as she asked, "Is that liquor I smell on your breath?"

"Liquor? No, Ma," Brian bawled, "just a glass of beer. I just stopped to chug a glass with the men. Hi, Pete, Agnes, Neilly!"

Rose eyed him sardonically, "Never mind your hellos or your little tete-a-tetes with your friends. You'll have little time for tete-a-tetes when the Army gets you!"

"True, true, that's why I'm enjoying life now, Mother darlin'." Brian sat down next to Pete and waited for Agnes to serve his stew. She did it without being told for this was a house where the women knew what was expected of them and did not question.

"Did you load any big ones today, Brian? Any secret stuff or any new weapons?" Neilly inquired eagerly.

This inquiry was enough to set Brian off on one of his long tales of a hard day's labor. Only Pete held these stories to be suspect, but even he would not openly question his brother's veracity. He was too amused with Brian's elaborations on the mundane and besides it was good to have Brian with them. He had his mother's forcefulness, softened by his father's wit.

Although Neilly glowed in the reflection of Brian's casual charm, it was his eldest brother, Pete, to whom he turned for counsel. For with Pete, Neilly could feel comfortable, free from the jibes of sibling humor. So it was that when Pete retired to his room to shower and dress for his usual date with Lillie Steiner, Neilly soon followed after him.

Pete looked in the mirror, questioning the closeness of his shave. He was aware of the admiring glances of young Neilly, as he was aware of the hurt and loneliness that pervaded the boy's personality. Pete flipped the ends of his tie and made a neat, broad knot.

"Well, that does it. Neilly, how do I look? Good enough to kiss?" He tousled Neilly's hair and smiled, "Not by you of course!"

Neilly pounced on Pete's bed, out of his brother's reach and shot back, "NO, by Lillie, of course!"

"Oh, go on you scalliwag! You know too much for a boy your age. By the way, how old are you?" Pete sat on the edge of the bed and Neilly stretched out on his stomach, his elbows bent and his face cupped in his hands.

"I'm almost nine," he answered, "and I'm twice as smart as Aggie. I just don't study so much."

"Well, you can say that again, Neilly. But don't be too hard on Aggie. She means well. She's a girl and you will find that girls are sometimes difficult to understand . . . a little difficult to understand, Neilly." Pete reached up and smoothed his dark hair, sighed and re-iterated, "Girls are a little difficult to understand."

"Do you understand Lillie, Pete?" Neilly inquired.

"Well, now you are getting personal, but being that I started this line of conversation, I'll tell you a little secret. No, I do not really understand my lovely Lillie," Pete answered and with this remark he looked as quizzical as Neilly.

"Do you love Lillie, Pete?" asked Neilly.

"Now you are getting personal!" Pete smiled at Neilly to reassure the boy that he understood the pangs of youthful curiosity. "But being that you are the only soul around this house who can keep his mouth shut, that is with the exception of Kathleen who took herself to the nunnery, I will place my confidence in you and tell you that I love Lillie Steiner and what's more, I intend to marry her." With this Pete gave Neilly a firm swat on the backside as if to reaffirm his own intentions. "And now I must be off and on my way to woo the fair young maiden."

"Wait a minute, Pete," Neilly pleaded. He jumped up and knelt on the bed. "If you don't understand Lillie, how can you love her?"

"Understanding women and loving one woman are two entirely different things. And that young man you find out when you are older!"

"I'm already finding it out right now." Neilly sunk down full length on the bed and Pete, remembering the boy's melancholy over the past months, thought better of his haste and hoped that Lillie would understand.

"Neilly, I think it's time that we had a long talk. What is it, Neilly? What's been eating at you?" Pete put the question into words, at the

51

same time dreading the poignancy that must follow such a question.

Neilly picked at the chenille runners of the spread, paused and then looked up to face Pete. His eyes brimmed with tears.

"I don't know, Pete. It's everything . . . Jackie's gone and Daddy's gone . . . Kathleen's so far away . . . and . . . and Mother . . . Mother doesn't want me, Pete. She just can't like me!" Neilly sobbed and Pete's eyes were moist with tears, tears for the living, tears for the dead, and tears just for the tears of things. He cleared his throat, wiped the tip of his nose and began, "Neilly, Neilly, you are suffering not only the pains of growing up, but the pains of being the last to grow up in a large family. I was first and it was hard, but, believe me, I wouldn't want to be in your shoes. Either way it's a lonely bit, if you're the oldest then you must stand apart to warrant the respect of the others, and if you're the youngest then you're set apart because you are the baby. And besides, you didn't choose a very appropriate time to achieve your manhood. It's been a desperate time . . . these last few months . . . a desperate time for all of us."

"I know that, Pete," Neilly broke in. "I know that everyone misses Dad and Kathleen and the boys and even Aggie cried at Jackie's funeral, but it's Mother, Pete. It's . . . it's Mother that I can't bear," and with this Neilly broke off in fresh sobbing.

"Neilly, Neilly," was all Pete said as he stroked the boy's back between the shoulder blades. He made no attempt to restrain him. He knew he must let it come out, for he knew that Neilly was right. It was his mother. It was Rose Flaherty Sullivan who was hurting her youngest son with the hurt he could not bear.

When the sobs had subsided, Pete helped Neilly to a sitting position and braced his shoulders with his arm. He tried to explain a fact of life, perhaps the most puzzling fact of life with which any boy has to contend.

"Now, we all know how you loved Jackie, Neilly. And you must have known that you were the apple of Big Mike's eye," Pete began.

Neilly started to challenge the latter part of Pete's statement, but thought better of it and nodded silently.

"And you couldn't have been more to Kathleen, if you were her own son." To this Neilly agreed. "And now, because they're gone you miss their interest, friendship and affection. But, Neilly, you must know that you never lost their love. You don't lose love. You know that, don't you, Neilly?"

"Yes, Sister Ursula and I had a long talk when Daddy died and she explained all that," mumbled Neilly.

"Yes, but all the explanations in the universe would not take away the hurt. Would they, Neilly? Nor will anything take away the hurt for any of us . . . especially for Rose Flaherty Sullivan!"

52

Neilly looked up and there was defiance in his tear-stained face.

"But why me? Why does she have to take it out on me? I didn't hurt her! I didn't kill Daddy!" Neilly protested.

"No, Neilly, I never knew you to deliberately hurt anyone." Then Pete lightened the mood, "Except for the time when you stuck Tessie Noonan's curls in the inkwell."

Neilly chuckled and Pete knew that he could proceed with a measure of logic as well as solace.

"Sometimes we hurt without knowing it. Take a look in the mirror, Neilly. What do you see? You're Big Mike Sullivan's son. You have his hair, his eyes, and his grin. The rest of us are black Irish Flahertys, but not you, Neilly. You're pure Sullivan. What's more, you bear Big Mike's father's name. That was none of Rose's doing, you know. She had you pegged Thomas William."

"What do you mean, Pete?" Neilly was puzzled. He thought that he had heard all the family stories but this story was entirely new to him.

"Oh, Mother sent you out to be christened in her beautiful antique christening coat with that awful matching cap with its yellowed ribbons and you were to be Thomas William Sullivan. But when he returned from the church, Dad handed you into her arms with, 'Meet our fifth son, Cornelius Vincent Sullivan.' I'll never forget the way he said 'our fifth son,' and you know, Neilly, Mother never said another word about Thomas William. Dad knew how to give it to her when he had to do it. Neilly, that's what you're going to have to learn to do. Give it to her—with respect—mind you, with respect. Every time she looks at you she sees Mike and it hurts, but, Neilly, you must never bend to that hurt. Sometimes, Neilly, women are like the winds that bend and twist the very trees that they helped to pollinate. If you stand firm, flexible in storm and crisis, but upright at all times, they will come and whisper sweet things in your branches . . . whisper sweet things, Neilly. . . . Well, that reminds me that I must be off to my own little whirlwind. Have I helped you, Neilly?"

Neilly smiled a slow, uncertain smile and said, "I think so, Pete. It seems to hurt less, anyway. How did you learn all this, Pete?"

"We all advance in wisdom and age, Neilly. Then again you can learn a good deal in books. You ought to read more, Neilly." With this Pete looked at his watch, bounded off the bed and opened the bedroom door singing softly, "Oh, Lillie, Lillie, whisper sweet things to me tonight."

"Pete, wait a minute," Neilly called after him and as his brother turned he said, "Thanks, Pete, thanks!"

Pete winked, smiled and was off to reap his own whirlwind. Neilly finished his homework, said his prayers, thought about his brother's advice and decided to let God worry the rest of the night.

Thanksgiving came and went as usual. In fact, it was so like any other Thanksgiving that Neilly felt guilty in its normalcy. He and Brian went to the annual football game between Brian's alma mater, St. Francis' Prep, and the local Jesuit prep school.

"We'll beat the tar out of those fancy pants," Brian boasted and the St. Francis team was soundly victorious. Neilly and Brian returned home at midday, exuberant in the spirit of the game. The house mellowed in the smells of Thanksgiving—turnips, creamed onions, pie and turkey. This year there was a five-pound box of candy from the boys of Mulvaney's Saloon, two mince pies from Mrs. Mueller's Bakery, two pounds of potato salad from Steiner's and pasta from Mrs. Cuneo. Neilly's eyes widened at the bounty and it was not until after he had tasted each treat that he connected it with the donor's compassion for his widowed mother. Even this realization could not detract from his delight in the delicacies.

When Miss Roderick arrived at two o'clock with her customary assortment of cakes and bonbons from Schrafft's, Neilly knew that the dinner hour was near. Miss Roderick was a hostess in Schrafft's who had befriended his mother when she was a young girl, "fresh off the boat," as they called it. Rose Flaherty was a hard-working eighteen-year-old, who made a courteous, smiling waitress, meticulous in appearance and service. Amy Roderick used to say, "If I had a dozen Rose Flahertys, I could make this place top-notch, top-notch!"

So it was that after Rose's marriage Miss Roderick came at Thanksgiving and on a few of her free afternoons. Usually she brought the components of high tea and Rose and she would enjoy a simple festive afternoon in the large kitchen. She took particular interest in Kathleen and Agnes, but Neilly and the other boys accepted this as a matter of course, since Miss Roderick chose to remain in single blessedness, a typical English spinster.

The Christmas season would have been uneventful too if it had not been for Agnes' theatrical debut and Pete's announcement of his future plans. The latter even was more meaningful to Neilly, who saw in Agnes' experience just an excuse to get out of doing the supper dishes.

It was on a cold night two weeks before Christmas, when Agnes was at rehearsal and Neilly was stuck with the dishes, that Pete came down from his room dressed for his usual date with Lillie. He said goodnight to his mother, kissed her lightly on the cheek and told her not to wait up for him. Then, as he turned to leave, he paused next to the refrigerator which stood by the entrance of the hall. He swung an arm on top of the refrigerator and waited a moment. Rose Sullivan knew this stance well. Big Mike had assumed it when he was puzzled, troubled or just thoughtful, and each one of his sons had unconsciously

54

copied it. However, she neither stirred in her chair, nor looked up from the pants that she was cuffing. She just waited.

"Mother," Pete began, "I'd like to talk to you."

"I'll go inside and do my homework," Neilly volunteered hoping to leave the rest of the dishes for Agnes.

"You stay where you are, Neilly, and finish your job," Rose answered. Then without looking up from her sewing, "Well, Pete, what is it?"

Pete knew this attitude for what it was. Whenever his mother had to come face to face with a reality that she would have preferred to ignore, she assumed an air of quiet, compulsive business.

"Mother, I intend to give Lillie a ring for Christmas . . . an engagement ring." Pete's voice was soft, but deliberate and without hesitation.

"H'm," was all Rose answered at first. Then she added matter-of-factly, "She's German, you know."

"Her parents are from Germany. If that's what you mean." Pete deliberately skirted the heritage issue. He knew that his mother would have liked to involve the Steiners in World War II and the fact that Frank and Mike, Jr. were fighting overseas. He looked at his newly shined shoes and reaffirmed his decision not to get into a stupid argument over misplaced patriotism.

Rose sidestepped her first implied objection and proceeded more judiciously, "Lillie's an only child, isn't she?"

"Yes," said Pete. His mother did not respond further.

"What has Lillie's being an only child to do with my giving her an engagement ring?"

"Oh, nothing, nothing, Pete. It's just that Lillie is used to having things so, neat and fancy and all . . ."

"Mother," Pete broke in, "if you think that Lillie is spoiled, just because she's an only child, you are dead wrong. She works hard keeping house, cooking and helping in the store and . . . ," Pete sighed and looked off. He was angry at himself for rising to his mother's bait.

"Did I say that she was spoiled? Did you hear the word 'spoiled' pass my lips? Pete you're too quick to jump to conclusions. All I wanted to know was if Lillie wanted a family."

Rose continued with her sewing, at the same time adopting an air of injured innocence.

"Of course Lillie wants children. We both do. Lots of them! Lillie hasn't liked being an only child. Why, just the other night, she was saying she'd like to have as many children as you have." Pete had not meant to divulge this last confidence, but after he had compulsively blurted it out he eyed his mother wondering at her reaction to the comparison.

"Oh, she said that, did she? It seems to me that you two have this

55

pretty well planned out! Pretty well planned out! I'm grateful that you even let me know about it." Rose's expression feigned gratitude, but her voice was tinged with sarcasm.

Pete said nothing. He looked from his mother to Neilly. But Neilly had remained facing the sink dutifully doing the dishes. Only the boy's hunched shoulders and his deliberate motions betrayed his tension and frustration. He was an embarrassed, unwilling spectator to this whole episode. It was the sight of Neilly that determined Pete to cut the conversation short.

"Well, goodnight, Mother. I'll let you know if Lillie accepts me in the morning," and with this remark Pete turned down the hall. He left the house whistling softly the strains of "Lili Marlene."

"Accept you? Accept you! Do you hear him, Neilly? Why, she'll jump right into his lap! Oh, damn it!" Rose wailed.

Neilly turned at his mother's profanity and he thought that he saw a tear on her cheek, but it was hard to tell. Rose sat sucking her thumb where she had stuck herself with her needle. Her only remark to her youngest son was, "Hurry up and finish those dishes and get to your homework."

The Christmas pageant played to a packed house of adoring parents. Neilly was surprised that Agnes performed so adequately, and he reluctantly offered his congratulations. Miss Roderick, who had come to witness Agnes' debut, presented her with a nosegay, and the whole family, even Brian, returned to the house for an evening of tea and left-overs from Schrafft's.

Neilly felt warm and secure in the big kitchen, even though he was aware of the strained silence between his mother and Pete. On the other hand, Brian was his usual exuberant self, and he beguiled them with stories of the docks and his dealings with the longshoremen.

Brian was the soul of all the Christmas preparations. His large salary, plus the long hours of overtime pay, gave him new stature, and he delighted in extravagant surprises for everyone. He bought his mother a string of cultured pearls and Agnes a fourteen karat gold charm bracelet. He sent packages overseas to Frank and Mike, Jr. and a substantial check to Kathleen's convent. He scoured the second-hand book shops for a decent copy of the *Britannica* for Pete, and he overwhelmed Neilly by presenting him with a genuine pigskin, regulation football from Davega's Sporting Goods Store.

Pete's gifts, though not as lavish as Brian's, were even more carefully chosen, but as Neilly thought later if Pete had brought them nothing but his Lillie it would have been more than enough. Lillie came for Christmas dinner, and Neilly revelled in the warmth of her well being and the vibrancy of her wit. He knew why Pete loved her; she made him laugh. She even made Rose Flaherty Sullivan laugh, and this was a major accomplishment for someone of German descent. Lillie brought a book, *The Knights of the Roundtable,* as a special present for Neilly.

The day had been full with festivities and at eleven o'clock, when Neilly was wending his tired way up the long stairs, he was struck with the realization that he had not missed his father. A wave of melancholy enveloped him as he thought of how his father would have cupped his chin in his big palm and kissed him on the forehead. This was a bed-time ritual between father and son, and the remembrance of it hurt and warmed Neilly. But once Neilly had retired to his small hall bed-room, he was caught up in the magic of medieval times and the tales of kings and knights and squires.

The days that followed Christmas saw a deep change in Neilly. He spent less time in the Independent Subway; he studied harder, and he was in every way a model student. Sister Ursula saw the change but said nothing. However, the family failed to notice any difference in Neilly's behavior because they were engrossed in a more serious mat-ter. Brian had been ordered to report to his draft board. The night Brian opened the notification, a quiet descended upon the Sullivan family. The silence perplexed Neilly. He reasoned that although they had all known that this would happen none of them had prepared for the actuality. He wondered how one *could* prepare for sorrow. It seemed to creep up on you when you least expected it. Brian's leaving was not like a knight going into battle. It was similar, but different. He watched Pete, seeking an answer to his query, but Pete's only con-tribution to family morale was in his quick embraces of his mother along with the words, "We knew that it must come. Didn't we?"

Little as it was; Pete's remonstrance seemed to console Rose, and she warmed to her first born, once more.

On the other hand, Brian was another matter. As the weeks wore on and his self-confidence waned, he became fretful and irritable. It was a difficult time for him.

Nevertheless, the sudden change in Brian's military status only re-affirmed Neilly's determination to persevere in his own sworn quest, the winning of Rose Flaherty Sullivan's esteem. He had decided that as a knight pursued a rare treasure to gain favor with his lady, he, too, must do something outstanding to please his mother. In Neilly's case, the object of his quest was easily set upon, for Neilly had striven for years to win the General Excellence Medal in his grade. Agnes had won it several times, but Neilly had only managed a second place on one occasion and a third place on two occasions. The medals would be awarded on the night of commencement, sometime late in January. This would be soon after the day that Brian would have to report to Camp Upton for training. What a consolation it would be to his be-reaved mother. At night, alone in his room, Neilly relished the thought of his mother's joy and surprise. This thought was his inspiration, and he persevered in his studies, even to the memorization of the first twenty lines of "Hiawatha" for extra credit in English.

The final examination was the history test, and it was scheduled for the day that Brian was to leave. Rose had pressed together a small family gathering the night before, but Neilly had resisted the temptation to stay in the kitchen and listen to the tales of Uncle Tim's immigration from County Clare, Cousin Deliah's bout with consumption, and Aunt Anastasia's winnings in the sweepstakes. He retreated to the quiet of his room and the accomplishments of the Second Continental Congress. Even the laughter from the kitchen failed to deter him from his studies, for deep in his mind's eye was the image of a small gold medal on a dark blue ribbon. This was his goal; this was his lady's favor.

Two days before commencement, Sister Ursula asked Neilly and Tessie Noonan to remain in the classroom while she escorted the lines of children to their appointed street corners. Neilly's heart surged with hope, for this was the usual preparatory method of announcing the winners of the medals. On the night of commencement one boy and one girl from each grade would be seated proudly with the graduates until their names were called. Then each one would step forward to receive his or her medal from the hands of the Pastor himself, Monsignor Charles Flynn.

Neilly's hopes were not in vain. As Sister Ursula returned to the classroom, she seated herself at the desk and began, "I know that you are very anxious and I won't detain you. However, I also know that you have worked very hard, especially you, Cornelius. Therefore, I am happy to inform you that you two will be the recipients of the General Excellence Medals for this grade. Be in the Principal's Office at seven thirty, Friday evening, January twenty-third. Wear your school uniforms, but be sure that they are cleaned and pressed and that your shoes are shined. Now congratulations to you both. I am very proud of you!"

Neilly skipped down the iron steps of the old school building, leaving Tessie and Sister Ursula to follow at a more lady-like pace. He flipped the lid of the mailbox and jumped the fire hydrant on the corner. He scooted up the street oblivious to the biting January wind, oblivious to the "Good afternoon," of Father Burke, oblivious to the calls of his friends who were playing hockey in the street. He bolted into the basement and immediately held himself in check. He had rehearsed this moment in his mind and had decided to adopt a casual dignity. He was instantly aware of the sound of voices coming from the kitchen. He could hear Agnes' giggling and the laughter of his mother and Miss Roderick. He welcomed this unexpected merriment and thought, "I'm glad Miss Roderick is here. It will please Mother even more when I tell her." He paced himself as he proceeded down the dark hall, and he entered the kitchen smiling, saying "Hello" to everyone and slinging his books on a vacant chair.

"Hello, Neilly, my boy. Come have some tea." His mother was exuberant. "What kind of day did you have in school? Agnes was just telling us some good news. She won the General Excellence Medal again. What is this? The *sixth* time, Agnes? Aren't you proud of your sister, Neilly? Such a little scholar! Have more tea, Miss Roderick?"

"Gee, that's swell, Aggie," and this time Neilly really meant it. However, he could no longer disguise his pleasure in his own accomplishment. He forgot his rehearsed mannerisms and blurted out, "Mother, I have good news for you, too!"

"Really, Neilly." His mother did not look up from the tea things. "Try these biscuits, Miss Roderick. I think that they're making them better than ever."

"Mother, I won the General Excellence Medal this term, too!" Neilly swelled in his achievement.

Miss Roderick beamed, Agnes sat with her mouth hanging open in surprise, and Rose Flaherty Sullivan sat transfixed with the tea pot lifted in mid-air. Then, blinking her eyes ever so slightly, she recovered her poise, lowered the pot and mumbled, "That's fine, Neilly. Very good, indeed."

She resumed her role as hostess and asked matter of factly, "Will you have cream or lemon, Miss Roderick?"

Neilly watched as the tea party proceeded as usual. He flushed in angry confusion, grabbed his books from the chair and bounded upstairs to his room. He flung himself on his bed and buried his face in the pillow.

"That's fine, Neilly. Very good, indeed," he mimicked his mother's voice. He pounded his fist into his pollow.

"I work my head off. I study as hard as any girl and I win the damn medal and all she says is 'That's fine, Neilly. Very good, indeed.' " He rose to a sitting position with the hot tears stinging his face, "I'll show her! I'll fix her! I'll . . . I'll . . ." But what could he do? He had done the only thing that he knew how to do and it had not made a particle of difference. Neilly lay back on his bed and wondered. He thought of Gawain, Lancelot and Galahad. He thought of Frank and Mike, Jr. He thought of Brian, a scared private in the Army. He thought of Pete who had defied his mother for his love of Lillie Steiner.

Neilly lay thinking for a long time. It was dark, almost six o'clock, when Agnes' knock roused him.

She tapped quietly and whispered, "Neilly, Mother says that it's time you came down for supper. Neilly, did you hear me? And . . .

and . . . Neilly, I'm truly glad that you won the medal. Really I am!"

"Yeah," was all Neilly answered as he rose from the bed and began to get cleaned up for supper. "Yeah, that's great," he muttered to himself.

He washed his face and straightened his school tie. He had forgotten to change his uniform and his mother would be angry, but he didn't care. He looked at himself in the bathroom mirror. "Well, you're certainly no knight of the Round Table. And you'll probably never be as brave as Mike or Frank. And you'll never be strong as Pete, nor as soft as Brian. You'll be Neilly. Not Rose Flaherty Sullivan's Neilly! Not even Michael Terrence Sullivan's Neilly. You'll be Cornelius Vincent Sullivan's Neilly. A man . . . your own man!"

With this new perspective Neilly began to feel better already. He combed his hair and went down to supper.

Little Violin

by John Marino

When I was five months old Papa died and Mama and I were left alone in that big house. I remember a large photograph on the parlor wall that seemed to look down on you while you were looking up at it. It was strange looking at this man's photograph who Mama said was my father.

After I started school and learned to read I would read some of the things he wrote in his memory book. They were simple words because he said them about me and to me. There were four snapshots of me pasted in his memory book—my son at the age of one month, my son at the age of two months, my son at the age of three months, my son at the age of four months. I would recite the words he had written under my pictures over and over.

When I was seven years old Mama and I moved to a small house in an alley way between Carson and Seybert Street. Across the street from our new house was a big ice plant. Wagons rattled out of the plant loaded with cakes of ice and covered with a khaki colored canvas. Selling ice was a big business in those days. The drivers didn't unharness their horses until after sundown. That's how busy they were.

After supper mother and I would sit on the front steps, look up at the sky and count the stars.

"There's the north star," she held my hand tightly as she pointed out the milky way and the big dipper. "God is everywhere."

"Uh huh."

She smiled and started to tell me again about the trolley car company where Papa had operated trolley car number 5. It was on this trolley car that Mama, on her way to the county fair, had met Papa. They married a year later. On Sundays they would ride this trolley car from Hazleton to Freeland and view the countryside, and every year they went to the county fair.

Around their fifth wedding anniversary the city council voted to replace the trolley cars with buses. The city was in favor of modern times. In the trolley car barn the trolley cars became huge mummies.

61

The smell of grease and oil remained in the old barn while rust settled between nuts and bolts of trolley car number 5—and Papa's heart.

One day as I was watching the morning sun come through my bedroom window I heard a horse scream.

"Mama, it's the ice plant. It must be on fire . . . fire!"

Mama ran to the window. "Be still—it's no fire."

I went back to the window and saw a man whip a horse: a little man with reddish porcupine hair. He weaved about while he whipped his horse.

Mama started to take in washing that summer, and when the hot weather came, the men from the ice plant started to come to our house for water. One day the man who had whipped his horse came for a drink. He liked it here . . . he told the others to stay away . . . he lashed one of them just to scare away the others. He drank water slower than anyone. One Saturday after a glass of water he headed toward Mama. He grabbed her hand.

"Drink another glass of water," Mama said.

He stroked her hair. She shoved him away and slapped his hand. He chased her to the corner of the kitchen.

"You've had your water. Go."

The door banged shut.

I ran to Mama. She smiled and patted my head. The next time that he came he brought Mama a beautiful sparkling bracelet which he took out of a black velvet box. She thanked him . . . after that day he brought groceries and opened the front door with his own key. Twice a day he would drive by and wave to Mama. He was still with us when the white snow painted the windowsills.

"Can I shovel the snow?"

"No, sonny, you're too small. Grow up first."

I wanted to grow and grow.

That Christmas Mama bought me a musical carrousel. The carrousel played "Brahms' Lullaby." The first time it played I almost cried. That Christmas they had a big fight.

"Youra littla boy musta go. Sen' him to youra uncle. He's a big boy. I wan' a son . . . but I don' wan' him . . . ."

"Oh, if only my husband were alive."

"God damn it! I wan' justa you! Youra littla boy is in da way . . . I wan' you . . . We parla Italiano so da boy don' undrastan' wat we say . . . ."

I moved closer to Mama.

"You littla bum. Get out of ourra way. Damn it da hell! An' dat utter bum you marry before?"

"Shut up!" Mama said.

"Get your littla son—youra littla pain in da neck out of dis house! Cry you littla bast, das verra good!"

"I don't want to see you again. Stay away from this house!"

She threw his gifts at him. He noticed my delight and slapped my face. I hit the wall. He grabbed my shiny new carrousel and stamped on it. I screamed and screamed. He bolted the kitchen door and grabbed Mama.

"I wan' some supper!"

Mama moved quickly about the kitchen—bread crumbs, garlic, olive oil, chopped meat and . . . spaghetti. I ran to my room and smelled the food . . . someday I'll grow up and give him a good beating. Nobody cared for him in the neighborhood. Why did he ever come to this house, that horsewhipper! Maybe one morning when he would harness his horse it would trample him to death. If Papa were alive he would have chased this man away. I wouldn't dare to think of having this man for a pop. I wish my Papa were alive. I bet Pop loved horses—even after he became a motorman.

It was the first day of the new year. I got up bright and early and ran downstairs.

"Happy New Year, Mama."

Nobody was in the kitchen. "Mama, where are you? Are you all right? Mama." I ran into her bedroom. She said nothing. She sat before her mirror and smiled. Mama was combing her long silky hair and looking into the mirror. She was a million miles away. It was then that I knew I had lost my Mama. I wanted to run away, but I was too young to shine shoes.

It was spring. The trees in the church yard across the street blossomed. The nuns sat, knitting and crocheting. The oldest remembered me best. She held me close and gave me candy. I almost forgot Mama . . . .

It was my birthday. Ten years is really old. My first pair of long pants. "Look Mama look!" Everybody asked me what I would be when I grew up. "A cowboy." That's why I went to the family theater every Saturday to see Tom Mix and his horse Tony. I was old enough to shine shoes! All the shoeshine boys liked Saturday evenings best. Our pockets jingled. All the men from the poolroom wanted to look snappy on Saturday night. With my extra money I would buy Mama a present from Woolworth's five and ten cent store. A handkerchief, or maybe a bottle of perfume that the salesgirl would recommend for the price I could pay.

On his paydays he would flash money in front of my face and hand Mama a gift. I wish she would refuse his presents. Once he dropped a dollar bill just to see if I would pick it up. I didn't. I knew that with his right foot he would crush my hand—like he'd crushed my carrousel.

One night they had a big fight. A neighbor phoned the police department. Mama was badly beaten. Furniture was broken. My face was sore. Black and blue marks punched and pressed my skin. I resembled a clown. He was locked up for sometime. Mama and I were together again—just the two of us. I started to take free violin lessons with Father Gullatti. I planned to learn a song for Mama. "Brahms' Lullaby." Mama was happy about my violin studies. "A nice instrument, the violin," she would tell me. Father Gullatti said I was good enough to be in the orchestra. We practiced in the church basement, preparing for Italian Day at the park. Finally the day came. Mama bought me a blue serge suit, like the other members of the orchestra. "Don't get your new suit dirty," Mama said before I left her to join the orchestra at the main entrance to the park. The city park was square like a baseball field. To the left were the concessions: popcorn stands, hot dog stands, shooting galleries and small games of chance. To the right was the carrousel encircled by patches of green grass. Zooming high toward the sunny sky and sloping down near the lake was the roller coaster. The stage where the orchestra played almost patted the lake. Father Gullatti raised both hands for silence. The audience gathered around and the music started to flow everywhere. When we finished they applauded. Before we were dismissed Father Gullatti reminded us that we were still beginners.

Some of the members of the orchestra joined their families. I remained on the bandstand a minute or so listening to the music of the carrousel.

Mama and I decided to take a boat ride. There were eight of us in one boat. The skipper started the motor and I listened to the humbuzz of the motor as we sailed out to the center of the lake. I slid my hand in the cool water. A girl about my age splashed water on my face. Soon, our mothers spoke. We too became friends. After the ride our mothers promised to see each other. The girl giggled. A little later we boarded a bus for home.

That Monday morning on the way to school I heard the townspeople whisper that that man was back in town. I couldn't wait to get out of school. He wasn't there when I came home. Mama fixed his favorite dishes. I couldn't eat the supper. He didn't come that night, or the next.

That Saturday night I shined many many shoes. I bought her a bracelet from Woolworth's. She kissed me, "Now eat your supper."

How happy I was. The attic was restored to a brighter look. I wouldn't be afraid of the dark anymore . . . except when the light was turned off, the room was still dark and strange. I heard and saw things that weren't really there. Noises you don't hear in the day time.

The next night I awoke—strange noises. I sat up and rubbed my eyes.

A beam of moonlight came into my room. I saw two dark shadows dancing. "Mama, Mama." Both shadows came closer. I was unable to move. The beam of moonlight vanished. Darkness. Darkness. On the arm of the tallest shadow was something long and white. It waved back and forth. They were close! "Mama, Mama." Footsteps. The door opened. The light went on. There was Mama and that little man. On Mama's arm was a white gown. The man had a hammer in his hand. "Sleep or I'll kill you." I cried and wanted to be smothered by my mother's hug. She was cold. I cried that night and the next.

It was Friday night and I had just left Father Gullatti. Dark clouds roved overhead. Lightning struck nearby. I looked up. The church steeple was all silvery. It started to rain hard. I ran and ran. Home seemed far away. It became darker and the rain came down harder. The gutters overflowed. My sneakers were soaked through and through. Lightning chased me. I was scared. I hugged my violin underneath my coat. I was closer to home and almost able to smell supper. The kitchen light was on. I banged at the door. The little man opened it. I stiffened. "Come in," Mama said. I wanted to break my violin. The man's eyes were hard and cold. I stumbled past them. Why must that man be there? The world is so big. Why was he home early tonight? I was going to play "Brahms' Lullaby" by heart tonight . . . for the first time . . . for Mama . . . .

Soon he was to be a fixture in our house. After many brawls he promised to make her happy. She believed him. I had to obey his commands and call him father. They danced and dined in the parlor every night. I was ignored. She was under his spell. I was unable to play the violin. Better to live in the fields, a barn or a haystack than in this tomb. I ate my meals in other homes: Mrs. Mervin, our best laundry customer, Mrs. Pantolini, who made big cakes with icing, Mrs. Alabate, who made the best apple pie, and Mrs. Kuntz, who always gave me a banana for dessert.

It was Sunday. I got up for early mass. I noticed a note in the lapel of my blue serge suit. "My dear boy—Mrs. Mervin will be over to take care of you. Love, Mama." Mrs. Mervin came with some groceries. She fixed my lunch and said, "Your mother telephoned me and explained everything and then some. That man, I can't stand him, but that's beside the point I guess. What has to be has to be. She married for your benefit, I guess."

A week later they returned. He banged at the door while I was playing the violin. We ate supper in silence. Would I be sent away? The neighborhood was gossiping about my future.

Three months later Mama decided to leave him. He complained about her cooking—too crisp on one side, no salt, less pepper. Mama's charm and sweetness failed to change him. Sweet syrup isn't extracted from stone. With him around her beauty faded. I watched his eyes while Mama combed her hair. He looked like a devil. Mama told me we would go to Mr. and Mrs. Cassie of Freeland, fifty-five miles from our home town.

He came home very drunk on paydays. One night he barged in laughing and cursing. "Send da boy away. Quick. I be back for you woman. I be back." He stormed out.

"Play lots of music for me."

"I play very little."

"The violin is clean. Keep it that way. And practice everyday."

"I will, Mama."

"It's all my fault."

"No, Mama, you were lonely."

"We'll go tonight to Freeland, I have friends there."

"I know. I remember."

"Nobody must know we're leaving."

We packed what clothes we had. We made our exit out the back way. The coal bin was filthy. We crept underneath the back porch. It was raining. Down the alley went our feet. Cats and tin can noises everywhere. If there had been a moon, the shacks in the alley ways would have been silhouetted against the sky. Someone was lurking behind a shack. If we could only see who it was. No cats purred. Footsteps came closer. We looked in all directions—back, front—"Look out, Mama! It's him!" His flashlight blinked at us. His club was large. He came closer. "It's you," shouted Mama, "Albano, the rabbit man." He clicked his flashlight. It was darker now than before.

"I won't hurt you or your son if you come in my shack. Come, come, the shack. I'll show you the rabbits. Your son can play with Whitey. The shack is warm. Why stay in a drizzle?"

The alley cats meowed.

He turned. "It's those friggin' cats." He screamed and sprang over the fence swinging his club. We started to run down the alley. Clickety-clickety-click. Our feet spanked the cement. That night we slept in a cheap dirty room.

Sunrise. Autos with wet bodies parked along the avenue. Familiar houses would soon be memories. The sun became warmer and friendlier. Church bells chimed six o'clock. A gas station man stared at us. Our suitcase became a burden. The avenue came to life. Women and men of all ages, carrying their lunches, walked hastily to the silk mill. Birds sang on tree branches. We reached the city park and sat down to rest. A man spoke to Mama. "The town is out to improve things, she really is," he said softly. A moment of silence. "Going away?" I sat still. Mama said nothing. "I'm sorry for asking so many questions so early in the morning. Only seven o'clock at that. Do you see Tom up

66

there painting the flagpole? Well, he don't dare to speak to anyone till he gets down on the ground. Well goodbye now."

Silence.

"What did the rabbit man want?"

"Nothing, nothing. Eat this sandwich."

"That hotel we slept at last night, it had a lotta bums in the lobby."

The bus station was crowded. We avoided faces. Mama pretended to make a phone call. I shrank between two phone booths. The bus driver shouted, "Freeland, last call for the seven o'clock bus to Free-land." We ran in the bus and sat way in the back. Finally the bus started. The clouds darkened. The rain started again, sweeping the highway and patting the bus windows. An hour and a half later the bus got up to Freeland. "All out for Freeland." We were the last ones out of the bus. Mama immediately called Mrs. Cassie.

At last we were in a friendly house. The cold rain pounded the slant-ing shingled roof. The warm kitchen said welcome over and over again. At supper time, Mrs. Cassie and her husband passed napkins and warm plates with chicken and potatoes. Her kindness made you forget that she was a funny woman with a big nose, heavy features and straight hair. Her blue wistful eyes gave you a feeling of happiness. You couldn't resist smiling back at her.

After a second helping of ice cream they insisted that we get some rest. Mama and I were to sleep in the same room. In such a home I could be happy.

"Could I take violin lessons here?"

"Tomorrow I'll buy you a new case for your violin."

"Mama, I . . ."

Someone was banging at the door. Mr. Cassie peeked out the front window. It was almost dark. A little man, soaked, stood there with shaking fingers. He knocked again and again. Mr. Cassie was frightened by the anger on the man's face. He telephoned the operator for the police. Mama and I and Mrs. Cassie went out the back way.

"Run to the bus station. Get away. Quickly, go! Go! Go!"

We started to run toward Main Street.

"Hurry, Mama, the bus station . . . run, Mama, run!"

The pale street lights gave little vision. It was silent except for dance music from a saloon, the heavy rain and our running feet . . . across streets, through a parking lot, a shack, and then—the shadow leaped like a panther. From his sleeve came the weapon. A shiny dagger. It was jabbed into Mama's breast many times. He fled. I knelt beside her body. Blood came from its wound, not like a fountain but like a steady stream. I held Mama close to me as the blood painted our gar-ments red. The heavy rain washed some blood into the gutter.

It was nearly dark. Another day had just ended. What was once a flower of the earth became a lifeless body. Mama passed away. Blood had taken liberty. I looked up and there were Mr. and Mrs. Cassie.

A few days later, Mrs. Cassie told me I was about to take a trip. She kissed me many times at the bus station. "You are going to live with your uncle, the fat one. He called here this morning."

The crowd at the bus station moved on toward the bus. "Now go to your seat." I thanked her for everything. "Take care of yourself." Those were her final words.

The town of Freeland faded away. The road became narrower—we passed a village, a town, a city. I was alone. The world seemed so much larger than before. I felt lost, deep down lost. "I'm going to live with my uncle." The words rode over and over in my mind. My belongings were in one large suitcase. The bus driver was very helpful. He smiled. I did too—for the first time in a long time.

"If you open the window the smell of the woods will come right in, for free too. After it rains the woods have a fresh green smell. Yep, she really has." While he talked I fell asleep hugging my violin.

I had a strange dream: I was a passenger on trolley car number 5, not a bus . . . blood flowing from a spring, down a mountain, to the sidewalk . . . I was back home. The wind whistled through the attic. I heard footsteps. A small shadow walked toward me. He took out a huge shiny dagger. I couldn't move or scream. Someone else screamed. I woke up.

"Wake up! Wake up!" I lifted my eyes. It was a passenger. "Better pick up your violin." I looked where he pointed. By my feet was my violin. I must have broken the strings in my sleep. Slowly I picked the pieces up. I looked out the window but saw nothing . . . nothing . . . .

The Adventure

by Harriet Sirof

The child fluttered in the doorway, hopping up and down with little excited hops. She ventured a few steps out into the darkness and then, in a rush of shyness, skipped back into shelter. She had never been out of the house so early before and she was overcome with the strangeness and daring of the hour. "Five-thirty in the morning," she said aloud to taste the wonder of it, and then realizing that it must be later because the kitchen clock had said exactly five-thirty as she left the apartment, changed it to "Twenty-five to six." Because she loved numbers she said it all, "Twenty-five to six in the morning, July seventh, nineteen hundred and thirty-eight." That sounded perfect.

The sound of the words engendered such security that she stepped out into the shadowy courtyard of the apartment building. The familiar courtyard where she played "Russia" and "points" during the day, bouncing her rubber ball against the brick walls, seemed as strange and mysterious in the pre-dawn light as if she were already in a foreign land.

She could hardly believe that today, this very morning, in just a few minutes, her father and mother were taking her to a foreign country, to Canada. She was a bookish and dreamy child as only children often are, and she was much taken with the romance of foreign places. Geography was her favorite subject in school and she always read ahead of the class for the delight of discovering the new countries without the teacher's interference. On the corner of the card table that served her as a desk she had pasted a listed of all the states she had ever been in: New York (where she lived), New Jersey, Connecticut, and Pennsylvania. When she came back from this trip she would add a country, Canada.

It was beginning to get light and she looked around for the sunrise, the reason for her permission to come down to the street alone. The walls of the courtyard cut off any real view of the sky and she was afraid to venture out alone into the deserted street. When she heard footsteps in the hall behind her she deliberately refrained from turning and pretended that it was a monster creeping up on her. She frightened herself and shivered in spite of the sweater her mother had made her wear. "Daddy," she called.

"Shh," he said coming up to her. "You'll wake the neighbors."

She fell into step next to him and they walked through the courtyard. She would have liked to hold her father's hand against the scary feeling of the deserted street, but he was carrying a suitcase in each hand. She stayed close to his side, taking protection from his presence, as they walked down Lincoln Place to the car. It was a 1932 model, bought second hand and not in very good condition, but the child did not know that. It was new to her, the first car the family had ever owned, and she thought it was wonderful. And this was the first automobile trip she had ever taken, and that was even more wonderful.

She watched her father strap the suitcases onto the luggage rack in back of the car. When he was finished she asked, "Where is the sunrise?"

"There it is." He pointed down the block to the intersection of Brooklyn Avenue where a section of reddened sky was visible between the two rows of buildings.

It was not what she had expected, but she looked at it with interest because it was the first sunrise she had ever seen and so was worthy of inspection. She wanted to ask her father a question, but before she could get it formulated in her mind he had turned back to the house. Her father was the one who had shaken her this morning saying, "Wake up Sleepyhead or you'll miss the sunrise," while her mother told him, "Let the child sleep," and now he was not even looking. She trailed after him looking back over her shoulder at the sun.

She wandered aimlessly around the apartment while her parents hurried purposefully back and forth carrying things and reminding each other, "Did you defrost the frigidaire, Dear?" "Are all the windows closed, Honey?" "Do you have the maps, Sweet?" and answering each other with annoyance, "I already told you I did, Dear" and "I am getting them now, Sweet." The child sat down at her card table desk and examined the three little dolls dressed in the native costumes of France, Italy, and China that her aunt had given her for her ninth birthday. She tried to imagine the native costume of Canada. Then she put the dolls back and took her rubber ball out of her pocket and began to bounce it counting out, "One, two, three, a-nation" and turning over skillfully.

"Stop that," her mother called from the kitchen, and she stopped. She leafed through her favorite Nancy Drew mystery, the one about the Indian Rajah that she had read seven times by actual count. Finally her mother called, "Where has that child gone to?" as if she were the one who was holding them up, and they left the apartment and closed the door behind them while her father got out his keys and her mother said, "Make sure you doublelock it, Dear."

The child had the back seat of the car to herself, or rather she shared it with a large thermos of lemonade, a picnic lunch, a bag of fruit "for tomorrow," an umbrella and two pairs of galoshes that would not fit into the suitcases, and her father's neatly folded jacket and tie. These assorted reminders of home made her feel both secure and adventurous, like Robinson Crusoe on the raft ferrying his provisions from the ship to the island. She also had three windows to look out of, two side windows to see where she was going and the back window to see where she had been.

At first, filled with the excitement of movement, she scrambled around looking first out of one window and then another, the three different views lending a special glamour to the passing streets. Then they were on the bridge, out of Brooklyn and into Manhattan. When the car entered the drive along the Hudson River she stationed herself at the lefthand window. She had been this way several times in her Aunt Edith's car and knew she was coming to the piers where the big boats docked. She was only allowed to have the window half open for safety so she stretched herself tall so that no glass barrier would be between her and the ships. She tried to guess which one would be in today. Perhaps even the Queen Elizabeth, the largest ship in the whole world.

"Daddy, look! The Normandy!" she cried. The Normandy was the third biggest boat, and therefore the third best to see.

"You've seen it before," said her father. "Just think, soon you will be in Canada. What an adventure that will be."

How could she have forgotten Canada even for a moment? "Will I be there today?" she asked.

"Yes," said her father.

"No," said her mother.

"We'll make Niagara Falls tonight," her father said, "so even if you aren't in Canada you will be able to see Canada."

"In the dark, Dear?" her mother asked. "You couldn't possibly make Niagara Falls today, Honey. It's more than five hundred miles."

"Less than five hundred, Dear. We'll be there tonight. I'm averaging thirty-five miles an hour and it's only seven o'clock."

"It's seven-thirty and you're lucky to average thirty. Less with stops, Honey."

The child was used to her father and mother contradicting each other and knew it would be some time before the truth came out, if at all, but she listened because she was anxious to know when she would first see a foreign country.

"Do you expect the Child to be able to take so much driving, Dear?"

71

her mother asked. The child squirmed. She hated when they talked about her. It always made her feel that she was to blame.

"The Child loves to be in the car," her father answered. The child tried not to listen. The George Washington Bridge was coming into sight. It was the longest suspension bridge in the world. That made the longest bridge and the third largest ship, all before breakfast.

Then the bridge and the river were gone and trees and grass were passing the windows. Her parents were silent, her father absorbed in his driving and her mother in her maps. The child said, "I'm hungry."

"See, Dear?" her mother said.

"We're going to have a breakfast picnic," her father said. "You never had a breakfast picnic before. Won't that be an adventure? Now you look for a nice place along the road to stop."

Every place looked nice, but none seemed nice enough for a breakfast picnic. She kept looking while she asked, "What do we have to eat?"

"Oranges and rolls and butter and hard-boiled eggs," her mother answered.

"Do I have to eat the egg whites?"

"Not on a breakfast picnic," her father said.

Her mother looked annoyed. "Do you have to encourage her to waste food, Honey?"

The child was still looking for the perfect picnic place when her father pulled over. She was not allowed to open the door herself (for safety) so she waited until her father came around to let her out. Then she stepped out to an unfamiliar place. She put her feet on strange grass. There was a scattering of trees a way back from the road and she headed toward them.

"Come here," her mother called. "You said you were hungry." The child looked longingly at the trees, but she had said she was hungry and now she was stuck with it.

"There will be time to explore later," her father promised.

The child sat on the grass and ate as quickly as she could. Her parents, sitting on the running board, ate as fast as if they too were eager to swing on the trees. Still chewing the last mouthful of roll and butter, the child wadded her wax paper into a ball, handed it to her mother and, receiving a nod of dismissal, raced to the trees. One tree had a long root stretched along the ground. She balanced herself on the root, putting one foot carefully before the other, pretending she was a tight-rope walker. Another tree had a strong straight limb only inches above her head. She grabbed the limb with both hands and swung her feet off the ground. She was a trapeze artist. It was more fun than going to the park, even better than going to Aunt Edith's bungalow last summer.

A voice from the car called her. She pretended not to hear, but it

72

called again, and she started reluctantly back. She scuffed her feet through a patch of tall grass, looking down because there wasn't much sense in looking up, and noticed that the grass was dotted with lacy white flowers. She bent to pick one and stood up again, thinking that they probably belonged to someone and you weren't allowed to pick them.

Her parents were in the car waiting for her. Her father got out and came around to put the child into the back seat. "There are white flowers in the grass," she said.

"Those are Queen Anne's lace."

"Could I pick some?"

"Well . . ."

Her mother poked her head out of the car window. "Do you want to make Canada tonight, Honey?"

Her father made up his mind, "Just one, quickly." The child dashed out, pulled one precious flower, and ran back to the car clutching it in her hand. As he threw the car into gear her father told her, "Those are wild flowers. You'll see plenty more of them and you can pick them whenever you want."

Her mother turned around, "Are you banging something back there?"

"No," the child said.

"Well, I hear something rattling."

Her father said, "It's probably the thermos sloshing, Honey."

Her mother returned to her maps. "It's twenty-four miles to Pough-keepsie," she announced.

Poughkeepsie had a nice sound. "Poughkeepsie," the child whispered to the flower.

"How far to Albany, Dear?" her father asked.

Her mother measured carefully. "Eighty-nine miles."

"Albany is the capital of New York," the child said.

"We'll be there by eleven-thirty," her father said.

"Not before twelve, Sweetie."

The child spoke softly to the flower, "Albany is the capital of New York, Trenton is the capital of New Jersey, Hartford is the capital of Connecticut . . . ." She could name all forty-eight capitals if someone gave her the states, but it was hard to name both the states and the capitals. She did thirty-nine, counting them on her fingers, and then she was stuck.

"Castleton-on-Hudson," her mother read from the map. "Six miles to Albany." Her mother read the name of each little town as they passed through and called the mileage to the next. At each town the child looked out of her window for signs with the town's name on them. She found "Entering Castleton-on-Hudson, Speed 20" and "Castleton Grocery." Her mother never seemed to look at the towns, just at the map.

"We'll be in Albany before noon, Honey," her father said to her mother, and then to the child, "Albany is the capital of New York."

For the first time it occurred to the child, "What is a capital?"

"Why, it's the place where the Legislature meets, where the men meet to make the laws. Like Washington, D.C. is the capital for the country, only this is for the state."

She was not sure she understood, but it seemed an intriguing idea. "Can we see them make the laws?"

"They don't work on Sunday."

That made sense. She watched out the window for "Albany" signs.

"We leave route 9 and pick up 5 in Albany," her mother said, so the child looked for "5" signs too.

She spotted a "5" and wanted to say so, but her mother was telling her father that she was sure she heard something rattling and her father was saying that he did not hear a thing and the child knew better than to interrupt. Her mother saw the sign, but it was too late. Her father got caught in a maze of one-way streets trying to get back, and they had to stop at a gas station to ask directions. They bought gas while they were there, and the service was slow. They hit heavy traffic going through Albany, and then there was two miles of construction on 5. The child counted three idle bulldozers parked along the side of the road.

"It is past one-thirty, Honey," her mother said accusingly as they pulled into a picnic ground for lunch. There were tables and other families eating and not much to explore, which was just as well because there would not have been time.

Then they were back in the car.

"Scotia," said her mother. "Amsterdam . . . Fonda . . . Herkimer . . . ." Her mother said, "You didn't tie the suitcases properly on the rack, Sweetie. I hear them rattling."

"That's just the end of the strap flapping, Honey."

"Utica," her mother said.

There were a great many Utica signs. The child counted twelve including "Utica Dry Goods" and "Utica High School," but she was wondering when they would get to Canada. She wanted to ask but her parents were talking about what the trip would cost and she knew that children were not supposed to know about money. She did know, though. She knew there was not enough. When she had wanted dancing lessons like her friend Cynthia, her mother told her that she was too young. "But Cynthia's three whole months younger than me," she had protested. "If Cynthia's mother wants to ruin Cynthia's feet, that is her business," her mother answered, but that night when her parents came to bed, long after she was supposed to be asleep, the child heard her mother being angry at her father because he did not make enough money so they could give their child dancing lessons like other children.

"Oneida," her mother called. "Sherrill . . . Canastota . . . Syracuse."

Syracuse was a big town. There were plenty of Syracuse signs, even the "Syracuse Funeral Home" and the child counted eleven passing taxis, but she was getting very tired of being in the car. She wished she had to go to the bathroom so she could make her father stop, but she knew if she said she had to, and she didn't really, her mother would be angry. She tried to picture Canada in her head, but her imagination failed her when she needed it most. She had seen it all when her father first told her that they were not going to Aunt Edith's for vacation this year, but were taking a trip to a foreign country. "It will be a wonderful adventure," he said, and the excitement in his voice made her see temples with bells, and canals, and a strange flag, and people in strange clothes, maybe even with slant eyes, though she knew that was China.

"Fairmont," her mother said.

"There's a diner, Honey," her father said. The child knew that diners were good places to eat. Her father had told her that the truck drivers ate there. He took her to a diner for supper one Sunday last winter when her mother had the flu. She had fried chicken and pie with ice cream on it.

"It doesn't look clean, Dear," her mother said and they drove past.

"Elbridge," her mother said.

"We're making good time," her father said. "At least we'll make Buffalo tonight. And Niagara Falls first thing in the morning."

"Never, Dear," her mother said.

The child knew that her mother was almost always right. Her father spoke as if wishing could make it so, and each time the child wished for her father's wish to come true, but each time her mother was right and he was defeated. Her mother was right this time, too. As they drove down the main street of Elbridge, the engine began to bang and the car bucked under her father's hands. "I told you all along I heard rattling, Honey," her mother said.

They left the car at the Elbridge Service Station, ate supper in the Elbridge Diner, and took a room in the Elbridge Guest House.

Later, the child wiggled around in the unfamiliar bed. Her parents were sitting on the porch below until she fell asleep and she could hear the buzz of their voices coming through the open window. She would have liked to go to the window to try to make out their words but the strangeness of the room kept her huddled in the safety of the bed. When her parents came in she lay still, pretending.

"Then we'll go to Edith, Dear," her mother said. "It will be hard on her, our not letting her know before, but she'll understand what happened."

"You wanted to go to your sister's all along."

"I wanted to do whatever you wanted, Sweetheart."

"You're glad it turned out this way."

"How can you say that, Honey? You know the mechanic said it would be suicide to take that old car any further unless you had the money to fix it properly."

"That would take all the trip money, and you know it."

"Well, Dear, if you don't have the money, why blame me because I like my sister's company?"

Her father had no answer. He was silent for a long while. Then he said, "The Child will be disappointed."

"At Edith's there's a lake for her to swim in and children her own age to play with. That's much better for her than sitting in a hot car all day."

"She wanted to see Canada."

"She's only a child and children get over things easily."

Only a child lay stiff against the unyielding mattress. She eased her left foot forward a fraction at a time. Her toenail made a scraping sound against the sheet and she stiffened again in fear of discovery. They must not know she was awake! Her whole body ached from her effort to lie still, but she was afraid to try to move again. She concentrated on the misery of her body. She did not know when she fell asleep.

She woke a long time later. The moonlight coming through the window was shining full on her face. It seemed to be telling her something. She slid quietly out of bed and padded barefoot to the window. The moon was low in the sky, round and big and beautiful. The child stood at the window and was comforted. "When I grow up," the child said to the moon, "I am going to a foreign country. To Canada. Alone."

East New York, 1953

by Susan Schwartz

I remember the warm and sticky candied yams that Daddy used to buy from the gray-haired vendor behind the steaming steel pushcart. That was when we still called him Daddy. Those were the days when he was Daddy and she was Mommy and I was The Big One and my sister was The Little One. Daddy used to take The Big One and The Little One to Blake Avenue to go shopping for Mommy. It would be winter. It would be cold.

Once upon a time, upon the time that The Big One and The Little One were both rather small, and for thirty years before that and for several years after, Blake Avenue was Brooklyn's open-air food market. Pushcarts brimming with fruit or vegetables or fish or nuts or sweets or cakes or breads were arranged in lines facing each other on opposite sides of the gutter. People would shuffle through the tissue-paper fruit wrappers strewn thickly over the asphalt path between the two rows of carts. Always behind the carts were middle-aged men, or old men and adolescent boys. I never saw a boy past adolescence or a man below middle age behind any of those carts. Occasionally, an old, old woman would be weighing off fruit or cutting bread, and she would always be wearing a frayed and dirty print head-kerchief. Years later I never let my grandmother wear a print head-kerchief.

All kinds of people shopped on Blake Avenue, especially on Sundays. There were old Jewish immigrants from Russia and Poland in greasy black coats, and there were second generation American Jewish housewives in dresses and high heels, and there were young Jewish laborers in patched knock-about pants and heavy jackets. Occasionally we would see some Irish or Italians, but for the most part, Blake Avenue, like the rest of the world, was Jewish.

Often as not, Daddy would meet a friend of his somewhere between the apples and the potatoes and they would stop to discuss the shop and the foreman and the landlord who never gave enough heat and how each would tell the other exactly what he thought of the landlord if the girls were not listening. And all the while The Little One and I would be hugging each other to keep from freezing and hoping that Daddy would hurry up and buy those potatoes so we could go home.

Home was where Mommy was. Mommy was wearing a full-length apron over her housedress and buttoned cardigan, and she was washing dishes in water that never got quite hot enough or stayed at the same temperature for two consecutive minutes. Or maybe she was on her hands and knees scrubbing the yellowed linoleum with detergent and steel wool. Or maybe she was crying and praying for Daddy to come home fast so he could get rid of the rat that was caught in the trap and making funny noises.

Finally, finally, Daddy would buy the potatoes. Then he would look down at us and say, "What! Are my girls cold?" and then he would take us to the steaming steel pushcart and order three hot, candied yams. We would all suck on the yams and warm our hands on them and The Little One and I would tell each other how much fun it was to go to Blake Avenue with Daddy.

When we would come home, Mommy would tell us to be careful not to slip on the freshly waxed floors. Then she would help us take off our coats and she would hug us and kiss us and make us some warm tomato soup.

Later, The Little One and I would have a nap, and Mommy and Daddy would have some quiet time together, time to discuss exterminating the roaches in the food cabinet, convincing a neighbor's cat not to drop dead mice in the hall, having both girls sleep in one bed so they could keep warm, sending the girls to college . . . .

Personal Relations

Counterpain

by Carol S. Shulman

Did you see me skipping today?
I skipped down the street, and then I ran a little.
And I was humming.
Did you see me?

Did you see me laughing today?
I laughed as I did when I was a child,
I laughed and I sang.
Did you see me?

I was happy today,
and I was carefree.
I did it all for you—
to show that I don't care
any more.

I hope you saw me today,
because I don't think
I could do it again
tomorrow.

Even after a Machine Is Dismantled, It Continues to Operate, with or without Purpose

by Sheila Ascher and
Dennis Straus

The author can't help feeling cornered in the summer home or cottage in the woods. The absurd wealth of nature that surrounds it is boring and repetitive, each leaf and pebble exactly the same and infinitely different from the others. To go on living here, one day after another, every 1440 minutes settling on every other 1440 minutes, over a vast, perhaps rotten bed of hours, seconds and centuries, must seem something like this.

```
                        1
                       111
                      11111
                     1111111
                    111111111
                   11111111111
                  1111111111111
                 111111111111111
                1111111111111111111
               111111111111111111111
              11111111111111111111111
             1111111111111111111111111 11
            1111111111111111111 1111111111
           11111111111111111111111111 1111111
          1111111111111111111111111111111111111
         1111111111111111111111111111 1111111111111
        1111111111111111111111111111 1111111111111111
       11111111111111111111111111111111111111111111111
      11111111111111111111111111111111111111111111111111
     1111111111111111111111111111 111111111111111111111111
    1111111111111111111111111111 11111111111111111111111111
   1111111111111111111111111111 1111111111111111111111111111
  11111111111111111111111111111111111111111111111111111111111
 111111111111111111111111111111111111111111111111111111111111 11
1111111111111111111111111111111111111111111111111111111111111111
11111111111111111111111111111111111111111111111111111111111111111111
1111111111111111111111111111111111111111111111111111111111111111111111
111111111111111111111111111111111111111111111111111111111111 1111111111
```

Still something, perhaps the author, seems to prevent Elizabeth from leaving.

One day Elizabeth borrows Walter's binoculars, which she finds in the living room, in a leather case. The sun is streaming through the bamboo shades and two dozen yellow rods of light slip off the smooth grain onto the slick cover of *Scientific American* and through the glass-topped coffee table.

She opens *Scientific American* at random and reads:

Mathematical Games

The rambling random walk
and its gambling equivalent

by Martin Gardner

He calmly rode on, leaving it to his horse's discretion to go which way it pleased, firmly believing that in this consisted the very essence of adventures.
—Don Quixote

The compulsive drifter who wanders aimlessly from town to town may indeed be neurotic, and yet even the sanest person needs moderate amounts of random behavior. A refreshing form of such behavior is traveling a random path. Surely the popularity of the great picaresque novels such as *Don Quixote* is due partly to the reader's vicarious pleasure in the unexpectedness of events that such haphazard paths provide.

Jorge Luis Borges, in his essay "A New Refutation of Time," describes a random walk through the streets of Baracas: "I tried to attain a maximum latitude of probabilities in order not to fatigue my expectation with the necessary foresight of any one of them." G. K. Chesterton's second honeymoon, as he describes it in his autobiography, was a random "journey into the void." He and his wife boarded a passing omnibus, left it when they came to a railway station, took the first train and at the end of the line left the train to stroll at random along country roads until they finally reached an inn, where they stayed.

Mathematicians insist on analyzing anything analyzable. The random walk is no exception and (mathematically speaking) is as adventurous as the wanderings of the man of La Mancha. Indeed it is a major branch of the study of Markov chains, which in turn is one of the hottest aspects of modern probability theory because of its increasing application in science.

A Markov chain (named for the Russian mathematician A. A. Markov, who first investigated them) is a system of discrete "states" in which the transition from any state to any other is a fixed probability that is unaffected by the system's past history. One of the simplest . . . .*

The author's optimistic zest for theory and abstraction seems to bore or irritate her, she shrugs, lays the magazine back on the glass table, slips the heavy binoculars from the leather case, lifts them to her eyes. By accident she's facing the windows and doesn't see a vast yellow-red blot that would have to be focused down to a wall with paintings.

*From "The Random Walk and Its Mathematical Equivalent" by Martin Gardner. Copyright © 1969 by Scientific American, Inc. All rights reserved.

She looks down through the windows into the underbrush and low trees. The "underbrush and low trees" become intersecting half curves: leaves, vines, branches, all steamrollered into a close-textured wall. Some dimension or depth or illusion of depth is removed. An illusion of lack of depth takes its place: distances disappear or flatten before and behind. Elizabeth, or the author, has this feeling: the binoculars sum everything up, perhaps a million years of tiny noises, deaths, aridity and fertile growth are packed tight and preserved like some sort of condensed food in dry ice or tubes of frozen jelly . . . .

Elizabeth may imagine that she's discovered another scale of things in the black, glassed-over tubes. As if she can project glass bridges into the distance, toward any desired point. The binoculars make her feel alone with space. Nearer to things and yet further from a sense of reality. The valley is sucked into the tubes and compressed into these discs that contain a million yards of space. The underbrush flattens into stiff arcs or fans, the air silvery along their edges. Fan presses on fan presses on fan on fan on fan on fan on fan forward back and side-wise.

The middle distance of dark green hills is even more compact and thick-textured. Not one speck of light shows through the hills.

Beyond the hills the compactness of things gives way entirely. Some broad space intervenes. And in that space the condensing force of distance loses its hold. As if the hand that gripped things has opened up. Blue distances, level silver-grey stretches of water are released. Her being follows this material line of development and experiences a disturbing sense of freeing and opening . . . . The view is like the one she had seen without the binoculars from the upper terrace, the lower terrace, the windows, the road, the lower terrace, the windows, the upper terrace, the road, etc. etc.

She wonders if she's free, why she's here, is this what her vacation was meant to be, is the real vacation beginning now, in the binoculars, is it all lies and fancy talk arising out of boredom, is William right for slipping himself like an extra suitcase into all the real and metaphysical baggage of these people who are returning to New York in two or three weeks, is there any freedom beyond the metaphoric one of an ideal and unlivable condition. These questions are packed into the steamrollered leaves, fans, trees, mountains, open spaces like glass in straw.

Or, she may not think or wonder anything, she's long past the point of examining the nature of her condition or of all these steaming heaps of haphazard and rounded geometry, it's only we who seem to require an explanation, or at least a puzzle that can be solved in our leisure hours, like a crossword of infinite dimensions.

Elizabeth descends to the lower terrace with the binoculars. The view is very much the same. Let's say: she continues to feel lost in an ambiguous condition—slipping into open space along the doubtful shuttle of a metaphor. Bird cries: raspy and broken or threadlike and musical: materialize swiftly and become visible in her lenses. The audible or musical becomes the visible or spatial, so that it becomes possible to feel or imagine one is gazing at musical notes turned to yellow glass threads, red globes, blue spirals, etc.

Despite the fact that she's half-dissolved in an ambiguous and open condition on the hot flat of the terrace, she may wonder why she takes pleasure or interest in watching what may be nothing but a banal or hothouse reproduction of the fertile nature of our dreams: the unexpected and exaggerated forms of life, for example, that appear like drops of paint against a curiously flattened landscape. She isn't a birdwatcher by nature, Walter's *Temple's Field Guide*, his conservation magazines, and so on, leave her cold. All these charts, graphs, crossing files of words like Energy (Thousand Electron Volts) and Time (Minutes) or Depth (Feet) or Volume (Cubic Meters), strike her as a technical escape-route from reality. Automotive magazines come to mind, or manuals of electrical equipment.

Or she may not be thinking about Walter and his magazines at all. She may be wondering what happens to birds when they die. Do they drop straight out of the air; rot in the grass; red, blue and yellow turning brown, black, grey; eaten by beetles, ants, flies, worms, larvae, bacteria, viruses; begin to resemble lumps of dung, then earth, then ash.

The screen door bangs on the upper terrace, breaking off her thoughts quite sharply.

A few seconds pass, the sound of shoes on the lawn, William appears on the lower terrace from the direction of the stairs, the lawn, the apple tree. His face is set and closed, as it has been on and off since they've rejoined. He has something to say but seems to be waiting for her to say it. She isn't willing to smooth the way: if he wants to "open up" it will be up to him.

The red-grey surface of the terrace becomes immeasurable.

"Walter took a look at my eyes. It may be nothing but a cold. But he isn't sure," he says.

It's true, each of his eyes looks something like a cherry pit. On the other hand, it isn't the first time he's complained or hidden behind his eyes. Perhaps if he said what was in his heart everything would return to normal, they would embrace. Elizabeth might even be willing to return or consider returning home.

She relents and smooths the way. Does he want to say anything? she asks, is anything bothering him, aside from his eyes?

85

Oh, no, he protests. Of course not, no. He just wanted to see, well, how she was getting along.

"Well, I think I'll see what's on the radio."

His tone has a familiar ring: vacationer's false heartiness or something in that vein. The air remains tense with possibilities that seem bound to remain unexplored, bit by bit it slackens off and he fades away.

Ellen appears on the upper terrace, calls and waves gaily. Someone is with her. Both of them are wearing dungarees. Ellen invites Elizabeth to come up out of the heat and sit with them under the tree, where she's put out a few chairs. She finds a chair and a whiskey sour waiting for her in the grass.

This apparent thoughtfulness surprises her. All solicitousness has begun to arouse her suspicions.

They talk about this and that—the new power station on the river, for example, where red-and-blue towers are just visible with the naked eye. Through Walter's binoculars one can almost spy on the operations of the plant, which, it's rumored in the community and in the conservation magazines, have something to do with atomic energy, count the number of bricks in the odd, dome-topped structure. Elizabeth says that she *has* counted the number of bricks and the number, supposing the back to be equal to the front, is 104,121. Everyone laughs over that, and Ellen's friend, who has driven down from her year-round home in the hills, objects that the number must be *much* greater than that, really, around a million.

Sooner or later they drop the subject of the power plant and the question as to whether the touch of the human added to the valley by the power plant and red-and-blue towers is ugly or beautiful and Ellen raises the question of monogamous relationships. She knows it's old hat, she says, but it seems to her the problem isn't a moral one but one of boredom and stagnation.

Boredom and dependency, the friend modifies.

Monogamous relationships are the result of fear, insecurity, etc. She sometimes worries about that. More recently than before.

"That you're dependent on Walter or that . . . . ?"

Both. More that Walter depends on her. But, after a while, you lose your freedom, boredom saps your energy and desire . . . .

Sexually, marriage or monogamy is a stupid convention, a real prison . . . . Both love and desire melt away with the years and what's left is a pure mechanism, lies, false sentiment.

Or pornography. Eroticism with no emotional overtones or undertones. She's not ashamed to admit that the sexual games one plays in married life are infinitely, let's say, *dirtier* than anything between lover and lover. Every new relationship is like the founding of a new society.

Everything is mysterious and invigorating. While in marriage eroticism has to be whipped up through the most bizarre fantasies.

Not that one can't continue to get a certain emotional satisfaction . . . .

The only solution, *obviously,* is for both partners to come to an intelligent understanding. Whereby one can satisfy one's erotic needs, let off steam, without all the bourgeois deception, stifled auto-eroticism, pornography, yet maintain one's relationship on an emotional plane . . . .

Yes. Doesn't Elizabeth agree that it's possible, and desirable, to conduct two relationships at once? After all it's pure bull that sexuality has anything to do with sentiment. Nothing could draw more attention to man's biological nature. What's more, an excursion or vacation is sometimes essential to breathe in new life.

Elizabeth doesn't answer, but neither Ellen nor her friend seems to care. The friend, in fact, begins to relate an anecdote of revitalizing infidelity.

Elizabeth's attention is absorbed by Ellen's dungarees, which are faded, particularly at the knees, where there's no blue at all; and a seam is open at the thigh, an inch of white skin showing softly through. She strikes Elizabeth as self-indulgent and false. She begins to wonder if the conversation is purely theoretical. Ellen's face and hair form a yellow aura against the hot masses of foliage and the hairy mound of the middle distance.

A few days later Walter, Elizabeth, William and Ellen go climbing. The climb is hot and exhausting, something like climbing a rope of thorny vines that hangs from a naked and blazing sky. Bit by bit they pass out of the familiar zone of black and silvered-over lakes ringed-round with green woodland speckled with brown, above that brown woodland speckled with green. Green light gives way to brown shadow, paths of salmon-red clay that are like bridlepaths sprinkled with tanner's bark. The forest is dotted with luminous flakes of yellow, and brown-green with decaying vegetable matter that resembles rotten sponges and steel wool soap pads.

Elizabeth feels more and more walled off by exhaustion and wonders if all this labor and heat is worth reaching some local tourist attraction, called "The Tip," "The Top," or, senselessly, "Le Temps," or "Le Tapis Vert," or "Tant Pis," which offers nothing but still another view of the valley.

It seems to her that all along the way Walter takes the opportunity to drop back, pass a remark—that such and such a rock is gneiss, or shale, or pegmatite—lend her a hand in the dry stream beds, or else fall behind altogether in order to watch her from behind.

She wonders about his peculiar behavior, which seems to be cut from the same cloth as Ellen's solicitous chair and whiskey sour in the shade, and finds it irritating.

Perhaps, she speculates, Walter has noticed her indifference or coldness toward William and thinks he smells an opportunity. He can see or thinks he can see that she's bored. Her detachment, keeping to herself, borrowing his binoculars, mooning on the terrace, sitting in one place for 1 hour, 4 hours, 14 hours, 31 days, 300 years.

The yellow-brown speckles and decayed vegetable matter give way to sunbaked rockfaces and stunted pines.

They reach a level space that may be the top. The trees, scrub pines and some other broad-leafed variety, are even more low and twisted, the thin soil and bare, broken rockfaces are densely crosshatched with blueberry runners. Blue-purple dots and pointed leaves. The footing is smooth and easy, but the bald rock is extremely hot. The four of them crawl around for a quarter of an hour, eating blueberries, pretending to find the tart and underdeveloped little berries delicious, Elizabeth holds a dozen or so in her palm. Some are a delicate mauve, others are a deep violet. She loses interest, walks a few yards and parts the branches of the tough and spiny shrubbery. For an instant she feels as if she's passed through a wall into blue and empty space. The familiar valley spreads out as something of a surprise, more vast and also more trivial than before. She sees dark green slopes a thousand inches or a hundred miles wide, swollen rivers of trees whose flow in time is fixed in countless spatial curves, a lifetime or a million lifetimes, all those mysterious, apparently inanimate existences one didn't have time to explore. In the central distance she discovers or postulates low-lying farmland, with its hard, shaved and sunbaked patches of red-brown. Here and there something sparkles like a coin.

She has Walter's binoculars with her and looks through them, perhaps wondering how many scraps of the human have, over the centuries, been hammered into this landscape like new nails. The sparkling coins, for example, may be aluminum silos or the silver fillings of murder victims who've been left to rot in the forest, but even with the binoculars she can't be certain. Instead four tremendous birds make wide pinwheels in the lenses, cut into and out of the mild silver of nothingness. The tubes pressed to her eyes block out everything else and she can't help feeling herself to be nothing but a mirror of the glittering emptiness of the atmosphere, the fertile desolation of the valley, three or four pinwheels of unreasonable fear . . . .

The others lose interest in blueberrying. They gather around Elizabeth and speculate as to kind and purpose of the birds. Almost without question, they're vultures, Walter asserts. And the way they're circling can only indicate one thing, a dead animal, and not a small one either.

They soon lose interest in that also. Perhaps all the hard work of climbing has nullified every semblance of freedom from cares or civilized-and-rational contemplation of nature and an unidentifiable craving is provoked. Or, Walter and Ellen have had a definite purpose in mind all along and only appear to make a spontaneous decision to walk a little further on. Elizabeth elects to stay where she is and look at the boring view for the next week or month or millisecond. William takes a hint and goes off to sulk. Everyone disappears. Elizabeth sits on the hot rock, her blouse is plastered to her back, she unbuttons two buttons at the top. A strong breeze blows out of the woods, propelling a moist and thermal shadow out of her body, over the valley. She feels cooler and weaker, though not quite ready to be picked apart by the birds of prey that are hidden behind some vast hump of rock and trees.

In five minutes Walter comes slipping back. He asks, "Ah, you don't intend to come up where *we* are, do you? You're staying here?"

That's right, Elizabeth answers. Or it *was* right. Now of course he's succeeded in arousing her curiosity.

Ellen's taking a sunbath, he explains, and she doesn't want any strangers, or even William, to . . . He stops, looks hot and sly. Well, if she promises not to tell William or to tell Ellen that he told, because he was just supposed to make sure no tourists were coming up the trail.

Elizabeth promises, out of indifference more than anything else.

Past those bushes, he says, there's another, even broader outcropping. One can lie down there very comfortably in the sun. Like a loaf of bread in a brick oven. Or like a brick red lizard. A girl who had hiked up here alone, and who was quite sure no one else was there, might very well choose the spot to sunbathe. Ellen is going to pretend she's the girl. She doesn't know he's been there the whole time, blueberrying, or contemplating suicide, and he's seen her go by. Right now she's taking off her blouse and her bra and she's lying down on the warm rock. He'll wait a few minutes, then sneak back through the shrubs and spy on her, maybe shoot some film. Then he'll have to decide what to do next. She may want to even out her tan and remove the rest of her clothes. Then he might sneak up and steal her things while she's sleeping, wait to see how she reacts when she wakes up, sees they're gone. Or else he'll just reveal himself and toy with his prisoner, whose naked back will be pressed up against a wall of open space. Or crawl forward and Ellen will pretend not to see him or pretend to be pretending she doesn't see him, turn over on her stomach, hoping he'll be satisfied and go away or enjoying this opportunity to have her rounded body examined from every angle.

Elizabeth doesn't feel much of anything. Or she doesn't know what she feels. Walter's motives are also a mystery.

Why did he tell her? she asks.

Walter seems puzzled. "Just like that," he says. Or, "Because you asked, how should I know!" Or he may smile and say, "It doesn't have to be *one* girl, you know . . ." It's even possible that the two girls have chosen this arid spot because of its isolation, they want to be alone, to lie side-by-side in the blazing sun. She looks at him uncomprehendingly, he hesitates, shrugs, warns her again about William and slips off into the shrubbery.

That night or the next night William is outside, possibly making a fire in the grate. Ellen is taking a bath.

Elizabeth is daydreaming behind a magazine in the living room.

Or it's just possible that her interest is actually absorbed in the Sunday supplement of a local newspaper, there's a two-page spread on a bizarre and grisly murder. No doubt there's some tale of murder or inexplicable brutality or sly exploitation every week, always in the same style: "Marie-Claire Janicek, a blonde, blue-eyed bundle of mini-skirted vitality, had high aspirations when she set out one day in her bright orange convertible. . . ." The article goes on to recount how this Marie-Claire, with her somewhat incongruous last name, sets out one evening to audition as a singer in a nightclub or cabaret in a nearby city. The place isn't much to speak of, it's pretty seedy in fact, there are strippers, possibly topless dancers or something like that, but it may seem to her to be a step in the right direction, you never can tell who might drop in and notice her, stranger things have happened, and if she lands the job her husband will be thrilled. . . . The reporter seems to make an effort to arouse one's sympathy or to gloss the ugly tale with a vaguely liberal social message: it seems, he or she points out, that Marie-Claire Janicek spent her girlhood in a small agricultural town, dreaming of the larger world. And so, when, after having put on her favorite purple minidress and tried her best to make herself into an object of love and seduction for all who heard-and-saw, or at least for the stocky owner of the Zanzibar Lounge, or the Eighth Wonder Cabaret, or the Malibu Club, she fails to get the job, she can't be more depressed. "Her booking agent and one of his employees walked the disheartened Marie-Claire to her car in the parking lot of the lounge. They watched her drive away and her agent noticed it was 10:35 p.m. Neither man was to know until much later that Marie-Claire pulled her yellow convertible into a gas station a few blocks from the lounge, on Bates Avenue, near the old Wheat Exchange, once considered to be a storage depot for underworld merchandise. It seems the car's tail-light needed fixing." Elizabeth or the author can't help feeling that the reporter leaves various psychological avenues unexplored in relation to this crucial point. The most obvious being the trivial, even absurd reason offered for Marie-Claire Janicek's stopping in the station, thus delaying the moment when she would return, empty of possibilities, to her mediocre suburban street, her home, her husband: to all the static elements of a life that's already begun to slide into boredom and death.

"By all odds," the obtuse reporter continues, "Marie-Claire should have arrived at the Janicek home before midnight. As the hours passed and his wife failed to return, Sam Janicek wondered if he should report her missing to the police. He paced the floor and finally fell into a fitful doze shortly before 7 a.m. Tuesday."

At 8 o'clock, a retired hotel clerk named Arbogast is walking his dog; he allows it to pull him into a lot or field next to a rectangular structure of unadorned stucco or concrete that seems to house a printing plant. Among the weeds, soda caps and pull-tags, flattened beer cartons, table legs, broken glass, bits of blue-ruled copybook notepaper covered with curls of scrawl like this: "in 1776 the colonists decided to live their own lives, threw off the yolk of the rulers and exploiters from across the sea . . .": he's amazed to see a naked blonde girl lying beside a turquoise-colored bulldozer about 10 feet from the edge of a paved parking lot.

"It was apparent to the first detective at the scene that the girl had been beaten, stabbed and strangled. She had been slashed numerous times across the throat. A single stroke had severed the larynx and the jugular vein. There was a circle of stab wounds in her chest. One knife wound had penetrated the heart. Several front teeth were missing; a deep gash stretched across the top of the girl's head.

"A Coroner's Deputy said the young woman could have died as the result of any one of the numerous and massive wounds. Later examination was to reveal that she had bled to death.

"Police said the killer apparently had used two types of weapons—a blunt instrument and a sharp one. Neither was found at the scene.

"The killer had stripped off his victim's clothing except for a silver shoe and the right leg of a beige-colored pair of panty hose. A dinner-type diamond ring on the third finger of the victim's left hand discounted robbery as a motive.

"Because of the small amount of blood found at the scene, investigators surmised that the killer had washed the body after death. Bloodstains on the pavement of the parking lot indicated that the body had been dragged from a car to the spot where it was found beside the bulldozer.

"The Office of the Coroner reported that first examinations of the body indicated that the girl had been killed between 11 p.m. and 3 a.m.

"In the absence of any pin-pointing clues to the identity of the dead girl or the killer, investigators swarmed out from the scene of the murder, questioning dozens of persons in the area."

Hundreds of detectives nose around, hoping some scrap of information will prove more real or unreal than the crossing highways, the littered fields, the small unadorned factories of stucco or concrete, the mediocre suburbs, the lounges or cabarets with their stocky owners who give two lines of grudging and useless information: "I wouldn't have known unless you told me that this girl was named Janicek. She used the name Cora Samuels. All these girls think it sounds better to have a name like that. . . . She left about 10:30. She was wearing a purple dress. She sang five numbers or so, I wasn't impressed, you could see she was disappointed, and she left. That's all." "Nothing else?" "Yeah. She had nice legs, but a lousy voice."

"Initially, detectives had no luck in their attempts to trace Marie-Claire's movements after leaving the parking lot of the Zanzibar. Then, thanks to the conspicuous color of her convertible, they got an unexpected break. A woman reported to them that she had seen the red car with a blonde in a purple dress at the wheel, on Monday night at a service station on Bates Avenue.

"What particularly interested the investigators was the fact that the gas station was only two blocks from the Malibu and three blocks from the vacant field or lot where Marie-Claire's body was found.

"Police interrogated the owner of the station, Arthur Hitchcock, and his employees. They learned that the night before a new employee, H. Ronald Anthony, had been on duty. Anthony, lanky, with a flat-top hairdo, had closed the station at midnight, on schedule, and on Tuesday had reported for work as usual."

The next morning, Anthony is brought in for arraignment. His wrists are hand-cuffed to the belt of his blue coveralls, he answers the questions that are put to him calmly and in a firm voice.

"At the hearing the assistant manager of the station reported that Anthony had worked the 2 p.m.-to-midnight shift. On Tuesday, the assistant manager had noticed one unusual thing. The clock in the gas station had stopped at 2:30. Then, on the following day, he had discovered that a tool—a punch—was missing from the station. He described it as about a foot long, 3/4 of an inch square at the top and tapering down to about 1/4 of an inch.

"And, he also testified, the station owner had called his attention to dark reddish smudges, apparently dried blood. They were on the wall near the clock, on the back of a company truck and on a tire. This macabre testimony," the reporter goes on, apparently feeling duty-bound after all this time to disassociate himself or herself from the ugliness and brutality in which he or she's imprisoned his or her readers, "was expounded on by a criminologist attached to the sheriff's

92

office and who is qualified as an expert in the field of human blood.

"At the service station, he testified, he had detected spots of dried blood near the clock, in a rear washroom and on either side of the door frame, on a broom handle and on a hoist used to lift cars. He also had found wet blood in a drain, and he estimated that large amounts— at least a pint—had been poured down the drain.

"In the tongue well of the black boots that Anthony had been wearing, the expert witness told the court, there also had been blood. More, he disclosed that the plastic window which had been torn off Miss Janicek's car bore bootprints—and he linked the prints to Anthony's boots.

"The implication was that Marie-Claire was murdered in the garage, perhaps in the rest room, and then was later dumped into the vacant field."

It may seem to Elizabeth that the article is never going to end, the reporter and the readers of the supplement can't get enough of the technical details of this more-or-less conventionally senseless crime, with its melodramatic roots in Marie-Claire's aspirations, her depression, her poor childhood, the psychotic background of the murderer, which is also developed at great length. It comes as no surprise that he lives alone with his mother in an old frame house, that 8 or 12 years ago, when he was a marine stationed in Korea or something like that, he slit the throat of or strangled a barmaid after 12 seconds of making out. The evidence was flimsy, his mother pleaded with the court, he was given a relatively short sentence and so on. . . . Everything fits into place: Even chance plays its foreordained role and Marie-Claire's aspirations and disappointment, in the guise of a tail light that may or may not be on the blink, drives her into the isolated garage at the moment when the psychotic marine is alone in the station. . . . Nothing is omitted, as if everyone had rehearsed his role for 1000 years.

All that's left is for the murderer to offer an explanation in his own words, no matter how irrational. Then everything will fall perfectly into place, the reporter will have done his or her job of piecing together a machine of psychological and circumstantial necessity that works to our satisfaction, and which comes to a definite end. The ex-marine is therefore questioned, perhaps in court, and he responds satisfactorily:

"When she first drove her orange sports car into the station, I saw her pretty legs. The impulse to have relations with her was very strong. I hadn't touched a woman since that girl in Korea. This girl in the car was a lovely, warm person, I could see that right away. I could see the possibility of romance. I looked into her eyes and saw the woman I had always waited for.

"I grabbed her by the arm and she sorta let out a gasp. 'Don't say anything,' I told her, 'or I'll kill you.' I kept her in the garage, but she tried awful hard to get out. I remember one time, after I'd taken off her clothes, and beaten her and choked her pretty bad, she still tried to crawl out. I was surprised. So I had to find ways to keep her quiet so I could wait on customers. After I strangled her again it still looked to me like she was alive. She had a smile on her lips and seemed to be trying to tell me something. She had a secret. I suddenly realized the truth about myself and this truth was the only thing—that she wanted me to kill her."

Does anything else happen, or is it ·possible that this ugly story is the end of the road, Elizabeth fades into the murdered Marie-Claire Janicek, or perhaps the story is really American, it's been adapted for a European audience and the girl's name is Marian Crane or Marie Samuels . . .? Walter may come in, drop into a chair, pick up a copy of something like *The German Journal of Conservation* or *The Modern Surgeon's Newsletter*. Minutes pass, the two of them sit there reading, there ought to be a fan that winds time into circles and distributes them throughout 100 years or 1,000,000 miles of space.

Walter looks up from his magazine and says sympathetically or analytically:

"You're bored, aren't you?"

"Is that the way it seems to you?"

He doesn't answer, and may even return to his magazine. He's reading an article about a river in South America. It seems that if a dam is constructed according to plans developed by local politicians and foreign industrial interests, the valley will be flooded like a bathtub, thousands will be homeless, in fact it will take no more than days or weeks for an entire sub-civilization to be lost forever, as if it had existed 2000 years ago. . . . After a few minutes he renews his efforts.

"Have you ever thought how fascinating it would be if we could all change places?"

Elizabeth says uncomprehendingly that she doesn't understand. "Do you mean the four of us, or everyone?"

"Everyone, the four of us, it doesn't matter. It would be like one of those comedies, say *Twelfth Night, or What You Will*, where a pretty girl has a twin brother, she's in love with her lord, the Duke of Naples, but the Duke is in love with a certain lady, he disguises the girl as a boy and sends her to the lady's place, to worm her way into her confidence somehow and find out who she loves or something like that . . . . The lady falls in love with her . . . . Meanwhile the twin brother gets mixed up in it somehow. . . . If William and I could change places, it would be just the same, like a play. . . ."

"What makes you think William will go for it?"

"No problem there, really."

94

"And me? Did it occur to you there might be a problem there, that you might not be the answer to my prayers?"

He laughs, says that he's surprised she fell for it, he was just pulling her leg . . . It's just that he's sometimes thought that nothing is more melancholy than literature in the face of life; unless it's life in the face of literature . . . Time is so short, one is never allowed to explore life's real depths . . . The only way out is for invention to be able, *actually*, to pass over into reality and reality into invention. . . . To wish or invent a circumstance, to fantasize and have it become actual. . . . And conversely to actually pass into the printed page. . . . He has certain fantasies, for example, he wishes would materialize and there are certain books he wishes he could pass into. . . .

And would others be aware that they were being let's say actualized or absorbed into these fantasies . . . ?

That's something he hasn't worked out. But offhand he thinks some intermediate state of awareness with loss-of-will would be best. . . . Everyone subject absolutely to the will and imagination of everyone else, while absolutely retaining his personality. . . .

Elizabeth may allow Walter to return to his magazine. Walter and Ellen have told her about themselves and about each other, all their queer little theories and anecdotes, and may become frightened. She doesn't like Walter. She doesn't like Ellen. She goes to the window and is surprised to find that it's already growing dark, not only in the forest, but from one of the universes to the other.

Oscar

by Luz Hubbard

One Monday morning, after my family had returned from a week-
end in the country, my neighbor stopped me as I was sweeping the
sidewalk. She came down her stoop with a determined air, and her
eyes were full of the things she wanted to say.

"Those kids were in your yard again," her shrill voice said, her thin
finger shaking under my nose. "I know where they live—in that rundown brownstone around the corner. Someday you'll come home and
find the windows broken and everything gone."

I tried to reassure her. "Nothing's missing yet."

"Dirty, filthy Puerto Ricans," she continued sputtering. "Living on
relief—taking our money—. Foreigners—why don't they go back to
where they belong?"

For a brief moment, these words disturbed me. A long time ago
when I was a child of eight, I had been told that I was a "dirty foreigner" because my mother wore a shawl. My parents were immigrants
from Spain and although I was born in New York City, much was still
new for them. But this was a long time ago and I was no longer a foreigner. The thought was rightfully buried as belonging to the forgotten
past. Still, her remarks about the children being in the yard troubled
me.

We live in a corner brownstone in Brooklyn. Only a five foot cyclone
fence separates our backyard from the street. My rock garden of herbs
is nearest the fence. Under some pussywillows and forsythias, I grow
iris. Two rows of tomato plants are bordered by marigolds, zinnias,
and petunias. During the spring and summer, the yard is bright with
color. In the center of the yard, we have tried to grow grass but a sandbox, a wading pool, and swings have long usurped the grass. The swings
have been the latest addition and the favorite playthings of my son,
Jonathan, and daughter, Barbara. Frequently we leave the backdoor
open or forget to lock the back windows while away. For the first time
since living in the house, I was concerned.

That afternoon, I took a walk around the corner to take a good look at that "rundown" house. Debris spilled over the garbage cans. Windows were wide open with plastic curtains flying out. Some children sat on the steps playing, shoeless. A baby toddled out from the hall nude and sat down among them. Wild, bongo music was being played at an ear-splitting tempo. What Mrs. Mann had told me was true. These people were dirty and ignorant, probably dishonest. I resolved to do what I could to catch some of their children in my yard.

One Sunday, several weeks later, the children had gone to Prospect Park with their father so I could get some sleep. I had had a miserable night and now had a mountain-size headache. From the bay window in Barbara's blue and white bedroom, I watched them go up the street toward the Grand Army Plaza. Barbara's blond curls bounced up and down while she held her father's hand and Jonathan's chubby legs had difficulty matching his steps to theirs.

I had just closed my eyes when I thought I heard a noise in the yard. I arose and glanced out the window. Sure enough, a little boy about nine years old with dark hair and eyes had climbed over the fence from the street.

Aha, I thought, I'll just watch him for a while and when he least suspects it, I'll run downstairs and corner him.

Wearing sneakers, he tiptoed through the tomato plants. He squatted to look at the yellow tomato flowers and the small tomatoes. I noticed his sweater was worn at the elbows and his dungarees had been patched over and over again. As he came down over the stone in the rock garden, he stopped before the vivid zinnias and bright marigolds. Holding the marigolds close to his nose, he sniffed deeply. The odor must have displeased him for he wrinkled his nose and then seemed to chuckle. Passing the petunias, he stroked the bell-like petals tenderly.

As he came to the sandbox, I leaned forward to see better and the curtains stirred. His dark eyes looked up, frightened. He stood motionless. A few moments later, he relaxed and sat on the rim of the sandbox.

I wondered what he was up to. Was it the sandbox, I asked myself. Was he planning some mischief in the sandbox?

I saw him cup the sand and let it slowly drift through his fingers. A pail and shovel lay nearby but these he left untouched. He sat there quietly. A boy in a sandbox.

After a while a great sigh seemed to shake him to his toes. He arose and stood by the swings. Looking around, he sat on a swing and began kicking his legs so that he could push himself out. The breeze blew his black hair over his eyes and I could see even white teeth as he smiled. I heard low, happy laughter.

He looked no more like a dangerous foreigner than my own son. Just another little boy on a swing. I thought back to the time when the girls on my block wouldn't play with me because I "talked funny."

And the day I was registered for school when the registrar refused to record me as "Luz," the name I had been given. She had said it was "too foreign."

I resolved to go down to the yard and talk with this little boy. I ran down the steps toward the kitchen and out to the backyard. My hurried footsteps must have frightened the dog, Laddie, for he started to bark. When I opened the door, the boy was climbing back over the fence.

"Please, *por favor*," I stammered in Spanish. "You don't have to climb my fence." Opening the gate to the street, I motioned to him to return. "See, you can come in and play in the yard. My son will be home soon and you can play with him."

At the top of the fence, he eyed me suspiciously. *"Solo quiero mecer.* I only wanted to swing," he tried to explain in a low voice.

I looked into his face and saw myself standing with my father and mother at the foot of the Statue of Liberty at Bedloe's Island. It was I who translated for them the words of Emma Lazarus as they listened intently.

> Give me your tired, your poor,
> Your huddled masses yearning to breathe free,
> The wretched refuse of your teeming shore,
> Send these, the homeless, tempest-tossed, to me,
> I lift my lamp beside the golden door.

With these words echoing within, I put out my hand to the boy on the fence. "Come," I said.

He took it hesitantly and climbed back. "Is okay?" he asked.

"It's okay," I told him, and suddenly we smiled at each other. Each of us had made a new friend.

From this experience of twenty-five years ago with Oscar Castillo grew a happy life-time exchange of friendship between the Hubbards and the Castillos. When the Castillos first came to Brooklyn from Puerto Rico, they had a furnished room in "that rundown house." This one room contained a bed for Señor and Señora Castillo, a cot for their daughter, Carmen, and a stuffed armchair for Oscar to sleep in. A two-burner gas stove, a broken-down refrigerator were the other "conveniences" for twenty-five dollars a week. At that time they received subsistence welfare payments, but as soon as Señor Castillo found steady employment, this assistance was not needed.

Within a few weeks, the Castillos moved from this furnished room to a four-room apartment a few blocks away. Oscar is now married and in the Air Force stationed in Virginia. He served in Vietnam after graduation from John Jay High School. Carmen, who became one of Barbara's best friends, also graduated from high school and found employment in the Social Security Administration. She is living in Isabella, Puerto Rico, with her husband and two children. The elder Castillos have bought a house in the Park Slope area.

Occasionally I go up to the roof of our brownstone in Brooklyn. From there I can see the upraised arm of the Statue of Liberty in New York harbor. I'm glad her "lamp" beckoned to my father and mother a long time ago, glad she continues to beckon to families like the Castillos. And I am especially glad I did not fail her altogether on that long ago day.

Some Minor Calamities

by Marion Lipkins Wiesner

Flour was everywhere, tacky tools and bowls, sticky and soggy, sat. Sara thought to herself, "When Al gets home tonight, I hope he'll be pleased with the meal." She was really happy in her kitchen. This was one of her favorite rooms and preparing good food was one of her main concerns. At times the kitchen looked like a deserted battlefield, with evidences of a monstrous, monumental maneuver, but after the resulting meal emerged, the war was more than worth the effort.

"It's fun being able to still surprise him about something after all these years," Sara said, to no one in particular. The only answer she got was from the radio, which kept her company now that the apartment only had the two of them to fill its new emptiness. "Better make time to fix myself up a little before I finish." Sara usually wore light-weight, well-washed old things to do her work in. Not very pretty to look at but so comfortable. This night she would see to it that she changed before Al got home. She could easily visualize the colorful and vivid dishes that would be served as if they were on view in an art gallery. Not often, though, did she see herself as an object of art. "What a mess I am, no makeup, hair's a mess, not to mention the lumps so comfortably settled here, there and everywhere," sadly but not sorrowfully she noted to herself again. "Maybe next week I'll start a new diet and not bake for a while." Her intentions were always good, but not often fulfilled.

This day began like most of the days. Through the fog of one of her morning dreams, Al's tapping reached her just as the warm, brown mellowness of the coffee crept into bed with her, gently prodding her out of her dreamland into the now. "Soup's on, Hon," Al quietly announced, "time to start." He was never abrupt or unreasonable, knowing that she was really "night people" and what a great effort it was for her to get out of bed each morning. She dragged herself into the bathroom, that hungover feeling weighing her head down and she didn't raise it till she was at the table reaching for her coffee.

Not a word passed between them, the radio as usual was the only sound till finally the coffee was finished, Sara spoke. "Hi, how are you,

Hon?" Al silently nodded his head as if to say "O.K." Sara yawned, "Me too, I guess. It's still too early to tell." "Maybe I should let you stay in bed?" Al laughed as he said it, "but I'd want to stay too." Sara grinned, "Funny, funny." "Seriously," Al said, "we don't see enough of each other, I know, and now that the kids are out of the house we should." "We should what?" Sara threw back at him angrily. She was fully awake now. "Oh, you know what I mean, we've sort of let things go the way they were when the kids were home." As he said it, he started to get up from the table. "Great, always leave 'em laughing," Sara grimaced. "Tonight we'll draw up battle plans, O.K.?" Al didn't think that was funny and as he put on his coat and hat said, "Please don't start anything, I just want us to talk and plan a little for the future." Sara just looked at him as the tears started down her face. He gently, but absent-mindedly kissed her on the cheek; it was a very old habit.

The door shut and Sara turned the lock, then went back to the kitchen for her second cup of coffee. She swept the wetness off her face with the back of her hand as she thought, "What have I done wrong now? It's always my fault." This time she put cream in the coffee and opened the breadbox to get a piece of cake to have with it. This was one of her eating times. There were crying times, sick times, telephone times and then there were cake times. It seemed to relieve the hurt a bit. If only there was a way to stop this hurt other than making it worse. "Maybe I should have stayed an old maid, then I'd be used to being alone all day and I could keep my own hours," Sara thought, "but how could I have gotten through all those years without someone to love, a husband, children? When they leave you, it's as if you have no reason for being anymore. Even knowing that Al is coming home at night doesn't fill the long hours of the day." The tears by this time had started to drop again, at first slowly then all at once she was sobbing and laughing at the same time. "What a nut I am, a classic from a 'Dear Abby' column," she thought as she fought to stop the avalanche. The tears were easy to stop but not the feelings that had boiled over and were too hot to do anything with yet. The cinnamon goodness of the cake and the creaminess of the coffee helped soothe her rankled nerves. She started to think about how the rest of the day was going to be. "I'll make something extra special for tonight and try to get myself fixed up for Al, maybe he'll be less upset about things after that."

Tonight would be America the Beautiful, a variety of New England dishes. Of course Boston baked beans and clam chowder were on the menu, and boiled beef and vegetables with a mustard sauce for the main course. Cole slaw that never saw the inside of a delicatessen, with a creamy dressing that never heard of mayonnaise, pickled beets and a large bowl of cottage cheese and a basket of biscuits would complete the main part of the meal. Dessert was as American as apple pie. It WAS apple pie and a good, sharp piece of cheddar served with strong coffee to complement it. Sara could just about smell the meal, it was that real to her already.

"I'll go shoppin' first thing while I can get the freshest of everything." The supermarket was a challenge to her. The bins and shelves were more than just cans, jars and produce to her. She seasoned and sauced, mentally stirring and combining, making herself impatient to get home and do the real cooking. A short tour of the market aisles, not letting anything distract from the planned meal, brought her quickly to the checkout counter. The checker knew Sara well enough to small-talk with her, "People from Boston tonight for dinner?" she joked. "No, just us mice," Sara smiled back at her.

The shopping done, the best part was about to begin. It was well orchestrated, she was the performer, the arranger and the conductor all at the same time. The years of rehearsals had made her a virtuoso. Instinctively her hand would reach for the right tool or the best spices and herbs to use. The timing was arranged so that nothing had to wait or overcook or undercook, the whole meal soon was cooking and baking. The kitchen was spilling in clouds through the apartment and the time for enjoying would be here soon.

The bell rang just once. She didn't answer as usually Al just announced he was home that way. "He's awfully slow coming up tonight," she wondered. Listening for his step, she heard a strange walk in the hall. As she went to the door to see why Al's step was changed tonight, she knew, "It's not Al. What's wrong? Where is he?" The knock was answered almost before it sounded. Sara painfully opened the door to Ronnie, one of Al's coworkers and opened her mouth to silently ask. "A terrible thing for me to tell you," Ronnie muttered almost as if to himself. "He's hurt?" Sara prayed. Ronnie's head nodded no. Sara's body shook as the blow of the dreadful thought hit her. "He's had a fatal stroke, we couldn't help him. We tried."

There were often some minor calamities. The closets were always stocked with emergency rations—in case of flood, war, and other unforeseen happenings. This was the worst that she could have imagined and it was not prepared for. "I didn't tell him" Sara said, pulling on Ronnie's arm. "All I had to say was I love you and he . . . ," she moaned, "I didn't say it, I didn't say it."

25 Minutes

by Howard Stabin

Thursday evening
   nine-fifteen,
While burning oil
and half a package
of frozen french fries
     for me
  I wait
and filled a tea pot.

"Help," he says
but not him
someone else
"No, thanks
   it's finished"
I think
He sings, it whistles
and whistles, he cries
The phone clicks
   Too late

I enter the smoke filled kitchen
burn my hand
on the tea pot handle.
   Refreeze
Friday night's chips
   for one
And scrub the burnt mess

...Thicker than Water

by Sophie Salpeter

She was awakened by a loud pounding. After a moment, she realized someone was banging on the door and, instinctively reacting to the fear of fire, hastily grabbed her happy coat and struggled into it as she raced to the sound.

"What is it?" she cried, as she fumbled with the lock.

"My father, my father, hurry." Marge finally got the door opened. Her next door neighbor stood with her fist in mid action, saw Marge, and finished the movement by grabbing her wrist and yanking her.

"Come quick, my father, he's dying," Florence wailed, pulling Marge along the hall.

"Wait, Florence, I've got no clothes on. I thought the building was on fire. Give me five minutes and I'll come right in."

"No, no," she shrieked. "You've got to come right this minute." Florence held her wrist firmly.

"All right. At least let me close my door."

Barely waiting for Marge to swing her door shut, Florence gave her a push; Marge found herself propelled on bare feet to her neighbor's apartment.

Once inside, Florence rushed her to the room where her father lay. Her husband, Lou, was sitting in the foyer at the telephone.

"It was the will of God, Sarah. What's to say? He had a long life. Yes, tonight we're meeting . . . ."

Marge found herself in the small bedroom with the old man. He was lying fully dressed on a rollaway bed. She sat down on the bed and gently lifted his long, white, patriarchal beard. She undid his tie and, with difficulty because the collar seemed lost in folds of flesh, opened the top buttons of his shirt. Not only was the old man wearing a worsted jacket with a woolen vest underneath, but in spite of the July heat he was also wearing longjohns. His pale skin was beaded with perspiration.

"Florence," she called, "get me a towel or some kleenex."

Florence came running into the room, her eyes darting wildly. "Why do you want a towel?" she shrilled with suspicion.

104

"Your father is sweating in this heat. I want to wipe him down."

"You say he's too hot? Wait, I'll get something." Florence ran out and returned with a basin of water. She began to sprinkle her father, splashing some on Marge.

"Here," she said, thrusting the basin at Marge. "You do it. I'm too nervous."

Automatically Marge took the basin and found herself flicking water at the still figure. Realizing she was acting like an idiot, she put the basin down on the small varnished dresser and went into the bathroom to get a towel.

As she was wiping the old man's face and his neck under the full beard, she could hear Lou's voice, ". . . so true, Jacob," he was saying sadly, "it happened so suddenly." There was a short pause. "That's right, your share entitles you to two votes. Come around six . . . ."

"Florence, Florence," Marge called. "Come here, will you." When her neighbor reappeared, Marge asked, "Doesn't he have pills or something? My mother always carries pills in case her heart starts acting up."

Florence stood there wringing her hands. "Pills? Yes, of course, pills. The doctor always leaves me pills for him. Margie, look under the pillow. It goes under the tongue." She pulled at her hair and ran around the small room screaming, "My father, my father, oh, my poor father."

Reaching under the pillow, Marge found a packet of digitalis pills. She took one out and gently pried the old man's lips apart. When she tried to separate his teeth, she saw with horror that the teeth were moving as one unit. Frightened, she jerked her hands away, leaving the teeth hanging half in and half out of his mouth.

She tried to get a grip on herself by remembering the soft way he would say good evening to her in Yiddish as he passed her with quiet dignity in the hall. When her hands stopped their trembling, she gingerly pushed the teeth back into place. Deliberately focusing on the teeth as inanimate objects, she finally pried them open. As her resolution deserted her, she quickly shoved the pill under what she hoped was his tongue. As she removed her fingers, the teeth clicked sharply together. She was sweating profusely and picked up the towel to wipe her own face.

As she sat there shivering, she saw his eyes open slowly. They were the palest blue and gazed at her solemnly. She began to massage his wrists. Slowly he smiled at her, a sad, apologetic smile. She smiled back reassuringly.

"Florence," she called softly. Immediately Florence materialized in the doorway.

"Your father's come to. Were you able to get the doctor?"

"The doctor?" Florence peered down at her father, then vaguely patted him on the head. "Lou's been trying for hours to reach him. Doctors, when you need them they're never around. I'll go see."

Marge could hear Lou chanting in unctuous mourning. "We tried our best for him. Marvin, you shouldn't have to know from these things. He couldn't have a better daughter than my Florence. Of course the factory will be closed, at least for Monday." He shifted to a whine. "Such an expensive apartment. We only took it so papa could have his own room. I know. I know the company paid his share. That's why I'm talking to you, Marvin. Your sister, who loves you as she loved your father, shouldn't have to worry about the rent at a time like this. Don't get excited, Marvin. We all have to make sacrifices. Calm down. We'll talk later. Yes, at six." The voice shifted again. "The will of God. But he had a long life . . . ."

Suddenly the doorbell rang and simultaneously there was a pounding on the door.

"Florence," Lou yelled. "Go answer the door. I'm busy on the phone."

Hearing many voices, Marge came out into the apartment foyer and saw four policemen milling around, one of whom was asking Florence questions. Then a tall, lean man pushed his way through and seeing Florence, went immediately to her and took her hands in his.

"My dear Mrs. Bratman," he murmured solicitously, "my answering service just reached me and I came over immediately."

"Oh, Doctor," Florence burst into tears. "My poor, dear father. You don't know what we've been through."

His voice was warm and comforting. "There, there. I'll take care of everything."

He started walking toward the old man's bedroom and discovered Marge standing there in her happy coat, barefoot, hair disheveled.

His nose lengthened in an imperceptible sniff. He turned to Florence. "Who is this?"

Florence was holding her chin and swaying back and forth in silent grief. At the doctor's words, she stared blankly at Marge. "Oh, her? She's from next door. A neighbor."

The doctor pushed past Marge into the bedroom and began his examination. During the process the old man opened his eyes and stared at the doctor with calm eyes. The doctor recoiled.

"Mrs. Bratman," he called angrily. When she appeared, he raged at her. "Your father is conscious. Why didn't you tell me sooner?" He busied himself with a hypodermic needle without waiting for her reply.

Marge watched in fascination while the doctor wrestled with the old man's jacket, woolen vest, white shirt and longjohns before he was able to insert the needle. While all the time Florence rocked back and forth, her eyes fixed in mute anguish on the doctor.

106

When he finished, he snapped. "We may still be able to pull him through. But," he shrugged, "at eighty-one it's hard to say. I'll arrange with the officers to get him to the hospital."

"Look, Florence," Marge interposed, "now that everything is under control I'm going back to my apartment."

Florence was still watching the doctor. As Marge was pushing her way through the crowd in the foyer she heard Lou saying, ". . . Dorothy, you've got a heart of gold. He'll get the finest care, no matter the expense. A father is a father. Yes, tonight at six. Here . . . ."

Before Marge could reach the outer door, suddenly she found Florence yanking her back. "Margie, you're such a darling. Do me a favor. They're taking Papa down the elevator in a chair. With the stretcher it won't fit. You have a blanket he could use? The doctor wants him wrapped warm. Such a hot day, why should he need a blanket?"

Marge kept her voice even. "Why don't you use one of your own blankets, Florence?"

Florence laughed with housewifely humor. "In July who has blankets out? All mine are stored away with camphor. Come, Margie, be a good girl. I promise to wash it out before I give it back."

"Okay," Marge said, remembering the calm, blue eyes. "He is a sweet old man. I'll get it."

After the blanket was tucked securely around the old man sitting in the straight-backed chair, Marge watched the procession. First came the two policemen, then the ambulance attendants carrying the old man, then two more policemen, with the doctor bringing up the rear. She wondered how they would all fit into the small elevator. As they progressed down the long hallway, Marge could hear Lou's voice, still on the telephone, droning through the open door, only to be drowned out by the sound of Florence's vacuum cleaner.

July July

by R. Racioppo

1

Mike and Mary chalky lovers
him is his chin and she is her size
they run themselves in doorways
and press in doorways

and not a word to Patty or Ben

doors are filled with feets of fours
Joey walks late and hears young sighs
Paulie plays a sax to Anna on a stoop
and the notes fall untold on her legs

2

Spanish bananas green in the window
a grey velvet fan tapping the air
sends it in circles over cans of meat
lights change at the corner.

July is on the milkcrates
undershirts are wet and wait for the weekend

the street is soft
Manuel spits
a cat gets up

Bodega Bodega

Raymond, His Wife, and His Women

by Vincent Campo

The clever, sharp, and subtle Raymond had solved one of man's most nagging problems: how to gain a slave-like devotion from women and his wife in particular. Through the intricacies of his nature, he had discovered that to keep his most precious possession, the love and complete enraptment of woman, a man must *never* commit himself or reveal his true emotions. Women must always be kept in a state of tension, insecurity, uncertainty and in continuous anxiety concerning their men's emotional intentions. Only thus can they be kept alive, vibrant, devoted and loving, notwithstanding what modern therapists and learned anthropologists might say to the contrary. Raymond himself never communicated his ideas in any form. He just lived them. One might say, if one were lucky enough to see Raymond in action, that he had computerized marital and extra-marital relationships to miraculous refinement. Considering the nature of the subject, this is no modest achievement. But before anyone starts mailing Raymond a Nobel Prize, we should first glance at his wife Judy, who had to bear the brunt of this apparently civilized advance into the unknown reaches of female space.

Judy loved and worshipped everything about Raymond. Her life-pulse depended for its rhythm on his very breath. So completely was she phased in with Raymond that his cough would be hers. A headache was not hers but his, endured heroically as his was not. The mildest reproach for not attending with the most scrupulous intensity his slightest enigmatic wish was enough to drive her to distraction, in private of course. When she was in his presence she attempted in every way to appear good-humored, smiling, content. That he never or rarely ever directly expressed any desire or wish made no difference. If he only had, she should have leaped in joy to fulfill all or any part of it. Yet she did the best she knew how, such as seeing to the little things, like fetching his towel as his hands searched after washing; his toothbrush, dental floss, cap off the toothpaste, all in handy reach as was the lather can, the razor with new blade inserted to be used at his convenience. As for his bath, she tended him with all the care and delicacy of a geisha girl, rubbing his back, lathering his neck and ears and hair with soft rinsings and towelings after; and then quickly everything back in its proper place, cleaned and sparkling. The bathroom was always free for his use, for she never took a bath or a shower while he was up and around. If she happened to be in the bathroom due to some urgencies of nature, she was sure to jump up, open the door for his leisurely passage. Not once did she think it was necessary to have a second bathroom. This was the way to feel his presence and for him to feel her own alert devotion. Her own things were never seen about. It was as if she owned nothing of her own either in the bathroom, bedroom, or living room, so deft was she in concealing what she imagined, and rightly, would be displeasing to his esthetic sensibility. But these were the mere tangibles. What about the intangible wishes and moods? How could she ever guess at them? That was one of her main anxieties if not preoccupations.

The logic of his moods gave Judy no rest and less security. She never seemed to guess the right thing to be done at the right time and therefore rarely ever, if at all, did she earn that longed-for eye of approval. The most seemingly innocuous statement he made would have her grappling for its ultimate significance with paranoiac fervor. What did he mean when he suddenly said: "I think I'll stay home tonight and read"? Did he mean he wanted to remain home and read a book? Or did he mean he wanted to stay home and read because he had to read this particular book? Or did he mean he wanted to be alone with her as a reward for something she had done? Or was it a rebuff for something she had not done or done improperly? Or did he mean he was tired and so was relaxing with any book, and then turn in early? Or had he intended to take her out perhaps to the theater, a movie or a party, but had suddenly changed his mind and decided to stay in and read a good book instead, for no reason? Or was he staying home to read a book while waiting for some important telephone call or a visitor? Etcetera, etcetera. There was no way of her knowing directly since he never informed her of his intentions until they were about to be realized. Thus was she ever in the air.

Yet even if this were indeed the intended punishment, it was beside the mark. For when he remained in, no matter what *his* reasons, she was overjoyed to have him in her presence. She could hardly believe it was true. His pipe, ash-tray, tobacco jar (better not forget the matches and lighter), pipe cleaners and scrapers were set carefully at his side of the arm chair, with the light flowing over his left shoulder. The hi-fi stereo was turned on with a set of his favorite records, seconded first by his nod, and the volume turned to his preferment. With love and devotion she spread out his slippers and sat as close to his feet as his shepherd dog, Shaggy, would allow, for he enjoyed petting the dog. This was a rare scene for Judy and as she kneeled with hands propping her face at a near distance she drank it all in with anxious contentment.

Though she herself worked on a woman's magazine, she came home rushing to prepare his meals which he expected at all times, even when he might at the last moment decide to eat out. She never knew if he was going to eat in, though he was punctual each evening, in order to feed and walk the dog. He preferred to attend the dog himself. When he did sit down to eat and was satisfied with everything including the dessert, she waited breathlessly for a sign. The best she could hope for was the absence of disapproval. If he had intended to take her out that evening but because of some culinary indiscretion, such as too much pepper in his mushroom crepe, he might well change his mind and either go out alone or stay in with a book. She never dared risk his ire by asking him directly what his intentions were. For long ago, just one month after they had been married, she had received a lecture in manners and he had not spoken another word to her for three days and two nights before he relented. Now he wouldn't even bother to lecture. He would just give her a look and then the grim silence.

They had their great moments together. They even went to parties. Raymond was a sophisticated man of the world. Judy could talk to anyone; she could even take on a lover or lovers. It was all one to him. So he had informed her more than once. Of course, he was sure she could not bear even the thought of another man. Indeed there was no one but Raymond for her. But woe if she so much as gave a covetous glance to the wrong kind of man. The wrong kind might be some man who in some mysterious fashion grated on Raymond. He never told her who or why he considered this or that man the wrong kind. It was understood or should have been. She could do whatever she pleased, of course. Implied however was that she ought not to place him in any embarrassing light, for if she did, her reward was any number of possible catastrophes: she would have to go home alone, or accompanied, if lucky, without him; or he would flirt or attempt a quick seduction of any girl available; or if she were the right girl, the three would go home together, while Judy spent the night on the living room couch sobbing softly so as not to disturb or distract him with the right girl in the king-sized bed.

And she could not protest. For to do so would have been to have violated an understanding made quite explicit before he consented finally to marry her. They must always be free to relate to anyone. None of the accouterments of middle-class marriage were to hinder their freedom of growth. There was not to be the intrusion of a third party in the shape of a baby to clutter their balanced nest. He had said, and

111

she thought very wisely, he didn't want to be caught in the aggregate greater than himself; having established his individuality by a great wrenching from the mass, he was not about to become its slave, symbolized by a suckling. He did not say, as well he might, an infant was a factor of unknown quantities in his calculations and also a greedy competitor for attention.

Now any man in his right mind may wonder if this seeming perfection might not be due more to some defective chromosome count in Judy than to any great skill of Raymond's. But there was nothing wrong with Judy. She was a perfectly normal, healthy, intelligent Vassar graduate, and no more insecure than any modern American woman of the day. As for Raymond, his achievement might well rank with Pavlov and his dogs. It must be emphasized that Judy and girls like her were no throwback to antediluvian times. They were modern, independent, full-bodied girls. They were not beholden to someone because of his power to dominate them, people such as promoters, agents, producers, bosses, professors, etc., who because of their position are able to drain compliance from them; these girls were free and the only thing that held them to Raymond was this tenuous something or other.

What he had done was parlay psychic instinctive skill with statistical modes of expectation. He had calculated that in any given social grouping where men meet women on anything like equal terms, there must always be at least one girl out of four, five or ten, etc., who would immediately be attracted to him physically. This calculation was based on confirmed experience. He was pleasant, youngish, dressed appropriately, well above the average in good looks, and there exuded from him an air of *je ne sais quoi*. Hence there was always a girl drawn to him like iron to a magnet, with no words spoken. In his wife's case, good looks and economic means would not have been enough. She had been born well-to-do, a child of parents of good stock and breeding (originally, that is, for several marriages later the original pair had drifted as far apart as Adam from Eve today). In the second place, it was the intellect framed in a body careless of rigid morality that had attracted her and women like her who in turn attracted Raymond. At the same time, Raymond seemed to live a life of higher principles, one guided by an esthetic sense of right living which added its own appeal to the rebel in such female souls.

Whereas the ordinary mortal, when he spots the girl of his dreams, or simply of his desires, will leap, contrive, concentrate his energies and furies to overwhelm her with attention, gifts, compliments, promises of eternal faith and love, etc., Raymond did the very opposite. The moment the girl he approved was attracted, he moved away from her, said nothing of significance, and after the initial impact of introduction, remained as far from her as nature and the social setting permitted. He

112

then put into operation every instinctive psychic device known to psychology, and the most useful would be that of passive projection.

To understand how projection worked for him, one need but glance back on one's own experience when he or she was struck down by love or infatuation. What made the girl so overpowering, so beautiful, so charming, so irresistible, and so possessed of those tingling qualities that tickle the poetic fancies in general? And that very same beloved moments, days, weeks or months later becomes an ordinary menstruating or pregnated blob with dandruffed, straggling, bleached hair, a mask for a face, etc? Obviously it was all in the eyes of the beholder. The girl is a girl objectively just as a man is a man. Therefore all Raymond had to do was just strut to the right psychic center to help set off that mysterious event more potent than anything bio-chemical or bio-physical; the bestower bestowing on him whatever there was to bestow. Very little conversation was required, thus no brilliant talk can be reported, for there was absolutely none.

Nor was that all. He took into account the fact that humans, including most women, desire to be looked on and approved. Strike here and the wound rouses not blood but panic. Being ignored totally is the worst wound, barely noticed a stab, fairly approved an insult, and so on. This was all programmed with diabolical efficiency.

Now add to all this the emotion of jealousy and Raymond had just about the entire gamut of feeling and sensation working full-time for him. His dog, Shaggy, had even taught him something. Once, Shaggy had refused to eat for several days and no amount of coaxing could make him eat; in fact the more he attended him the worse he got. Just when he was thinking the dog would die of starvation, a woman's dog in the apartment next door sneaked in and immediately went for the food. Shaggy watched for a moment in puzzlement. Then Raymond began to pet the intruder and offered him biscuits, when lo! Shaggy grew menacing, leaped and barked his displeasure, demanding his quota of attention and the rejected food and biscuits to boot. Such knowledge was never wasted on a Raymond.

At the final stage of conquest, he had floating about in full view of the targeted one girls who were already assimilated, or about to be assimilated or dissimilated. In Judy's case, one of her close friends had prepared the ground for him unwittingly. She had ever praised him, giving intimations of his wonders, so that as she was dissimilated, Judy thought she could succeed where her dear friend had failed. Raymond, in truth, wasted a lot of psychological thrust in the initial stage of Judy's wooing. But obviously there were intermediary stages that had to be negotiated in order to gain the end-all: namely a girl wholly and solely devoted to his well-being; one selflessly dedicated to him with love, while he remained true to himself or his masculine spirit. This meant

113

that the girls attracted had to be willing to share him in full knowledge that the others were sharing him too. Thus if they were not jealous or envious of the girl on whom, above all others, he bestowed his favor at any given time, they would not have been human, or they wouldn't have been fit.

Of course there had been casualties of the unfit, girls who had fallen out of his magnetic sphere. But that would easily be explained as a matter of survival. In the process of selection the unfit falter and die by the wayside of oblivion, while the fittest survive; and the fittest seemed to be Judy, his wife. She thrived on competition, she accepted complications; she endured everything so long as in the end she had Raymond or a wraith of Raymond. After all, doesn't science say we are more space than matter? How much matter does a gamma ray hit going through a heart? She had at least the status of an X-ray.

Now this could hardly be cataloged as a story if the matter were to end here. How would a future Raymond or Judy profit in the succeeding line of evolutionary thought? So without further apology, allow me to continue the story.

After eighteen months, plus twenty-four premarital, the limit of endurability was about to be reached. Judy had cooked up one of her best meals. Then she had set beside the dessert dish a pair of first-night theater tickets which she had wangled from the editor of the magazine. After enduring an entire array of anxieties as to whether he would eat in the first place, find the meal faultless, down to the special dessert, she had the additional anxieties as to whether he would take notice of the tickets, then approve their use, and go to a party after. He seemed quite satisfied and content, petting the dog and playfully teasing him with bits and morsels, when he finally deigned to take notice of the tickets. He studied them with approval, and even smiled.

At this signal, the joy and gratification in Judy were surpassing. She forgot restraint and showered on him kisses and hugs, ignoring Shaggy's warning growls. Out came her evening gown, so little worn, while Raymond wore his turtle-neck. Just as they were having a departing drink, the telephone rang and an ominous flutter beset Judy's heart. Yep. A woman's voice. He changed his plans entirely. He had to go out, but she could attend the theater and he might pick her up after, maybe, and with that left.

Poor Judy had no heart to go anywhere alone. She flung herself down on the couch and cried and cried, and the dog, disgusted, skulked away under the bed. After crying more than her usual share, something began to grow out of the hurt. It was nothing like a nuclear blast, but something more modest like outraged injustice. Injustice always demands justifiable action to justify itself. The action presented itself in the form of a telephone ring. One of her husband's close friends, not hers of course, was calling. It gave her an outrageous thought upon which she acted immediately. She invited him over that very moment. He was delighted to drop his paint brush and canvas and dash over two city blocks. The doorman after the usual confirmation let him by and he elevated himself to the eighteenth floor.

"What's the matter?" he asked, after kissing her proffered cheek.

"Ah, Stevie, it's so good to see someone. Come in. Come in. How about a drink?" and she handed him one already made.

"What's the matter? Anything wrong?" he said, noting her red eyes.

The dog had poked his head in and retreated. Everything was fine in that quarter. Then maybe something had happened to Raymond, though that seemed impossible.

"Drink up. Drink up. Here's another one."

"I have enough here, thanks. What's up?"

There was nothing she could really explain. What she required was justice. And Stevie's presence. But there was a problem. How could she hope to keep a man as cultivated as Stevie entertained and interested? She was being forced to the brink.

"Stevie, how about a quickie?" she said, dead pan.

"What?"

"How about a quickie? In the bedroom? Now."

Steve stroked his triangular mustache, gulped down his drink, and repeated: "What?"

"I know you're an artist. But does that mean I must draw you a picture?"

"One moment, Judy. I understand that part without pictures. I've always admired you and . . . ."

"Good, let's go then."

He rose to escape but now knowing how to shed himself of the glass, was caught. "I just can't. You see, you are Raymond's wife. He's a very good friend of mine, as you know. I know damn well if he were in my place, he wouldn't give it a second thought. But I am not him."

Judy experienced rejection again deeply. Obviously not only was she a bore but she could not interest him physically. Ordinary, commonplace men, yes, no problem. But with distinguished talented men, she had nothing to offer. This was one further devastating proof of her inadequacies. But things were churning inside and a couple of drinks hadn't helped matters much.

Steve saw the hurt in the girl so he attempted to soothe her.

"I know the scene, and what's behind your suggestion . . . ."

"What makes you say I'm suggesting? I'm saying, man. I'm saying how about a quickie?"

"It's like this. I just don't like to do this to Raymond."

115

"Now what in the hell is so goddamned sacrosanct about Raymond, I would like to know!"

The words had barely escaped. They astonished her so that she could not believe they were hers. So dumbfounded was she, she said: "What did *you* say?"

Stevie was so shocked by the outburst that he actually for a fleeting moment, and perhaps because he really thought them himself, imagined he had made the utterance. "What did *I* say?"

It took some time before the whole thing refocused into its own proper perspective, and Judy marveled that the world had not come to an end. Steve was realizing that he had a most delicate situation on his hands. To refuse to oblige Judy would hurt not only her vanity, but add another psychic affliction to her already scarred soul. He felt he had to explain both to her and himself why, because she was Raymond's wife, she merited this special treatment.

"It's like this. I don't like being misused. You pick on me because you know Raymond and I are close friends, and you'd like to break us up to satisfy a female outrage. What's more, I know you'll get the greatest satisfaction in telling him I was your partner whenever the occasion suits you. And you would hope this would hurt him. Better yet, make him jealous. He would then desire you more, not less. That's why, isn't it, you offer only a quickie, and not a ritual affair?"

This was indeed extremely interesting, thought Judy as she harvested this crop of information about her motives. Everything Stevie said was as logical as it was reasonable. She was amazed too that she had not been able to think these things herself. It was a man's view, without a doubt, and as always perfectly to the point. She liked this explanation so much she decided to adapt it as her own. But it had one drawback. The explanations were regressive, not progressive. Stevie was about to leave, probably exhausted from his deep reflections and she would be abandoned to her misery once again alone. Having a man there, even Stevie, was extremely comforting. Besides, she knew how much this was going to affect Raymond. She had Stevie's word for it. To turn to someone else other than himself for anything however trivial, would be very annoying to him. To add a sexual ingredient with one of his good friends who might be categorized as the wrong kind of man would be a factor of some interest.

"How about another drink now?"

"No, thanks. I'm going."

Steve just hated these moments in the lives of couples more than anything. When a wife chose to leap to such extremities, it was a matter of brinkmanship. He wanted no part of it.

But on no account was she prepared to let him off so easily. In her

116

mind she knew it would be no use trying to reason with him, for her powers of persuasion had atrophied from disuse.

"Suppose I undress?" she said and began to do so.

"It won't do you any good. I'll just sketch you like any model."

"Fine. Okay, sketch me then," she said, naked as the day she was born, and pointed to her own sketch pad by the easel.

As Steve sketched furiously from various poses she herself initiated, and as she got used to the situation as it unfolded, she began to think. Stevie had only given her *her* reasons why he wouldn't sleep with her. But what about *his* reasons? Was he just rationalizing? Wasn't it rather unusual for logic and reason alone to keep a man from taking what a naked woman was offering? What great power had Raymond over this man's natural instincts? She really hated to distract him from his concentration, but she simply had to know more.

"Stevie, I want the truth."

Steve was now sketching with studied concentration. Truth was in his art, not his tongue.

"Why is it that because I happen to be Raymond's wife, you refuse to consider me as a sex object?"

"Well, you see, Raymond and I were good friends even before college. He was a fair artist himself before he made so much money at it in advertising . . . ."

"Stevie, I know all that crap. Answer my question please."

As an artist he could concentrate on his lines and proportions with the greatest intensity, and at the same time; only in such moments could he converse fluently, for the truth in the one medium seemed to free him in the other.

"Well, it's like interfering with a great experiment."

"I don't understand."

"On your back more, please. Thanks. I have always marveled at how he managed to hold and keep more than one attractive girl at a time. It's always bugged me."

"Really?"

"Face me more. Spread your legs out just a little more. Thighs too. That's it. Thanks. It's the way he operates on you dames."

She had never thought of Raymond exactly as a surgeon, though it might have been better if she had. Of course, she was too involved to be able to see herself.

"Well, go on. How does he operate?"

"You ought to know better than anybody. I mean does he ever compliment you for anything? Never a thank you even, right? You never know, do you, where you stand with him? He comes and goes. In the old days, before you married him, and how you managed that

117

is a mystery to me, he might have five or six steady girls, if you know what I mean, at one time. They could all be with him at one party. I'd see them wander around like broken-hearted dolls, yet at his beck, they'd jump with joy into his arms on any condition."

"What's so strange about that?"

"If you don't know, there's no way in the world I could explain it to you."

"What about the experiment bit?"

"If at such a party with all these girls scattered around lonely, I asked one to bed, they wouldn't hear me. But even when I managed to take one out all she would do is talk about Raymond. Then I'd see he had invested an awful lot of his psychic time on these girls. You know, you are not the only one of his girls that have offered themselves, but when it comes down to business, I felt as if I was spitting into one of his experimental jars and fouling everything up."

"I see. You mean if you went to bed with me, you'd feel you were fouling things up for him, is that it? Very interesting. Very."

"Not only that. Right now, just sketching you, I feel a traitor. Take your arm away from your breast. That's it. Thanks. One thing I never quite get is how a girl as attractive as you knowingly could marry him. I mean, you knew the circumstances."

"Why did I marry him? Simple. Because I couldn't live without him. Do you know what that means? Not to be able to live without him? I wanted him on any terms. Just to be with him is the greatest. When he was with the others, I was almost crazed with agony and doubt. Do you have any idea what that must be like? The despair? Why, you don't know if he cares for you at all, or that he will ever come back to you and he suddenly calls, or the door opens and there he is? It's like life restored at death. After we were married, I could bear some of my agonies when he was with the others because I knew he'd have to come back to me. At least, if for nothing else to get the dog or his clothes. That would give me a hope. Do you know what a caress or a kiss is like when you feel as I have many times, it might be the last?"

"There! You see? That's just what I could never dig. How does he do it? My own lack of success with women is legendary."

"That's not what Raymond says. He says you're great."

"Is that so? But we're not in the same league. I'm nice to girls. I pay them all kinds of compliments. I treat them almost as equals. I'm faithful. When I'm in love, I like nothing better than to confess it. I pay them all kinds of compliments even if they don't deserve them. I'd do anything for them. Even cook. Yet with all that, they seem to lose interest in me. The moment my back's turned or another male beast shows up with pretty teeth, they're gone. But with him . . . Am I boring you?"

"No. No. Not at all. This is the first time I have had an occasion to talk to anyone like you about him. Please, go on."

He was sketching madly now. "He treats you like dogs . . . ."

"I wish," she said, wistfully.

"No matter how badly from my own narrow point of view he treats you girls, you jump into his arms. You love him. You adore him. You worship him. You serve him hand and foot. You're faithful . . . What are you laughing at?"

"Go on. Yes, go on."

"Well, you know the rest better than I do. Why go on? You've explained it already yourself."

"That's amazing. I never realized it."

"What's that?"

"I never thought that a man like you, cultivated and talented, treated girls any other way than Raymond does. This is the first time I ever heard an artist, like you, say you'd treat girls like equals. That you'd be faithful to one. That you'd tell them you love them. I thought that was old hat, like poetry or the old movies. You're not just saying this, are you?"

"Even if I'm only saying it, it's true nonetheless."

"You mean, if you were in love with a girl and married her, you'd be true only to her? You wouldn't care about any other girl?"

"When did I say that?"

"Just now."

"I wouldn't go that far. I've never been married before."

"But you would be faithful to one girl? Yes, I think you could. That's amazing, indeed."

"You're distracting me. Hold still. Where was I?" he said, and then finished off the vagina with a flourish. "I'm finished."

"Oh, Stevie, you're not going to leave me like this? Now? What will people say?"

"You're not exactly in a position to broadcast. Give my regards to Raymond, will you?"

Just when she had been making such a courageous recovery, the slam of the door opened all the wounds again and one in particular: insecurity. She wanted so much to be reassured by Raymond, for him to be there with her now. Just to be there. What could she tell him now? Not even Steve would have her. I offered myself but he didn't want me. She could see Raymond's grimace. Nobody wanted her. She was lucky to have even a shadow of Raymond to love. She was an utter nothing. How horrible for him to be chained to her. Tears fell and she seemed utterly crushed pitying Raymond. Then her tear-drowning eyes caught sight of the sketches. There was something about them transcending the normally narcissistic that made her start. She

119

began to study and compare her body in the mirror to the images of it sketched. They were beautiful representations. Each sketch had been made in a manner that revealed things about her she had never imagined, dreamed, or realized before. If the artist in Stevie could see this, it must have been in her in the first place. It was not something projected from the artist's imagination entirely. It was as if Stevie the artist was saying something to her about herself which she should know as woman. And so she lost herself in the exquisite revery of herself through the medium of the art in the sketches.

She was no longer crying. There was a slight disassociation of self as she calmly tacked the sketches along the living room wall. Then training the light reserved for Raymond's favorite Picasso lithograph onto the sketches, she quietly retired for the night.

Raymond returned exhilarated. Shaggy leaped up, lovingly tender, and Raymond allowed himself to be lapped and licked. After feeding the dog his rations, he took him out for his late walk. As the dog sniffed and leaked and squat and sniffed, Raymond feasted his mind on the glories of Suzan at the magic moment of initiation. It had come off supremely well. She had survived the critical shock of his marriage beautifully. It could have been premature, but it had worked out just the same. If it hadn't been that Judy had hugged and kissed him, revealing her exuberance at the prospect of an evening together, which had to be squelched then and there (the phone ring really a god-send), he might have easily endangered the precarious balance of their marital bonds. Yielding at that moment would have altered the pattern of devotion. Only in frustration was desire fired to sublime heights. Judy did not merit this disservice. Now this evening, in which he was sure she was abed waiting for him, he would bring to her a spark of fire he had left blazing in Suzan's bed. Suzan had been difficult, being young and spoiled. It had taken lots of patience to reach this stage. When she called to invite him to a little gathering, held for him really, he had spent most of the time half-listening with a bored air to her friends' discussions of art and politics. But he had injected his icy comments here and there, making them all well aware of his existence. The other women, Suzan had taken good care of that, were not his type, so that more than usual he had desired to have her in his presence. But he had to be firm, grow properly distant and indifferent whenever she did come near. It had been altogether very exhausting. Before the party broke up, when she was yearning for his company, he had moved to leave. How distraught she had been, begging him to stay. This really was the ideal moment to further reinforce her desire by breaking away. But she had so much warmth and beauty in her, the situation was so ripe with possibilities, and her pleas that if he remained she would make it worth his while that he had relented. Without a word from him, after the others had left, she had lost no time at all in undressing and lying abed naked, inviting him to her. He had fondled her, kissed her gently, building to a moment between longing and distraction. Then when she had expected the climax to his sojourn, he had disengaged himself tactfully and shrewdly, making certain by this gesture that he was not acting out of any moral belief, but for her own sake, mysteriously suggested, of promises of more delights to come just because of this suspension. In spite of her seeming boldness, driven to it more out of desperation than desire, she was rather inexperienced. But the potential was there. Gracefully she would resign herself to his needs, happy to see him whenever he wished. Fortunately she was socially active so that she could bear those idle hours and days without him. And whenever he did make his appearance, she would cherish him the more on his terms. Now he was ready to please Judy. He was full-fired with his recent successes and his present anticipation.

As he was about to enter the bedroom, he noticed for the first time the sketches on the wall. He studied them with enormous interest. Then, taking them down one by one, he set them on the easel, retraining the light on his precious Picasso lithograph. Full-stepped, he entered the bedroom.

"You needn't tiptoe. I'm fully awake."

It was curious that she should think he was tiptoeing when he never did. But what had surprised him more was the odd tension in her voice. Slowly he got undressed, enjoying his nakedness in the mirror, and then slipped into his pajamas. He couldn't find his slippers, and thought Shaggy must have hid them for they were always duly set out by Judy.

"I see you didn't go out tonight."

"You knew I wouldn't."

This was not like her at all, and he didn't like the tone she was using. It irritated him. Thoughtlessly, more as a test probe than anything else, he said: "By the way, those sketches you made of yourself are not bad. You're improving." And no sooner had the words slipped out than he had misgivings.

"I didn't make them. It was Stevie."

This too was surprising. All kinds of possibilities suggested themselves. He decided to brush his teeth, and to his annoyance found the cap on the tooth-paste. He knew he should not have complimented her. True, the work was not hers, therefore the compliment did not apply. But it gave her an opening. If he had said nothing, or reprimanded her, after all where were the slippers, and the damn cap tight on the tooth-paste tube? that would have squelched her to passivity. It was a lapse he did not intend to repeat soon. Now what was Steve doing here? He was supposed to call. He knew that he should have had him call at the office, not here. All right. She took his call, and one thing leading to another, he showed up here. Did he invite himself when he learned he was out? Very likely. Or had she invited him? Also possible. Of course she was entitled to do as she pleased. But this? When he had left her, she should have been mired in self-pity, locked in and grooved with thoughts of him and nothing else. Now why had she posed naked and deliberately set up the sketches for him to see? In her idiot female psychology she imagined he would be jealous. Annoyed, yes. But jealous? No. With Steve? She had never done anything like this before. Why now? Obviously in her anguish, she thought she was about to lose him forever, and just then, Steve's call. Damn. He should certainly not have called here but at the office. Definitely. He was always like that. He knew nothing whatsoever about women. He spoiled them every way. Paying them compliments, making them feel important. Giving them attention. Discussing things with them as if they knew what they were talking about. Swelling their heads. He does it all the time. Never learns. That's why he rarely ever invited him over. He was angry. He ought to teach her a good lesson. Too bad now he had not climaxed the night with Suzan. There! If he hadn't been thinking of Judy . . . . It would have been premature to spend the night. But what a counter-stroke it would have been. All her preparations would have been wasted if he had not appeared the entire night. Her anxieties would have eaten away all the cuteness and angles she nourished in the shadows of her female soul. Steve he would cut dead. He was out. Now to straighten her out. Not a word. Not a sign from him. Total indifference. He might even spend the next couple of days away in his apartment, still his nest. To bed.

Judy had been measuring her thoughts to the words which she let out slowly, deliberately, just as he was kneeing the mattress.

"Ray," she said, and the coldness stopped him dead. "I want you to leave. I want a divorce."

The sketches, Steve sketching her nude, his compliment, the tone of finality in her cold voice and the consequences of all these at once leaped at him with claws. The shock of it sent him back on his feet away from her and the bed.

"Now? At this hour?"

"Yes, now. It's my apartment."

The shock was over. So be it. He'd take his dog. And his Picasso too. Immediately, without another word, he hurriedly dressed while his thoughts tightened stiffly about his head. He began packing a suitcase. Yes. It was over. He could feel nothing but loathing. He was fuming inside. A terrible anger was building in him. Somehow he had to get it out of him before he left. He had to strike back. This was something new for him. Never once had he ever even reprimanded her, though

122

God knows she deserved it. The fact was, he had never given her the satisfaction of an overt reprimand. But this time. This last time . . . .

He was at the door, holding the knob. With the ice-honed edges of his thought, he let out with all the might of his impotence: "Why did you wait until I was undressed? You could have told me before."

With that said, he slammed the door, not hearing her last words or caring less. He had realized his fatal error. Yes, even as the dog and the lithograph were controlled by his left hand, and the suitcase by his right, he knew he should not have complimented her about those wretched sketches.

As for Judy, the words he had not heard were simply: I didn't know myself until I saw you, naked. I owe it to Stevie. He gave me eyes. Yes. Stevie . . . .

Blow Job

by Michele Cusumano

Sun streaks across the bed
bodies soft with sleep
My breath is flowing down
through me
as you put your head between my legs

Hair brushing the inside of my thighs
pressure of your mouth against my pubic hair
tongue on my clitoris
My mind is empty, my body taut
opened up and disarranged
I'm coming

When it's over and I've fallen apart
hold still
I want to feel each drop of blood
returning to its proper place.

A Woman of Thirty

by Thomas Hubschman

She was beginning to enjoy herself. Her qualms about the long trip to Norfolk, subject of half a night's argument with John, who insisted that she owed it to her brother, had dissolved with the mists of South Jersey. Whatever made her think the children could not get along without her, for just a single day? One day apart from John and them, one day in almost five years. And to think she had felt guilty about going.

The landscape grew more and more rural, and finally the unaccustomed scene of farms and cattle began to bore her. She dozed, her head gently jostled by the headrest. The motion of the bus became something visual: a receding plane, an undulating arch. She fell into a deeper sleep and dreamt she was home again, having decided not to go after all.

It was the man beside her, touching her arm gently to say "coffee-break" that roused her. From his expression she suspected he had put off waking her until the last moment. She only realized now that all the way down the Turnpike he had been taking glances at her, brief but significant glances.

"These places are all alike," he said, following her with his tray, paper napkin and cafeterial dinnerware past the gluey pies and rubbery jello. "They change the name when you cross the Delaware, but the food's the same."

She smiled to show she appreciated his friendly observation, but she could think of nothing to say in reply. His attention made her uncomfortable, though there was nothing to suggest he intended anything but to be an agreeable travelling companion. She asked for coffee with cream and sugar, recalling that in her single days it would have been black and without the slice of pound cake, and wondered that she could have grown so timid in just a few years.

The man sat down at the table beside hers but did no more than smile until she offered her own comment about the food. It immediately seemed very bold, a married woman with three children, speaking to a stranger when they would ride a hair's breadth from each other for another three hours. She had hardly realized she meant to

125

say anything until it came out, just like that. But she could not have carried it off more naturally had she never left her desk at Bache.

"Going all the way to Norfolk?" he asked, cutting into his pie as though it had a French crust.

"For my brother's wedding," she replied. "And you?" He swallowed unselfconsciously but kept his eyes lowered. "Washington," he said, with no trace of regret. "A business trip."

You see? she told herself, though her expression showed only that a traveler's pleasantry had been exchanged. She got up a few moments later, leaving the man to his own heavily creamed and sugared coffee, and with a brisk, independent stride crossed the parking lot to the bus.

The wedding was a hasty, almost makeshift affair spliced between two lengthy tours of duty for Ed. Still, it was very well attended, and, watching him make the appropriate responses in a shaky but still melodious voice she recalled her girlhood fancy that, if he would have her, she would not have hesitated to marry her own brother. The memory was embarrassing, but she was forced to admit that the same boyish but unmistakably masculine charm remained.

But, as if she needed to be reminded, more than one of the young guests—young by the advancing standards of a woman approaching thirty—confided to her at the reception that Ed was not only the best-looking ensign Norfolk had ever seen but was the best-liked as well; not only by the Old Man, but down below, too, by the first- and second-classers. Such reports were not new to her, only she had forgotten how pleasant it was to hear them, even more so than if they were given in praise of herself, for there was no need to make a denial. Four years is a long time and even the handsomest men grow fat and the wittiest become dated.

Finding he was the same magnetic Ed also relieved her from describing him to the young officers and their dates who had crowded into the hotel suite. There was nothing to tell. Instead, it was they who reminded her of his exploits on the gridiron, his splendid record in the service and (aside) his phenomenal popularity among women of all ages. She had only to listen and modestly agree. She need not follow him with her eyes about the room as she might have ten years ago. Since nothing had changed, nothing need be explained.

The best man, an ensign on the same ship as Ed, gave a florid but manly toast, and everyone took that as a signal that they might now return to the more relaxed conversation they assumed at less formal occasions. She noticed that the men—particularly the single men—stopped introducing themselves as "great friends of Ed" and steered the conversation quickly to their own interests, with only a brief introductory remark about recognizing her right off as the groom's little sister.

126

One young man in particular, a handsome officer who looked to be half a decade her brother's junior—a nice age for a man of his youthful looks and charm, a younger Ed in many ways—began to monopolize her. The directness of his inquiries about her life—the life of her interests and tastes, not the life of her marriage and motherhood—were amply redeemed by the sincerity of his smile and his engaging, confidential manner.

He was apparently on intimate terms with her brother but spoke of him merely in passing. She suspected that, despite his friendship with Ed, he really knew nothing about her. He did know the story of Ed's football days and had a surprising stock of tales about his footloose youth. But he also assumed, incorrectly, that she had been an intimate of those athletic glories and mischievous capers, when of course she had only admired them from the sidelines with the classmates of the girls' school she had attended.

The generosity of his attention was most flattering, was in fact embarrassing. But it was the kind of embarrassment, full of flattery and half-denied pleasure, that she had felt on her first dates as a young secretary. She could not bring herself now to accept it merely as her due, but she felt herself giving into it even less guardedly than as a single girl without responsibilities to one man and a family.

She accepted a second drink—a vile punch everyone pretended was excellent. His clean, pink hands seemed newly manicured beneath the immaculate cuffs of his shirt, which in turn showed all the whiter for the dark blue of his uniform. He was hardly the rough sailor, seemed even younger than his twenty-six or twenty-seven years. His complexion, the soft pink of a baby, emphasized his youth. Were it not for his unfailing self-confidence and the insistent expression of his eyes, he might be taken for a cadet.

"You're with a brokerage house?" he asked, fixing her with his cool blue vision.

The question took her by surprise. It had never occurred to her that he was paying her so much attention because he believed her still unmarried. She casually crossed her right hand over her left and estimated the significance of a truthful response. Her fingers fluttered across the wide gold and pearl band—almost too wide to be taken for a wedding ring.

"No," she replied, wondering if what she was saying were technically a falsehood. "I left the brokerage house a long time ago."

"Really? And what have you been doing since then?"

She looked directly back into his strong gaze to see if he were joking. Some of the clients, men with families, who knew very well she had married, used to continue asking her out, pretending they hadn't heard. She had never hesitated then to give the polite, even vaguely regretful refusal which would check their advances but maintain their

127

good will toward the company. Why did she hesitate now? She had seen that insistent gleam before—in the eyes of those same men she had turned down during the few months between her marriage and first pregnancy. She twisted the ring around her thin finger, sliding it up and down from the knuckle to the first joint. It had always been a size too big. She had expected to put on weight but only did when bearing a child.

"Oh," she said, her shoulders jerking nervously, "things." His smile widened, as though her words and the accompanying gesture were only a feminine stratagem. He inclined his head confidentially, as if he were asking a child for a withheld secret.

"Ed's spoken so much of your talents, I'm certain every man in New York must be looking to grab up a girl like you."

"Not at all," she replied, feeling the warmth of his skin on her own. "There are plenty of girls to fill the jobs in New York. Don't let the classified section of the *Times* fool you. It's just that good secretaries keep moving around, and of course a new one has to be hired every time one gets bored—or married."

"That never occurred to me," he said. "You see, I never have any fear of my typist leaving for a better position." He inclined his head again, and she felt this somehow gave another meaning to what he had said.

"So you've moved on to something else?"

"Well," she said, relieved that the deception was coming to an end, "yes, I have."

"Better? More lucrative?"

"Well," she laughed, seeing the tubs of wash she had left for John. "I wouldn't exactly say more lucrative."

"But satisfying."

She bit her lip thoughtfully. She didn't want to seem flippant, as if she didn't take her role as a wife and mother seriously.

"Well, yes," she began, studying the leg of a nearby table. "I guess I do consider motherhood a valid way of fulfilling oneself."

She looked up to confront those marble-blue eyes—but they were gone.

"Here," he said approaching from behind with two fresh drinks. "Have another one of these. Personally," he added softly, his lips just inches from her ear as his eyes darted about the reception in mock concern for privacy, "personally, I think this is the vilest stuff I've ever tasted. With all due respects for your brother."

The proximity of his warm, insinuating voice sent a thrill down her spine. She accepted the glass and allowed the empty one to be taken. She thought of repeating what she had said, but the words would not come, seemed hopelessly out of place. She wondered if he had not

128

actually heard her before going for the punch, but his eyes were wandering leisurely over the scattered guests, and he sipped his drink with the indifference of one who takes things as he finds them.

Well, what harm was done, she thought, cupping her hands securely around her glass. After all, she had told no lie. And what difference would it make? It wasn't as if she had agreed to go to bed with him.

But the idea of going to bed with him gave rise suddenly to a vivid image of the reality, the young man sitting at the edge of a bed—her bed—naked to his potent but hairless organ, holding a drink and smiling as if he had known all along this final intimacy was inevitable.

She put her glass down and blinked three times to see if she was really that far gone.

"Sit down?" he asked, taking her arm, and escorted her to a small sofa. "I know how you feel. This stuff is dynamite."

Once seated, pushed together by a stout woman who immediately began exchanging pleasantries with the young man, she decided she had made a mistake in sitting down with him. He soon finished with the older woman and turned his attention—that total, insinuating attention, as though he were always trying to convince her of something—back to herself. His broad shoulders, wedged between hers and the woman's, pushed firmly against her. Their thighs pressed together as though they were already lovers.

"Well now," he said. "Feel better?"

"Yes," she replied, showing a weakened smile. She had no idea a man's body—a strange man's body—could excite her so. She felt alternately thrilled and weakened as she felt his muscles tighten and relax as he crossed his legs or pulled at the crease of his pants. Thank God he thought she was just feeling the punch.

She looked up and saw that the people and objects in the room had merged into one amorphous organism, vibrating with the dull insistence of her own pulse, a mere protoplasm, indistinct and somehow inconsequential without her powers of consciousness to define its separate parts. She reached across his arm to flick the ash of her cigarette in the crystal tray he had balanced on his blue knee. Her breast brushed against his arm, pressed it, one second, two—did she dare?—gently rolling the grey ash in one of the crystal grooves, all the while dragging out an observation about the values of a military education.

She sat back, the gesture half-forgotten, and arched her wrist, letting the cigarette burn as if it were merely an ornament. For a brief moment the young man seemed to draw back, actually move slightly away from her. But then he relaxed, and by relaxing pressed himself more intimately against her.

"Tell me," he said, speaking in a measured, carefully balanced voice, in a manner somehow lacking much of the insistence that had characterized it before. "From what you've said I can see you have refined tastes. I would imagine you're an art lover and go to concerts. Am I right?"

The compliment—and yet somehow it struck her that she had heard, or should have heard, the same words before—thrilled her almost as much as the presence of the flesh. Her breath caught short and she choked on the first words of her reply. She laughed, tapped her bosom, as if it were the smoke, and tried again.

"I try," she said, vaguely wondering why she was talking in such a husky voice, giving strong emphasis to every word. "I *try* not to let *life* pass me *by*."

"I thought so," he said, looking very much as if he really did think so. "Let's see," he continued, drawing back again and squinting as if to take a bead. "I figure you for a Mozart fan. Very intellectual stuff."

"Oh," she said, casting her eyes down at her lap where she noticed an old stain. "I'm afraid not."

"Beethoven."

"Nooo . . ." That on a rising note with a smile.

"Okay. I give. Who's your favorite composer?"

She brought her vision to his face for a moment, then looked off into the room, where the blue protoplasm of her consciousness continued to hum and throb automatically in tribute to her ability to perform two separate, complicated functions at the same time. She was aware that she was presenting a furrowed brow, indicative of the careful consideration she was giving all the musical immortals.

"Well," she said, cocking her head to the side—his side. She did it casually, even though she could sense his flesh just millimeters away. Her vision fell on a disjointed piece of protoplasm gesturing in a corner of the room.

"I suppose I would have to say Sigmund Romberg. Does that," she said, fairly rolling her green eyes as she turned her head, "does that surprise you?"

He met her gaze directly.

"Not at all. In fact, what a coincidence. Romberg is my own favorite."

"Really?"

"Yes. In fact, I have quite a collection."

He described his stereo in some detail. She listened attentively, understood nothing, watching Proposition rise from the horizon of his rhetoric and advance rapidly towards her.

"Oh," she replied, smiling woodenly. "I'm afraid I couldn't. You see, I have to catch a bus in just a few hours."

"Then come now."

She was amused by the insistence in his expression, disconnected now from the irresistible appeal of before. There was a kind of fear in those blue eyes, despite his ever-present smile, so full of fine, white teeth. She would gladly have kissed him right then, just because they were so white and his gums so pink and healthy.

"Nooo," she cooed consolingly. "Some other time."

Her eyes left the officer and focused on the reception. Definition was returning. That piece of blue protoplasm gesturing in the corner was her brother. "Thanks just the same."

She excused herself, gathered her purse and stood up. At first it seemed she would not stop ascending. But by the time she had smoothed her dress across her abdomen she was settled at the altitude to which she was accustomed. She inquired of an unattended maid of honor the way to the ladies' room and found as soon as she entered the lavatory that she was getting sick. The colored matron stood unperturbedly outside the stall while she threw up.

A wracking headache replaced the nausea. It came on all at once as she sat on the tile floor, her arms straddled across the porcelain toilet. The suddenness and violence of her illness had not given her a chance to think, but now, with only the splitting headache to occupy her attention—a pain so intense it was like two rough stones banging together inside her head—she felt a slow, threatening tremor, a kind of electricity rising from the depths of her abused bowels: She knew she must leave at once for home.

"Dare anythin' ah ken do, Miz?"

She looked up at the matron, a stout, black woman with small slits for eyes. She studied those eyes and the woman's expression, looking for some sign of sympathy. But the matron seemed to be looking not so much at her as at merely another fixture of the lavatory, one for which she felt a responsibility neither more nor less sympathetic than what she felt for the porcelain sinks and the white tile floor.

"No," she replied, self-pity—since there was no other kind available—filling her eyes as she laboriously brought her body to its feet. "Thank you, I'll manage."

A discreet knock sounded at the lavatory door. The matron opened it cautiously and exchanged words with a male voice. A moment later her brother was standing at the stall, his new blue suit still as crisp as when he had walked down the aisle.

"Under the weather?" he asked, giving her the old smile but checking also to see how badly off she was. She stood up, smoothed the abdomen of her dress and threw her shoulders back. But her head reacted just as if she had struck it against the wall. She cradled it in her hand and groaned, sagging, as if she would return to embracing the toilet.

"Here, let me give you a hand."

131

She allowed herself to be assisted, half-carried in fact, out of the lavatory, through the lobby and past the gathered guests, who watched with what seemed lightly disguised amusement. He brought her to an empty bedroom and insisted that she lie down on one of the twin beds. Then he sent someone for a seltzer and sat down on the other bed, watching her with the kind of concern she had longed for a few minutes ago. It seemed to bathe her in warm consolation. She reached for his hand and gave it little pressures of gratitude, watching his bright eyes for signs of affection.

"Easy does it, old girl," he said in a warm resonant voice, full of memory. It might have been fifteen or twenty years ago, when she had fallen from a tree, and he was there stroking her forehead and smiling reassuringly, with that absolute confidence which made even the pain a kind of pleasure; it might have been the night of her prom, she in desperation, then tears, because her gown was the wrong size, or rather that *she* was the wrong size, too flat-chested to hold it up, having insisted on a strapless against her mother's advice—then his reassuring smile and tactful flattery, insisting she would be crowned queen.

The force of the memories brought her to tears. She squeezed his hand and looked deep into his eyes to see if he understood how profound and intense was her love.

"All right, old girl," he said, gently patting her hand. "All right now."

The door opened a few inches, then half-way. A woman's head appeared. Then the head became a figure, dressed in a white bridal gown. She relaxed her grip on her brother's hand and fixed her eyes on the ceiling.

"Is there anything I can do?" the woman said, approaching her brother. They exchanged a significant glance, the kind one exchanges over the bed of a sick child. Then the woman looked down at her, taking in her disheveled dress and a foot now missing its shoe.

"How are you feeling now, dear? Any better?"

She forced her eyes as far as the white veil—the veil and gown seemed somehow just a costume—but could not bring herself to look directly into the woman's eyes.

"Yes, I think so," she replied. "Thank you."

The woman continued to study her, as though she were not someone in a position to judge her own condition. Ed drew his arm casually around the woman's waist, and they considered their ailing guest together.

Under their scrutiny she stiffened, was compelled to look away. "Yes," she declared finally. "In fact, this is silly. If you'll leave me, I'll just straighten up a bit." She looked up at the woman, bending her lips into a smile. "Really," she insisted, winking both eyes. "I'm all right." She looked at her brother, saw a doubtful concern still weighing on his handsome face, and gave him a warm, indeed reassuring smile of her own, with a one-eyed wink just to keep the woman guessing. "It's that rotten punch your husband served," she declared, as though it were all a joke now. "What did you put in it, naval gasoline?"

"That was Eric's doing," he confessed gravely to the woman. "I knew I should have seen to it myself."

The woman pursed her lips and frowned at this expression of responsibility. Still lying on the bed, she wondered what appeals this person could have for her independent-minded brother.

"Which one is Eric?" she asked.

"Eric? Why," he replied, "Eric is that ensign you were sitting with when you took ill."

On the bus, riding through the darkened countryside of Maryland, her head still throbbing lightly despite the aspirins she had taken, she watched a quarter-moon jump from one side of the road to the other, despite the bus's steady progress northward. The landscape, flat scrubland powdered silver by unbroken moonlight, grew gradually more familiar as they left Baltimore behind and sped toward the Delaware border. She had so far avoided unpleasant recollections of the afternoon, preferring to lose herself in a sleepy thoughtlessness. But now as the bus crossed an unfamiliar river, she began to cry.

The small lights above the heads of the dozing passengers were all turned off, and she gave in willingly to the sobs that shook her breast, pressing a crumpled tissue against her nostrils, her gaze fixed on the flat, repetitive landscape. But it was not until they had passed the first roadside restaurant in Delaware that she found an image for her grief.

She had been a bad girl. "Unfaithful" was too strong. But, realizing she could not face that accusation, tears flowed all the more freely. She thought of her children, not suspecting her unmotherly behavior far away from them, and the thought, the image of their trusting faces, to which she returned again and again despite the pain it caused, elicited greater sobs, sobs too strong for a public conveyance.

She tried to think of John. But she could only see his figure, vague, unwelcoming, somehow ready to challenge her. Then the faces of her brother and the young ensign intervened. She thrilled again at the officer's smile, but when she recalled the unvirtuous pressures she had exchanged with him on the sofa, her nausea came unsettled again and threatened to overcome her.

She rested her head on the back of the seat. The heavy, elderly woman beside her was sleeping with her mouth open. Her flowered hat had fallen part way across her blunt, aged features, making her elaborate application of cosmetics seem grotesque, funereal.

There was nothing to do but sigh, the deep broken sigh of someone who has been weeping for a long time. In the darkness outside the bus there appeared the arch of the Delaware Bridge, and beyond it the scattered lights of New Jersey. She drew a deep breath and closed her eyes in gratitude for those welcoming beacons which she could still contemplate behind her closed eyes. And even the bus, as it sped up the bridge's windy approaches, seemed like a rescue ship sent to ferry her safely through the night.

Transitions

In the Funny Version of My Life

by Alan Rosenberg

In the funny version of my life
my mother gets to hold flowers
a wreath is hanging on my door
and I spin through the treetops
inside a tire
pretending to be a bell

High School

by Norma Beverly Cohen

she was lost in a world of
silence where wish flowers
daily floated sad and
lonely upon the indifferent
air. she felt herself solitary
as a stone or a sea wave
when it breaks invisible
in anger angry spraying
dissolving and as though
by the slight swaying of
a wand disappearing to
a state beyond mere
sand or a sound screaming
against what can not be heard.
perhaps the wind it was would
lift the fierce the knightly
night-like ghost of splash
of dream permeating her
last breath her last quiet.
now could she care. the thought
of death flooded her dreams
calming the fire flaming
her desire nurturing her
despair.
death the great dream
seemed the one unknown
most yearned for most
wondered about. death the great
dream seemed the only
answer to her loneliness
to her poverty that wanton
child of thought like a grief
wandering wild through
all her youthful years.
and yet—and yet—
her thoughts found themselves
becoming the red the gold
the bronze the green leaves she had

138

while sitting the side of a small
library window seen dancing
free from the branches of a
wind and rainy day became
the shells and tinted pebbles
she had one day of escape
from her home and school
gathered from where the sea
had touched retreating
leaving there only the frame
of its diaphanous imprint.
her thoughts found themselves
changing. were they phoenixes.
perhaps they were young gulls
eagles grackles learning flight
dreaming on to those hours
the hour when soaring
would be breathing
breaths of uncare
through wind and light.
or were they clouds, owls, flakes—
her mind could not answer.
for she only heard the music
a music of silence
like white islands of eyes and shine
swirling drifting her days
while somnolent disquieting
her nights.

Thirty-Day Leave

by Terry Berkson

The dimly lit market place was deserted except for Max and Schlango and a half dozen more Germans from the gang. The sound of a rock tripping over the cobblestones and heels chasing after it mingled with cries of laughter and excitement, as the simulated Fussball game progressed to the far side of the square.

In the distance, two meandering GI's approached in the path of the game. The rock was kicked past them, and chasing after it, the Germans crashed through the GI's, pushing them to the side. "Hey, you stupid Rads," called one of the soldiers. "Who do you think you're pushing?"

"Yeah, who do you think you're pushing?" echoed the other.

The Germans halted, turned, and walked towards the GI's. When they were several feet away, they formed a circle around them, and Schlango stepped into the middle. The soldiers looked scared and stood with open hands at their sides, scanning the circle for a kind face. "We're sorry," said one of the soldiers. "We were only kidding," he said, forcing a laugh.

Max stood apart from the circle. Though he was a GI, he did not care for GI's. Schlango and the others were his friends. He could always count on them.

He thought back to the first time he had met Schlango. It was at a little Gasthaus called the Pfisterer. He had entered meekly and seated himself at a small table in the corner. The Fraulein came and he ordered a beer, watching the people dancing in costume for Fasching. Seated a couple of tables away was a tall, broad-shouldered fellow with black hair and pronounced features. He was rolling a cigarette and, when he caught a glimpse of Max observing him, good-naturedly offered a rolled cigarette, and Max accepted. In return, Max bought the fellow a beer and the fellow invited Max to join him and his friends at their table. He noted their boot-shaped beer glasses, a name etched into each glass. The name "Schlango" was etched into the glass that stood before his new friend. His own was plain, and, due to the lack of a toe, held less beer. "Where do you get a glass like that?" Max asked.

"Oh, they're special," said Schlango. "They are only for us."

Almost any night Max went downtown he could find Schlango and his gang there, drinking beer, playing cards, or talking Fussball or Autorennen. He would come in and approach their table, ritually knocking twice, and everyone at the table would knock twice back and greet him with, "*Grüss Gott!*" or "*Wie geht's, Max?*" If there was anyone new at the table, Schlango would introduce him to Max, saying, "This is Max, a good friend from me," and Max would be immediately accepted, even though he was a GI.

They went places in a group. Sometimes it was to the auto races in Hochenheim, or to the Schwimmbad in Biedigheim, or to a Bierfest. Schlango always made sure that there was room enough for Max to come along. Already, more than once, Schlango and Max had fought back to back for some small principle, magnified by the beer they were drinking. One time they caused a riot, and Max had to be smuggled away before the military police arrived. Schlango, remaining behind, was arrested by the Polizei and spent ten days in jail, besides having to pay a two hundred marks fine.

Occasionally, some GI's would stray into the Pfisterer, only to be ignored by everyone. Max would silently scorn their ignorance of manner and dress. They would gawk at the two attractive girls that were waitresses and try to buy drinks, but after being ignored for a prolonged period of time, they would get disgusted and leave. Max had told Schlango about an incident with Myers and how the brunt of the whole thing had fallen on him, and Schlango understood fully why Max had no use for GI's. This endeared Max to the group even more.

Still most of the time was spent on duty. Only the nights and some of the weekends were free. The pettiness of the men was magnified before Max's eyes and he shrank into a spore-like shell, having as little to do with them as possible. Finally, he requested a leave to Italy. The night before he left, he went downtown, and said goodbye to Schlango and the rest of his friends at the Pfisterer.

Spring came closer with the passing of each mile on the train. Although it was still winter in Germany, it was already warm in Italy. The countryside was painted with the colors of spring flowers, yellow most of all. Max's spirits soared to the half-time rhythm of the wheels on the tracks.

Finally the train sighed into the station. Max reveled in the new freedom, for in Rome spring was in full bloom, and the warm sun melted the winter garments from his back like butter.

Not having much money, he found an inexpensive pension on Via Montebelo near Stazione Termini. The room he shared with four others cost only four hundred lire a night, and an extra one hundred lire for a hot bath, which he did without.

He found the pension very pleasant. It was filled with students from all over the world. One of the occupants in the room was an American that they called Thomaso. His rugged features made him look more like a boxer than the sensitive person he was. He knew Rome well, for he had attended the seminary for two years before he decided to discontinue his studies. Thomaso knew good, inexpensive places to eat and many interesting places to go. He knew the language and the customs well, and he had many Roman friends whose society it was Max's good fortune to share. Every day gave birth to myriad adventures. It was a joy for Max to wake up in the morning knowing that the day had such good things in store.

Thomaso enjoyed showing Max around Rome, and, as they visited different places, they talked a great deal. One day they were visiting a little house next to Piazza Di Spagna where Keats had lived and died. When they came out into the street again they turned right and mounted the steps. They sat down halfway and bathed in the warm afternoon sun. "How come after two years you decided to quit the seminary?" Max wanted to know.

"Why do you ask?"

"It seems like a big step."

"I guess it was many things."

"I'm sure something in particular must have moved you."

"Well, I couldn't accept a lot of things they were teaching. I was always knocking heads with the teachers."

"That sounds like how I feel about the army. Wish I could quit and live on the economy with my German friends."

"Don't be foolish. When I quit the seminary, that was it. But if you quit the army, they'll always be after you."

"What are you going to do now?" Max asked.

"Well, you know, I've been painting. I put some of my work together and sent it to an art school in Vienna. If they like it and accept me, I'll attend school there in the fall."

They both got up and walked down the steps again. "Let's take a bus over to St. Peter's," said Thomaso. "I haven't been to the Sistine Chapel for a long time. There aren't many people there at this time of day."

They found the chapel almost empty and, after looking at the ceiling for a long time, Max said, "I suppose it's worth a stiff neck, appreciating Adam's innocence."

"We could lie down on the benches along the side as long as the attendant isn't here."

"This is the way it should be seen," Max said, stretching out.

142

"I'm going to Vienna next week," said Thomaso, "to stay with the Massiczek family. When I decided to quit the seminary, a friend arranged for me to visit with them for a while. They were great in helping me to find myself again. You should come."

"Oh, I don't know. I was thinking of going to Sicily."

"They're a wonderful family. Vati is a doctor of philosophy, and Muti was a history teacher. All the children do something like paint or play piano or violin. We always go for walks, and in the afternoon, at tea, there are wonderful discussions and, often at night, we sit around the piano and sing chorales. There are always interesting people stopping in. You'd love them and I know you'd be welcome."

"Uh-oh, we better get up. Here comes the attendant," Max said.

Thomaso's description of the Massiczek family was too good to resist, and the following week Max found himself on the train to Vienna. Tom was in especially good spirits and they talked and joked for most of the trip. Tom drew many sketches of people on the train. It amused Max to see how self-conscious they became when they realized they were being used as subjects.

The Massiczeks lived in the suburbs of Vienna, on Adolfstorgasse, not far from Himmelhof. The house, which had been built by Muti's father, had a tower with an observatory. In the daytime one could see the steeple of St. Stephen's Church from the observatory, and at night one could see the heavenly bodies the steeple reached for. There was a big backyard with a high wooden fence and lots of tall trees populating the land as it sloped down away from the house.

"Make yourself at home, Max," said Muti, in charming English. "We don't have regular mealtimes. They're too confining. So whenever you're hungry, go to the kitchen. There's plenty to eat." She was a handsome woman, tall and thin, with soft eyes and graying hair. Somehow she made Max feel at home only moments after he entered her house. Thomaso was like one of the family.

The next day was Easter Sunday. In the morning everyone walked down the hill to church. The sun was shining and a soft breeze lifted the newly budded branches of the trees. One of the children was singing in the choir. The music fell upon Max's ears ever so sweetly. For the last couple of weeks it was as though a dark cloud had been swept from above his head.

For the special day, dinner was served at a huge table in the kitchen. Muti told Max how the Russians, during the war, had stationed themselves at her house because of its high elevation and the big accommodating kitchen. Thomaso went around hollowing out Easter eggs and returning them to their hiding places. The poor children discovered the eggs, only to have the empty shells crush in their hands as they cocked their heads in singular wonder.

The following day, when Thomaso finally got the old Morris running, he and Muti and Max and the children all scrambled in, and they set out for an ancient fortress high in the mountains overlooking Vienna. After much coaxing from everybody, the car labored over the last hill and they were there. The elevation provided a wonderful view. The tiny city took on an orange glow from the retiring sun as the Danube, like a ribbon, wound its way through the concrete maze. Tom, having seen the sight many times before, ran off with the children to make new discoveries.

"Sure is beautiful," said Max.

"Now that's the old part of the city," said Muti pointing off to the right. "And there's where the Danube used to run."

"There's so much history here," said Max.

"Yes," said Muti. "This fortress was used to ward off the Turkish invaders six hundred years ago."

"The Turks are rugged soldiers," said Max. "I heard about them in the Korean war. They had guns, but they'd charge out of the hills and terrorize the Chinese with knives as long as your arm."

"Yes," said Muti, "but even more ferocious were the Viennese young men that the Turks captured long ago. They displayed *Janitscharen*."

"What's *Janitscharen*?" Max asked.

"It's the denial of what you are."

"What do you mean?"

"Well, when the Turks captured the young Viennese men, they gave them a choice—to die, or to enter the Turkish army. Those who entered the army were always under suspicion and, to prove their loyalty, they fought more courageously than the Turks themselves."

"Even against their own people?"

"Yes, they butchered their own people the worst."

"That *Janitscharen* was a terrible thing."

"Yes, these men went against what they were. We must never forget our origins. Come, it's getting late."

On the way home they sang a travel song and after the tenth time, Max knew it well enough to sing along:

> Karamba karacho karutschi
> Die schönste Zeit ist futschi
> Karamba karacho karutschi
> Für immer immer futschi
> Wir fuhren ins Land der Kastanien
> Ins sonnige südliche Spanien
> Dort traten wir eine Senorita
> Ihr Name war Julia Pepita

The next morning Max had to board a train back to Germany. He was sad to go. Thomaso and the family accompanied him to the train station. It was as though he was parting from his family.

"You must come again," said Muti, "but next time for longer."

The whistle blew and Max mounted the steps.

"I forgot to tell you," called Thomaso. "I was accepted at the art school."

"That's great," yelled Max as the train lurched ahead. They remained on the platform, waving until the train turned them out of sight.

It was a long ride from Vienna to Ludwigsburg. Most of the time Max thought back over the vacation to the time spent seeing Rome and then Vienna with Thomaso and the Massiczek family. Often he hummed, *"Karamba karacho karutschi."* It was better to look back. There was not much to look forward to. The army would still be there. It would still be the same. The men would still be the same.

But then there were the Germans. There was Schlango and his friends at the Pfisterer. "I'll be glad to see them again," he thought. "That's something to look forward to."

As he expected, Max found everything about the army the same. At the end of the day he skipped chow, washed and dressed as fast as he could, and set out for the Pfisterer. He could not wait to tell Schlango and the others about the good time he had and the fine people he had met.

Max turned left from Wilhelmstrasse on to Kirchestrasse and all the welcoming familiar sights came into view: the bakery, the souvenir shop, the back of the old church. But the most welcoming sight of all was the little yellow sign with Pfisterer printed out in red letters. He entered and stalked the usual table, knocking twice on its surface. Everyone knocked twice back, and then Schlango looked up from the poker hand he had drawn, and his face came alive when he saw that it was Max who had knocked. "Oh, Max, my friend. Come and sit by me. How was your vacation?"

"Wunderbar," replied Max.

"A beer for Max," cried Schlango to the Fraulein. Everyone looked toward Evelyn as she brought the beer. She set it down before Max and he flushed with embarrassment as tears flooded his eyes. Before him stood a boot-shaped glass with "Max" etched into its side. All lifted their glasses high and Schlango said, *"Prost,* Max," and the others echoed the same.

"Prost," returned Max in a broken voice. After a few beers, they left the Pfisterer and set out for a Gasthaus on the other side of town.

Now in the market place, one of the GI's was holding his mouth, as blood ran down his arm. The other soldier was lying on the ground

145

holding his groin. Max's mind flashed back to Vienna. "It's the denial of what you are," said Muti.

"That *Janitscharen* was a terrible thing."

Max ran and pushed through the circle. He grabbed Schlango by the arm. "Stop this," he said. "Let them alone."

"Stay out of it," said Schlango, pushing him away. The beer glass fell from Max's hand and broke into a thousand pieces.

Max went in and secured another hold on Schlango. "Stop it," Max said as Schlango cocked his arm to hit him. "If you're my friend, you'll stop this."

Schlango dropped his arm. He motioned to the others and the circle disintegrated. The Germans walked towards the far end of the square as Max helped the soldiers to their feet.

"Thanks for breaking it up," said the GI with the bloody mouth.

"Yeah, thanks to you my glass is broken," said Max, as he turned and walked back towards the Kaserne.

Rites of Fall

by Dorothy St. Pierre

Detachment

To fall is to separate oneself
    from something else
Which may be air, reality, or will

A leaf from a tree falls
As the season from the sun

The wood of the tree is warm with late light
But each leaf, alone, drifts to bitter chill

What was above is adrift
The earth lifts to its horizon
    and turns away

There is so much of space
Where the long slant of autumn slides
    beyond the day

Consider how your light is spent
Then fall slow or fast to night

I burn I burn
I do not wait

Adrianne

by Michele Cusumano

Prosperous
owner of the junkyard near the canal
fathered five children
All grew up straight and obedient
except the fifth
Adrianne

Fourteen when I first saw her
in a long maxi-coat
with the shortest of school uniforms
tantalizing underneath
Her head a big bush of brown hair
curling around sparkling eyes
Beautiful Adrianne

At fifteen a friend OD'd
died in her arms
Adrianne ran
fearing the police

Sixteen and getting beat up
by her old man
for coming home at 3:00 AM
(we heard them yelling from two houses away)

Seventeen
She moved away
mother cried
father followed
caught her with her lover
brought "the boys" to break his legs

Fighting in the hallway
yelling in the street
Everytime she lay down to make love
the police were knocking at her door

148

E*I*G*H*T*E*E*N*
School and family left behind
Adrianne lives now for John The Writer
who is creating something Wonderful
while she pays the rent
by waitressing
on 42nd Street

An Old Man

by Geri Reilly

an old man
whose hands shook when he spoke
to stop and ask me directions
i said south
and he told me of the old times
good times, he said, too many years ago
before the war
which war i asked
before the others came
and the streets were safe to walk down
wore a straw hat
which he tipped when he left
to go north
and he stopped and asked
some directions.

I'm Eighteen

by Sandy Hayden

I'm young. I'm eighteen.
I'm old—speaking of how much I've done.
Maybe I'm only a child to the aged,
But at the same time a symbol of time for the infant.

What if my mind surpasses my age,
And no one believes how much I'm capable of?
Will they try to disprove my worth?
Or say it never existed?
Will their fear of my expanding mind
Cause them to destroy it?

But maybe my thoughts are too childish!
Will this be accepted and helped to be improved,
Or will I be laughed at and forever taunted?

What if I'm just what's wanted?
Perhaps I can live without others judging me—
But everyone knows perfection is non-existent.

I'm eighteen and aware that I can be what I want,
Just as long as it fits my age.

Education

by Barbara Krasnoff

The halls are dim, dank, damp
(Alliteration is an important form in poetry.)
A fitting testimonial to the
teaching?   (A question mark indicates a question.)
which is attempted
here   in the dimness

It begins
I will learn   know   it is
                                        good
                                        it was
                                        good
                                        we are
                                        good
                                        the enemy
                                        the Indians
                                        the different
                                        bad

    ("Although the Negro worked hard, he was generally happy and
contented. His simple and childlike nature was easily satisfied.")

                                    one times one = one
                                    the theory of inter
                                    an equation = zero

I   you   he   she   they
  drag   drag   drags   drags   drag
(Verb form is very important. We must speak properly!)

I will learn

                      please!
                      please!
(An exclamation mark indicates strong emotion.)

THERE ARE SECRETARIAL POSITIONS AVAILABLE FOR WOMEN, WITH CHANCES FOR PROMOTION

To what   where   who   how   what   where   who   how   what
where   who   how wh
it is   it was   it will be   they are   they were   they will be
we are   we w

I will learn   not
(A negative comes before a verb.)
I will not learn
(A period ends a thought.)
I will not learn.

Loneliness

by Barbara Krasnoff

apart from   all
who are there
waiting
in the dark
frightened
enclosed
in my mind   alone
apart
in a crowd
      that smiles
          and laughs
             and jeers
                at the one
they dance
two together
no one else   allowed or wanted
talking
many together   in the light
of their blindness . . .

I wish I were blind.

Sam the Sorry Zebra

by Nan DiNapoli

Sam was a young and playful zebra. But it seems he was always into trouble—like the time he went quite far from his home past a large lake. His mom had told him never to go far from the lake. She kept warning him that there were dangers there. Sam would look very serious, with his head tilted to one side, his eyes wide with a look of wonder, and his perfect stripes showing proudly.

No matter how many times his mom told him not to go far he just didn't obey. He would find himself wandering off. Oh, it sure was exciting to just keep trotting far from where he lived. Many times he would ask Toby, a little bit of a bear (and next to Sam he looked even smaller), to go along with him. Sam had other friends also like Maurice the giraffe and Hilda the reindeer. Maurice would grumble and tell Sam, "Now remember what mom said!" Even though Maurice was as young as Sam, he sounded so much like a grandpa. And Hilda the young reindeer would always sound like screeching birds and sing out, "Don't—go—past—the—lake—S-a-m." Oh, this would annoy Sam, as she always seemed to spot him trotting off no matter how careful he was not to be noticed.

Well, one day it was very hot and everyone in the village just sat lazily around. Nobody even wanted to play. Every once in awhile Toby the bear would walk or wobble down to the lake. From a distance Sam could see Toby splashing water all over. Maurice and Hilda watched also. Without talking or looking at one another they started dragging themselves to the lake. Nobody planned to sleep there but it seems this is what happened. Everyone started yawning. As Sam made himself comfortable, he fell into a deep slumber. The last thing he remembered hearing was the cry of a bird far off. It was a peaceful sight with every-one sleeping and looking so cool. The stars shone so bright that the lake looked as though sparks were slowly and softly shooting up and down. At a quick glance Sam's stripes glowed. When dawn arrived all that could be heard was the swishing of tails and the twitching of faces, as though the animals could not make up their minds whether to get up or not.

Sam was different. He got up as though someone had thrown a jug of cold water on his back. Then morning was gone. Everyone in the village was busy doing something—even play looked very busy in this village. Sam, as before, began to wander off. This time he was extremely careful not to be spotted by Hilda. Boy, he felt so wonderful once he had passed the lake. He loved his village, family and friends, but to Sam wandering was such fun. As he slowly turned his head to look back to see just how far he had travelled, he noticed how far he had gone. He stopped awhile to chew on some leaves. As he chewed he gulped and was choked up thinking how alone he was and so very far from everyone. If you could look close into Sam's eyes, you could see traces of fear. It wasn't that he didn't know how to get back. Well, deep down this is what he hoped—he could find his way back! He thought he could hear his mother saying, "Don't go further than the lake, Sam. There are dangers there."

"Well, anyway," Sam thought to himself, "I better start going back, it's getting dark." And the land was now cold. First he walked down one path, then he turned back because it looked as though that was the wrong direction. Then he started to walk a different path, first trotting fast, then all of a sudden slowing down. It was getting darker. He saw high mountains at a short distance. The snow caps showed quite clear. He would have enjoyed this sight if he were surrounded by friends and family. He was so tired now and all he wanted to do was sleep. He spotted a cave and entered half way so he could just see the mountains. The cave was warm anyway. Two big drops fell off his face as he fell asleep. Perhaps he had had a good cry.

When morning arrived Sam felt a little better. He was on his way home again, so he thought. As he put his quick graceful trot in motion he heard a flapping of wings and he felt a soft breeze. He glanced up and saw a frightful sight hovering over him. It was a bird, not a bat, as he first thought, because he realized bats dislike bright daylight. He tried going faster, but the unfamiliar bird jumped on his back, clawing at poor Sam. Sam tried kicking, shaking his head, but that terrible bird still kept hurting Sam. Then another bird whom Sam knew at once because it was an eagle came swooping down and began tearing and pulling the horrid bird off Sam's wounded back. It was quite a battle. The eagle with its very large claws and wide wings won of course.

Finally the eagle spoke to Sam, saying, "What in the world is a young one like you doing in this strange land?" Sam explained. "I see," the eagle said slowly. "By the way, my name is Victor. I'm the king in this land and I know at once when there is trouble. We have a problem here with those wicked birds. I've been here a long time and still can't figure out where they come from. To get back to you, I'm sure you're lost."

In a heavy but soft voice Victor said, "I will help you get home, at least half way. It is important that I stay in my land as my family and friends depend on me. I don't understand why you young beasts do not heed the warnings of dangers from your moms." As the eagle took Sam along, Sam began trotting faster and faster since Victor flew very proudly and with lots of strength until they reached a certain spot. Then Victor said, "I will leave you here. Go down that path and don't take another or you will have problems." Off flew Victor as Sam stood and watched this beautiful and kind bird. Sam thought to himself, "When I grow up, I must return to Victor's land. I can learn much from this eagle."

As he began trotting again, he noticed a slight graying to the sky. He thought, "Maybe there will be rain." Suddenly the sun shone quite bright and he forgot about the gray sky. All of a sudden Sam tripped and fell. He hurt a bit, and once down, the fatigue that did not bother him when he was moving took over. He decided to get up though when a huge cloud came in front of him. First it moved back and forth like it was trying to tell him something. As it came closer he noticed this cloud had shapes for eyes, nose and mouth. Sam was too stunned to move. Who had ever seen such a thing—a cloud that looked so much like a person.

This cloud, or whatever it might be, spoke! With a roar it said, "You didn't obey your mother, Sam." You could see tears roll down Sam's sorry face. The cloud continued, "My name is Basil. I came by to punish you just enough to make you remember not to disobey."

Sam, weeping and choked up whimpered, "Must you punish me?"

"Yes, I must. There are things that cannot be explained until one is older and wiser and knows of sorrow and pain."

Then Basil the cloud made a roar more kindly and said, "Your punishment will not be painful, nor will it be with you all your life. It will be with you for less than a year. By that time you will understand better and respect an adult who tells you of dangers and you will obey. I'm going now, Sam. Please don't hate me. Maybe someday you will thank me." It floated and disappeared.

Sam jumped up and started home. He forgot about what Basil the cloud had said. He felt once he was home he would feel better and be able to face anything. As he trotted he noticed a small lake. He went for a drink of water. As he drank he noticed his reflection. He looked up and saw the awful truth—his stripes were gone! Yes all of them. He just fell to the ground, kicked the dirt, and said, "What in the world will I do without my stripes. How can I face my family and friends?"

He lay there and wept. Sam looked so different without his stripes. He thought, "After all my family loves me, and my friends too." So he got up proudly and started off. He thought to himself, "This is what Basil the huge cloud meant by punishment. So I must be brave. I *must!*" He noticed the large lake where he lived. "Oh, boy, I'm home at last!" he thought.

As he came closer he saw his cute little friend Toby the chubby bear. He called out, "Toby, Toby."

Toby was wobbling along so fast and looked so cute trying to go faster so he could reach Sam. As he came closer, Toby yelled out, "Where are your stripes, Sam?"

Sam yelled back, "They are gone for awhile, Toby."

When Toby had calmed down, Sam explained everything and said, "I hope you will help me face everyone in the village. And another thing, Toby, I want to pretend I'm not facing all these things. It must be *our* secret, okay?"

"It's okay with me, Sam, but how the heck are you going to explain those missing stripes?"

"I'll just tell everyone I ate some strange leaves that did not agree with me, and I ran into a kind bird who told me in time my stripes will return," said Sam.

As Sam faced everyone in the village, everyone was so happy to see him. Later on of course they wondered about his stripes. Sam and Toby sat together as night fell near a cozy fire. Everyone listened to *some* of Sam's story as Sam's mother gave her young one a slight kiss. Sam and Toby glanced at one another knowingly.

As Sam's mother put the fire out everyone returned to his sleeping place. Every once in awhile Hilda the reindeer would glance shyly at Sam and Maurice had a look of wonder thinking about Sam. The stars sparkled as everyone slept and Toby whispered, "Good night."

Violence

A Handy Guide for Walking the City Streets

by Terence Malley

for Joan Templeton Carpenter

Grow all your fingernails
as long as you can;
if (as is likely)
yours have been gnawed away
practice stiffening your fingers,
practice jabbing out
at eye-level.

Whether or not you smoke
    normally
cup a cigarette
lit-end toward your palm;
practice wide sweeping motions
aimed at an ear or neck.

Even though you seldom read
    these days
carry a book
(a thick hard-covered one is best);
swung downwards
across the bridge of a nose
or upwards into a windpipe
the edge can kill.

And always wear
a signet ring
heavy enough to cut flesh.
Be sure it has
a hollow compartment.
This can be filled with
some quick-acting powder
(many are available).

There are indignities
you will not
be able to bear.

Cooked

by Richard Lann

God
the burger's just
a piece of crud

bingo—
you're a card
your number's up!

why, plug my holes
say cheese
and force a grin

we're frying men

Only the Dead

by Denis McKeown

Only the dead have seen the end of war,
Said the Greek. There are only the quick and the dead;
In war the choice is filled with equal dread.
My wounds are red, my body beaten raw;
My mind is bitter—my youth forever lost.
The burning sun cuts through the ceiling branches,
I wonder at the war that once used trenches.
I think: When did I see snow last?
When did I breathe free, no huddled masses
Men with many faces, the dead, the quick?
The young one breasted with the pongi stake?
Where the Christ, was there ever Moses?
Is God now blinded to us here in Hell?
Is there really life? Is Mother well?

Apocalypse

by Jeanette Erlbaum

G. O. Davis was convinced that she was a very hung-up person—and probably mad. She was convinced of this for an inexhaustible number of reasons, one of them being her colossal ego, which, she felt, had been nurtured in part by the accident of her initials. Some of the other things that had convinced her of her probable madness were her endlessly shifting points of view on an infinite range of subjects; her belief in the messianic mission of Jews in general, but of herself in particular; and foremost, her regularly predictable apocalyptic visions.

One of her frequently recurring visions was that of the world-wide ascension of the black man over the white. She saw the terrorized white populations of Europe and the USA and of stranded colonial outposts the world over being nightmarishly converged upon by the colored hordes of China, the fierce multitudes of Black Africa, the lumbering dark hosts of India and Arabia (not to mention the swarthy mobs of Latin and South America) and, not least, the belligerent blacks of Harlem, Bedford Stuy, and Brownsville.

From an objectively moral point of view, she felt that when the time for the bloody black holocaust arrived, it would certainly be about time. But physically she quaked with fear. And exactly where the role of Jewish messianism fitted into that picture she was not very sure at all.

It was not only the morbidness of her apocalyptic visions that oppressed her, but also the secret inadmissible conviction that she was endowed with strange powers of prophecy. And the visions assaulted her at all times, both awake and when she was asleep.

In the years that the Russians were unloosing one poison-flooded bomb after another into the atmosphere, G. O. Davis could see nothing but a hair-raising parade of human deformity hobbling continually before her eyes. And at the time that the thalidomide scandal had come to light, G. O. Davis envisioned the hapless products of human corruption massing together into a society of freaks and avenging themselves horribly on mankind.

164

The first time that she had awakened screaming from one of her visions, her husband had wiped the sweat from her teeming brow tenderly and had cradled her gently in his arms. But when nightmare had followed irrational nightmare with grim monotony, he finally lost his patience.

"Goddam, Gloria," he had said at last. "You're driving me insane!"

"I'm sorry," she replied contritely. "I can't help it."

"Why don't you have a baby?" he demanded then. But G. O. Davis didn't bother to reply. He cherished a foolish notion that maternity would distract her from the anxieties which were plaguing her. But she had made him promise even before they were married that they would never have children. Bringing children into the world was unthinkable, considering the present state of affairs, not to mention the appalling overpopulation of the planet as it was.

Occasionally, she vacillated on this point. In a way, it was perhaps her duty to flesh out the skeleton of European Jewry, to demonstrate that Judaism was a phoenix, rising from its own ashes, indestructible. But ultimately she always yielded to a larger nobler view of herself as a humanist first and a Jewess second. Jews took up as much room as anyone else—relatively speaking—peculiarly spiritual though they were. And she could not, in all conscience, contribute intentionally to overcrowding.

Often—not terribly often because she was of firm resolve—she felt sorry for her husband. He had developed a pitiful habit of ogling children at every opportunity so that she sometimes had to drag him away. (Once a kidnapping charge had been lodged against him by a neighbor in the building. But her three-year-old had turned up under his own bed when the police had begun by searching the apartment.) Still one had one's responsibilities to the human race.

In her more down-to-earth moments, G. O. Davis felt very grateful that her husband loved her. In fact, she found it almost incredible. Between her vocation as a welfare worker and her avocation of carrying the burdens of the world on her shoulders, she had little time for housework. She ran a rather shoddy ship. And she had a terrible habit of misplacing things—even money. Especially money. He was definitely an angel, G. O. Davis felt, in her more down-to-earth moments.

But when she was especially harassed by one or another of her visions, she felt he was a terrible nuisance. On occasion she even wished that he would go home to his mother, particularly when he snored prosaically in the middle of her dreams. And when he would have the gall to ask her to mend his socks. Goddam—you could get four pair for a dollar at John's on any day of the week! And why should he complain about TV dinners or frozen french fries? Just because his mother had nothing better to do than slave over a hot stove all day? Or sew zany patches on her husband's boxer shorts?

He probably would have divorced her actually, she finally decided, if not for the fact that she had managed to convince him of her powers. Pathos, their dog, had had a litter of five pups and on the morning following their birth into the world, G. O. Davis had peered at the furry little creatures with all the stifled maternalism of her pent-up breast and pronounced incontrovertibly at her beaming husband, "They're going to die." And in her mind's eye she saw them wasting away tragically, one after the other.

He had struck her then, flush across the face—as if she had ordained their death, rather than merely foreseen it. She had straightened her shoulders and, not for a moment losing her dignity, she had said simply, with not a little condescension, "That won't change anything."

And indeed, exactly as she had prophesied, Pathos' litter bit the dust one by one before they had even tasted of life. And, thereafter, her husband treated all of her visions with trembling respect, often echoing her nocturnal screams with some of his own.

"I think you should see a doctor!" her husband shrieked finally after she told him that she had envisioned her mother-in-law being raped by a Black Panther.

"I think you should ask for police protection," she had replied earnestly.

"You're crazy!"

"The dogs," she reminded him gently.

"When is this going to happen?"

"How should I know?"

Her husband had called her mother-in-law then and urged her to remain indoors, even though she never went out because of her crippling arthritis.

"How's your mother?" G. O. would ask meaningfully from time to time.

"Fine," he replied finally, carefully avoiding her eyes.

"You're sure?"

"If you're thinking about that crazy dream of yours," he sneered, "it didn't happen after all."

"She's ashamed to tell you," G. O. Davis said with conviction. And her husband had seemed to stop and think about that.

"About the dogs," he said finally. "I'm sure it was only a coincidence."

"All of them?"

He got up and began dialing his mother's number.

"Hello, Mom?"

"Yes, Mom. Look, has anything unusual happened to you lately?"

166

"Ya, out of the ordinary, Mom."

"No, that's all I wanted to know. Thanks, Mom. Good-bye."

"What did she say?" G. O. asked.

"She said a colored salesman tried to get in yesterday, but she shut the door in his face."

"What did I tell you!" G. O. Davis said, slapping the table triumphantly.

After that she grew dizzy with her own prowess. When Martin Luther King was assassinated, she recalled her formerly enigmatic vision of a black man being nailed to a cross. And when Bobby Kennedy was shot down by an Arab, she said to her husband, "Remember: I told you so!" though she had not really told him anything at all.

She began to wonder again why he didn't divorce her. The poor dear had gotten into the habit of turning ashen every time she opened her mouth. Then she decided that he was probably a masochist and, that being the case, she was really a very good wife for him after all.

On the other hand, maybe he wasn't a masochist. She was really very good company. And who could wish for a more entertaining wife than she was? However, she felt compelled to ask him regularly in a timorous little girl's voice, "Do you love me?" And she knew that throwing herself at his mercy often, as she did, endeared her to him, in spite of all her faults which weren't actually faults. Were they?

She almost blew the lid off their marriage again though, when she told her husband that she had had a vision of her father-in-law committing an act of sexual infidelity with the black janitor's thirteen-year-old daughter. He had raged for a solid week after that revelation, and she had decided finally that she could no longer entrust him with any of her visions, even though she had meant to honor him with all of her confidences. His shoulders were simply not broad enough to share the burden of prophecy.

By now G. O. Davis had permanently abandoned the notion that she was mad. Of course, prophecy often went hand in hand with madness. But it was the sightless public who thought of the prophet as mad, while the prophet himself knew better.

Since she had stopped sharing her visions with her husband, she noticed that he was now much happier. He took to mending his own underwear inconspicuously. And he pretended not to notice that she was feeding him frozen french fries, even smacking his lips over them in ostentatious gratitude.

One day he went so far as to offer to take her with him on one of his business trips—this time to Maryland—which formerly she had always been happy to let him go off on alone. They had a day left to visit Washington, D.C., and tour the Capitol.

She was deeply shaken by the unexpected magnificence of the city.

167

She was transfixed by the Capitol building with its eagle-capped spire which pierced the blue Washingtonian skies above the pristine waters of the Potomac. She felt irked with her husband's holiday levity, and each time that he impinged on the sobriety of her thoughts with his hoarse laughter, she fixed him with a withering stare.

As they began climbing the long broad staircase of the Capitol, so white and so flawless, G. O. sucked in her breath. Surely its classic elegance was not unequal to the glory that was Rome. (She shed silent tears over the lost glory of Rome.)

A guide began rushing them in whirlwind fashion through the building. He led them through the crowded statuary room and through the empty chambers where the Senators met and where the members of the House convened. He led them over marble stairwells and along the painted English porcelain-tiled floors. He encouraged them to ogle briefly the giant crystal chandelier in one of the lesser rotundas, awing them with statistics on the number of crystals and the difficulty of replacing burnt out light bulbs. And her husband seemed joyously relieved that she was oohing and ahing in a rhythm with all the rest.

It was not until the guide led them into a room filled with countless panels painted with scenes of historic significance that G. O. Davis began to feel one of her visions coming on. And it was not actually until the guide pointed out that the artist had thoughtfully left several panels blank to be filled *en futura* that her head really began to swim. It began to swim because it was so eerie to her that the artist had left several panels blank to be filled in. It was eerie because she could see that he had left only a few panels blank. And if America was to go on forever, as she had really always hoped that it would in spite of her terror of the black holocaust, then how would those few panels ever be ample to record its glorious history? Unless the artist too had been some sort of prophet and had left only a few panels blank because he had foreseen that no more were required. Oh, she could just scream! But really she couldn't. Because her husband would never forgive her, in fact he was already looking at her quite strangely.

She continued to stifle her screams when all the historically significant panels began tumbling down in colorful heaps of crumbling plaster, and when all the Senators and all the members of the House began dispersing like ants and fleeing in uncomely disarray. But she just couldn't help ducking when the crystals started popping and the light bulbs began bursting all around them, and when the magnificent floors began to give way, and when the statues began tipping and the marble pillars began toppling. And she couldn't help crouching catatonically when the glorious white dome itself and the great eagle, too, came crashing into the pristine waters of the Potomac.

She still did not scream though, until the great marble tombstone of the Unknown Soldier that they had visited earlier, reappeared in the middle of the giant rotunda where Abe Lincoln had lain in state, and the stone tumbled and the grave began vomitting up the grisly dry bones of the Unknown Soldier which sprang together miraculously, fleshing out and yielding a faceless black monster with stunted flap-like arms that began advancing towards them menacingly. Then she just had to scream, and though she saw her poor husband's mouth drop open in dismay, she still could not stop.

And she just kept on screaming.

A Poem about Nothing You Don't Already Know

by Mikhail Horowitz

Batman in the ghetto;
breaks heads with a

        Louisville Slugger

Unmarked tanks
patrolling them

        "hippie communions":

    MARIJUANA
    YOU USE IT TO GET HIGH
    WE USE IT TO GET YOU.

No jive. A black man
Strapped in a metal chair
is watching a lobotomized
jury—all cast from
"The Ox-Bow Incident"—
chuckling and weaving their curious

        lanyards

Luz

by Thomas Glynn

She had to walk with her bag because she couldn't find a taxi and that's when she started to hemorrhage. The cut had been fresh that morning and now the strain of the bag had pulled it open again.

Goddam, she thought. Fuck love.

It came slow and at first she didn't know. She thought she might have peed her pants or it was hot and she was sweating, but this was too sticky. And then she looked down at her dress and saw the stain, faint at first, not like blood at all but like raspberry juice or the popsicle stains you used to get when you were a kid.

She set her bag down and tried to take her hat off and cover up the front of her dress but she found she couldn't walk that way. It was too uncomfortable. And besides she had to stop the bleeding. Not that it hurt but who knew how long it would go on. Your insides might drain out.

She didn't know much about the body, bones and names of the organs and all, but she knew a lot about the groin, about ovaries and tubes and the vagina. I ought to by now, she thought. I sure as hell ought to. And why do I keep going back to that cheap sonofabitchin nurse. Stuff yourself up with cotton she tells me. Or go horseback riding and take cold showers. She tried everything but in the end she went back to "motha." God how she hated that woman. Motha loved to get inside you and scrape. She was always short on novacaine. She talked to you while she scraped. Always the same. Men were no good. They fucked you and ran. You grew their seed and then had to have it cut out. No goddam good, motha said, her face pasty like a billiard ball with water on it as she worked the scalpel inside burning your woman parts and drawing out pains you never knew you had. Wise up kid, motha would say. Don't let men stick that stiff ugly thing inside you. It makes you dirty and you smell like rotten fish. There are other ways, Luz honey. Motha can tell you about other ways. You be a five-time loser already, baby. One more time and you sure to die, Luz dearie. You bleed to death somewhere out in the street.

171

She was still bleeding. She could feel it. It was down to her stockings now, below the knee. She was embarrassed. She didn't want to bleed in the streets. It was such a cheap way to die.

It started to rain. Not enough to stand in a doorway for but enough to get wet. She wiped some hair from her forehead (You turnin dark at the roots, honey, motha said. Let me do your hair. Please. I like to do hair). The bag felt slippery in her hand, and her dress clung to her fat legs. The rain brought out the stain, widening it until it was the size of a large blood pancake. It was beginning to hurt. Even her veins.

She set the suitcase down. A taxi went by and she waved and yelled at him but he looked over once, quickly, and sped by. He wasn't carrying anybody.

Some kids came by, giggling. They looked at Luz and continued to giggle. They started to run. One of them turned back and yelled: "You're bleedin lady!" Then they laughed harder and continued running.

Luz sat on her bag. She could feel the handle coming right up through her ass. She tried shifting but everywhere she moved that goddam handle stuck her in the butt. She had to sit for a minute. She had to think. She could feel herself bleeding, like she was menstruating and had no kotex. It was warm and sticky. She remembered the last time George did it to her, when she was having her monthlies, and he pulled it out all bloody, like a brown banana.

She wished she had kleenex or something to blot up the blood on her leg. It oozed through her stockings, hanging outside her hose like little globules of red spittle. She looked in her purse for a handkerchief but all she could find was an itty rag the size of an airmail stamp. She tried blotting up her leg but all she did was bloody up her hand. Fuck love in the asshole. Look what it got you. And the last time Herbie had been on her he said, "Baby, your breasts are sagging and you got bad breath. Can you lend me fifty?"

It started to rain harder and she moved into a doorway. It smelled of cat shit. She got blood on the handle of her suitcase. The bottom was soaked through with rain. She looked up and noticed a woman looking at her from a third story window. The woman had a pillow on the window sill, and leaned out, though not far enough to get wet. She turned her head back and yelled at an invisible husband, "So bring me some no-cal, Sam, I should die of thirst. Open, and three oreos." She turned back and watched Luz in the doorway. A bottle dropped from the roof above her, shattering on the sidewalk. There had been something in it, a pale colored liquid. Whatever it was had wet Luz's shoes.

Luz looked up at the sky. A rain like this could go on for seven years. Like a case of syf.

She itched. She scratched. She could even smell herself. That was when you knew you were dirty.

She reached into her purse and took out a cracked diaphragm. Memories of Ocean City. The nice Margaret Sanger lady had told her all about putting it in, taking it out, washing it off, sprinkling a little talcum on it (treat it like you would a friend, honey, it's the best one you ever got). Shit! Who had time for all that? Long Island teeny boppers maybe, or Westchester once-a-weeks, but not Luz. Sometimes she left it in. Sometimes she let it lay on the dresser, moist and crawly. Sometimes she washed it out but that damn talcum was just another expense. It got old before its time. Like everything Luz used. Like Luz. It was about to crack and she never knew it. Not until that night. And even then she didn't know it. Not until her monthlies got late. They had been late before, but never that late.

Fuck love in the asshole anyway!

"I likes the color of your stockings, honey," someone said, walking by.

Luz looked down. They were peppermint striped. Candy. To lick. She looked across the street. The woman had a pillow on the sill. She rested her elbows, and two mashed potato breasts on them. She was sucking on something. It would be chocolate. Luz knew. She heard a voice above her. "Don't forget to get the electric toothbrush fixed!" A little kid came running down the stairs. He almost tumbled over Luz. She was about to say something when the kid said, "Hey lady, why don't you watch where you're sittin?"

She looked at him. He took the end of his sleeve and picked his nose with it. "I mean, you can eat a pound off the ground lady." He skipped off, imitating a faggot.

"Sam you got the batman on? Sam? I'm sitting by the window so tell me."

From somewhere, Cousin Brucie was jerking off on the AM. It was the older men she should have stuck to. The Des Moines pretzel salesman who liked to run around in his birthday wearing a pair of boy scout boots (lace all the way to the top, pocket in the right boot for a Fulton Barlow). A retired disc jockey who got it up to half mast, and then only with a German shepherd in the room. She tried a bull mastiff once. No soap. Some people had their specialties.

The mouth. That's how it always ended up. You could taste everything in the mouth. Food, sex, disappointment. Even blood. She was bleeding inside too. She could taste it. She stood up, her dress pulling up at her thighs. She reached down for the suitcase and lifted. The handle came up. The suitcase stayed down. Shit! The way they made these motherhumping b's you couldn't use them for two weeks before something went. She sat down on the case, holding the handle in her hand. What was she supposed to do with it? It hurt. She could feel it inside, like a corkscrew unbending itself, waking up. It curled and uncurled, like a worm, making its rusty way through her organs. No one ever knew, when you talked about pain (say, honey, you should have my piles in Kansas City), what it was like. No one had what you had. If she could call Big John, he might come. She looked at the rain mixed with blood. He might come. Big John might. What she did for him must have been worth something. She looked around for a phone booth.

"Sam, with more salt. You call this a pretzel?"

There wasn't any phone booth around.

Red rain. Wounded rain.

She was tired. Her head ached. Motha had told her to get some sleep after the "removal." She was all hopped up on aspirin and five other kinds of amphetamine, along with some under-the-counter barbiturates. She could feel her eyeballs. It felt like she had sand underneath her eyelids. She had to get a taxi. To go somewhere, where there was a bed. And a door that could be locked.

Two teen-age boys came by, their hair teased, doing a bad imitation of two teen-age girls. They floated, giggling, holding an invisible poodle. Next came two teen-age girls, doing a much better imitation of two boys. One of the girls was short and had dark, closely cropped hair. She was wearing a tanker's jacket, open down the front to reveal a sweat shirt. She was heavy in the ass and stomach, no breasts, sort of humped up shoulders, and had a razor scar on her chin. They stopped to look at Luz.

"You all right honey?" the butch said.

Luz looked up. Somewhere there were words, but she couldn't bring them up.

"Can we do something for you, baby?" butch continued.

Luz opened her mouth and her lips hurt when she tried to smile. Nothing came out, just bad air.

Butch put her hand on Luz's hair. "My ain't you got nice hair," she said. She turned to her girlfriend. "Here, honey, feel her hair. Feel how it be soft."

Her girlfriend just looked. She felt her own hair, patting the side. "C'mon George, let's go," she said.

"Shut up, you dizzy bitch," the other one said. She slapped her face. "I'll goddam tell you when I'm ready to go. Now feel her hair like I told you."

Eyes wet, she extended a pale hand and placed it on top of Luz's head, gingerly, as if she expected to get bitten.

"Now don't that feel nice like I say?"

"Sure. It feels nice, just like you said."

174

Luz looked at both of them.

"Say, honey," butch said, "isn't that blood?" She took her boot and spread a drop of it around the sidewalk. "You like to bleed, honey?" she said.

She made fists and stuck them into the hip pockets of her jeans. It started to rain harder. She zipped up her jacket and pulled up the fur collar. She leaned over, her face inches away from Luz. "Do you like to get hurt honey? Do you? My, you be a big one. So nice and big. What size you take? Thirty-seven I bet. And d. You don't have to say. I bet you're nice underneath. Wada y'say honey? Would you like to get hurt? Would you like to have her watch?" She pointed to her girlfriend. "I could do it good honey. I could really hurt you good. Here, feel my muscle."

Luz was silent.

"Cat got your tongue honey?"

The other girl put her hand on butch's shoulder. "C'mon George, leave her alone."

She ignored her. "I could really stomp you something. I could make you cry, hair and all." She waited for an answer.

"It's too late," Luz said.

Butch stood up. The rain had plastered down her hair. There was a drop of water that ran down her nose and tried to hang deliciously from the tip.

"C'mon George, let's go. I'm hungry. You promised me. Let's go."

Butch spread her legs apart, jammed her fists in her pockets, and looked down at Luz. Then she grabbed the other girl by the arm and they left.

Luz, don't cry no more. She kept saying that to herself. Over and over. It don't get you nothing. You lose water. Your eyes get red. And no one cares. Not really. That ought to be the way it is.

She couldn't get up.

She tried but she couldn't.

It wasn't raining as hard, but the rain was coming in waves, as if someone were dumping troughs of water over the roof above her in rhythm.

She shifted her weight so what was left of the handle didn't shove her in the ass.

She looked in her purse. There was money there. Some. It wasn't like she'd have to hit the streets or anything. She could pay her own way. Charity from no one. Take your lousy lecture and shove it. Can pay my own way. Wipe that smile from your face, you slut. I had my principles. I didn't beg for it on the street. You knew what you were getting with me. I had my friends. Respected. I was clean. Everyone knew.

She tried to lift. Up, with the legs. Move. Walk. Run. Before they catch you in the streets. My God, at least have a room to bleed in. At least that. Don't be the kind that has to bleed in the street.

C'mon Luz baby. It's been worse. Move it before they cut it. Before they plant it. Before they wear it out. Remember how it was in high school. Even then the bush was rich and black. Big. Guarding two tight petals. Rose colored. Smooth legs. She never wore a bra. She had the most beautiful smell underneath her arms.

Somebody dropped a bag of garbage from above. It hit the sidewalk like a paper watermelon, shattering grease and glass and rubbers whose tips were filled with cum.

Luz expected the moon to come out. She thought of all the songs she could remember that had moon in them, and then she thought of all the moons she could remember. She couldn't remember any. She couldn't even remember what a moon looked like. It had been years since she'd seen one. Light bulbs she could remember well. Moons not at all. There were flowers and pears and prints and sheets and she'd have to get up and go into the bathroom wearing a cheap chenille robe, pink, with something fluffy on the edges that always collected dirt. A clock ticked. The plant whistle was blowing. The sheets felt cold and slimy, as if they'd been washed in grease. There was no door, just a curtain clipped to brass rings hanging from a wooden bar across the doorway. It was heavy, velvet. When someone pushed it aside the rings made a sound on the wood she could still remember. EEEeeeee. The curtain would flap back and forth. In the wind, even though there was no wind. She had friends and used to go for long rides in the country and duck dinners (OK, not duck, but chicken). She was remembered. Then. Yes then.

My God, look at it come out!

Like a little brown river, but thicker, and much more even. She never knew she had so much. She felt silly, sitting here watching it come out. She felt like laughing. It wasn't hers. It was too much. It was like watching a balloon deflating, a liquid balloon. And all that's inside you. Never think about it really.

She started to giggle.

Really, it was the funniest thing in the world. She wanted to swallow it. She wanted to swim in it. She wanted to float in it. All she could think of was how years later the suitcase would be stained a dull brown, black really, but very faint, and someone would ask someone else how that got on there and the first person would say, I don't know really it's always been there, and Luz just laughed some more. She threw back her head and howled.

Someone shouted from a top floor window to shut up.

Shut the hell up!

They dropped another bag of garbage.

A business man came walking by, staring. When he was satisfied that she was conscious, he kept on walking. Her left leg was asleep. She shouted at it to wake up but the only reply came from the top floor window. Another bag of garbage. Those people must do nothing but eat and shit Luz thought.

Beautiful.

She had never felt so cool in all her life. Everything was cool. Everything was flow. She was flowing liquid. Nothing could touch her. Nothing could harm her. Someone came by and she put her hand up to her mouth, giggling. She had a secret. How could she tell them? How could she begin? Where?

That was the secret.

You had to flow. Everything was flow. Hitting liquid never did any good. You had to be liquid. She could feel herself becoming liquid, especially between her legs. Her bush was crusty and matted, but soggy. Red soggy. Brown soggy. She put her back against the door. Everything was cool now. The rain had stopped. It was cooler. She could see her breath, small little smoke like clouds that hung about her nose, almost reluctant to leave.

In the sky. The sun. Or was it the sun? But those colors. You couldn't find those colors anywhere else. To say blue and grey and gold and red was to say nothing at all about those colors. They were slipping, sliding, falling into the universe. Everything was beautifully cool. So cool. She laughed because she couldn't explain to anyone why it was so beautiful, and so cool. No one really knew about this kind of cool.

Some kids came over and watched her slump.

So very very cool it was cold.

On the Spike

by Ben Wilensky

There were two men in the room,.staring at him. "Get dressed, Beebee," one of them said, the white man. "Move!"

The white man stood at the foot of the bed with a smile on his face, like he was saying, Go, Beebee, run. Shoot out of line. The other man was brother black, dick partners. "Ya', baby, tell *me*, so white friend here don't crush your nuts. C'mon baby, talk."

"You messed up, Beebee," the white man said, rubbing his knuckles. "You done for."

Shee', the man see too many movies, oh Chris' it's time. He could feel the pain rolling in his guts. "Move!" the white man gritted his teeth. He smacked Beebee across the face with his report book.

Beebee pushed himself up onto the bed, trying to see the face of the colored john, but the john was sitting in darkness. The lamp was by his bed. He was going to be sick. When he turned towards the lamp chain, the white man hit him again. "C'mon, Beebee," laughing out of the corner of his mouth, "turn on the light, make a run for it. Go on, sweetheart." The white man jerked the covers off his body and pulled the lamp chain at the same time. "Goddamighty, look at them spike wounds."

"Lay off muthuh," Beebee said, edging off the bed, "I'm movin, I'm movin!"

"Not fast enough, nigger."

He felt the pain, dizziness. Christ, it's time. *Jesus.*

"You got a warrant?" Beebee choked.

The white man smiled. "Warrants are for people. You're a nigger. You're a dead nigger."

The black john was silent. He was studying, studying hard. He had to do it right. He was black Judas.

"Won't work," Beebee said, gasping. "Throw it out in court . . . 'legal search and seizure. Muthuh," he tried smiling, "You got a bad arrest on your hands." Every time he opened his mouth, the pain increased. Soon he would throw up.

"All of a sudden you're a lawyer. Well not this time, Beebee. This time your black ass is shit and I own it. Move, nigger!"

178

"Nuthin . . . you got nuthin . . . ." Jesus, it hurt to breathe. Stop kickin, dammit.

The white man sucked on his teeth and spoke very slowly. He was grinning. "I count ten bags on the night table, one cooker, two spikes. In the bathroom, five ounces with the talcum powder. You're a big man, Beebee," he said, booting him again.

"Yeah, you find that stuff here, I kiss yo' ass."

The black john lifted himself out of his chair. His voice was pained, sympathetic. "Make it easy, baby."

"We waited for you," the white man grinned. "You're gonna start yellin your head off. Give us a break and you get one too. Where's the piece?"

"Shee . . . muthuh, nevah use a piece," Beebee said, and then he remembered. He kicked the white man and bolted for the door. Jesus, Jesus! The bullet would go into his brain like an ice pick.

When he reached the stairways, he was sick.

He was dragged out to the car, dragged up the long flight of steps leading to the precinct house. It must have taken him three years to climb up the mountain to the metal cage. Dear Lord, it's always the cage, peering out through the wire mesh, it's home, I'm home. The pain was coming faster.

The white man grinned. He was holding the yellow sheet in his hands, reading and smiling, reading and smiling, and then he said, "Beebee made another mistake. Bad boy, should never kick a cop, should you Beebee? Beebee's a bad boy."

The colored john sat, dapperly dressed, looking sad.

"Lessee now," the white man said, scratching his head, "You're fifteen bags a day now, right?"

"So?"

"Where you get the bread?" the white man snickered, bringing up his knee.

Beebee grunted. "Thasswheah," he said.

"Old John the Rabbit," the white man sang out, "he got a mighty fancy habit."

The glaring yellow light made him dizzy. He looked in the colored john's direction. The brother turned away . . . lit a cigarette.

"Let's see now," the white man went on, reading from the yellow sheet, "in '49 knife, '50 knife, '51 gun, well now, made the grade, didn't you coon? '52 A and R gun, possession, '53 possession, simple assault, ah yes, some bleeding heart judge reduced it, lucky Beebee. '55 knife, reduced . . . six years . . . '62 possession, A and R knife, pending . . . '63 A and R pending . . . what else is pending, you dirty black shit?

179

Your time's run out, bad ass, you're dead. Now where's that piece?"

The ball spasmed in his guts, it ripped him, he felt blood, Jesus, it was ripping him up.

"Prove it, prove it, prove it, white fuck, you prove it."

The white man moved to the cage and dragged Beebee out by the hair. He went to the back and began stomach kicking him around the squad room. "You think you gonna beat it, you think so? Not this time, not this time, coon, not this time. Where's the piece . . . where is it?"

He was born screaming, with shit pumping in his blood, screaming from his eyes. Break em break em break em.

"Drink it!"

His head snapped. Sweat dripped down from his eyes. He licked it. Salt or blood, salt or blood? Salt.

"Come on son, drink it," the black john said. "You black, I'm black, all the same, don't give that sonofabitch any lip. Give him an excuse, he'll smash you like a bug."

The brother had watched while the white john had done all the work. Black feeling the pain of black, feeling the kicks of a white man's boot, feeling the veins whimpering.

"Drink it."

Beebee took the container of coffee and tried to swallow. He was sick again, but there was nothing left, not even bile. "I suck you' miserable white ass, oh you dirty, mm, oh, mm, just one . . . just one . . . ," he couldn't open his mouth. Even when he blinked, it killed him.

"Name is Sam," the black john said.

"Oh yeah, Sam," Beebee whimpered, "SamSam, the pants too long, evah long, Sam, them pants killing me."

"He's mad this time. He's gonna do a job on you."

"Let him, let him. Doin it fo' years. Killin the nigger. Got long shoes, that dick, white muthuh fuckin bastid. He stand on my head fo' yeahs chokin me to death . . . gimme one, gimme one, oh Jesus." He let his head fall against his chest. His eyes closed up. Then like a sleepy clam digging itself out of the sand, he gasped, involuntarily . . . his body whimpered, shook.

"Where's the piece?" Sam said, apologetically. "Look, kid, he don't care you black, he don't care you come from shit. I do, son. I'll get to the judge, I'll talk to him. I'll get you five, Beebee, I swear. That white man gonna get you dead. I mean it son. If you don't open up to me, he gonna carry you out inna hearse."

"You get me . . . you get me shit," Beebee whimpered. "You suck that white man. He stomp you, and you suck. He kick you, you suck. You suck, Sam, you black like me, you got the gut pain like me, you shit Sam. Oh God, Sam, you weak nigger."

180

Calmly, eyes clear, Sam sat back in his chair and lit up a cigarette, sucking the smoke as far down into his lungs as it would go. He had his report back before him, and the yellow sheet was spread out. 3:25 A.M. He was getting hungry. Five more minutes Brodsky would spell him.

"You makin a mistake son, that's all I can tell you."

"Shee' Sam, same one I always made. Don't got a piece, nevah needed one. C'n breathe a little now, feels bettuh, gonna hold out fo'evah."

"Two more hours you'll be screaming. But Brodsky don't want that. He gonna beat you to death."

"Burn that white muthuh fuckah. I want a lawyer." Beebee shouted, "I want a lawyer."

"You robbed a grocery. You shot a man. I want that piece. I want to help you. I can get you five."

"Yeah I know, ol' judge tol' you pick up that pickininny wid his piece a' action, gimme five. Judge black? Is that it, Sam? No piece f'um me, Sam. You and that white trash get shit f'um me."

"I'm trying to help you," Sam said with dignity. "You don't know him."

"I know him, Goddamighty, *I know him*."

"We can wait. We can wait until you start screaming. I wanted to save you some shit."

Beebee looked up into Sam's eyes. He started to cry. "Oh Sam," he said, "you weak nigger."

Brodsky returned with two containers of coffee. The detectives sat around their desks sipping, shrugging to no one in particular. They were tired. When they belched, you could tell there was acid in the coffee.

"Sackin' out." Sam shuffled to the door, held onto the door knob. He looked at Beebee, then shook his head. "Al, take it easy on the kid," then he moved down the hall.

"Sure," Brodsky answered him, finishing up a swallow of coffee. His stomach backfired, and his eyes turned into asiatic slits. "Why not? Have some coffee, coon." As soon as Sam's footsteps had died away, Brodsky smashed his knee into the kid's groin. "Where's the piece, kid, where's the piece?"

Beebee cried and shook his head. "Just one, gimme one."

"Where's the piece?" Brodsky droned, whacking away with his forearms, "where's the piece?" over and over again, voice indifferent, methods indifferent.

"Cut it out, you bastard."

181

"Sure kid," Brodsky said, bringing up his right knee. He paused to sip his coffee. The coffee was pure acid. "Bum stomach, ya' know?" He pushed his forearm against the kid's jaw. "It takes you slobs all night before you give in, and by that time my stomach's gone to hell. Be a good boy. You think I enjoy this?"

Beebee panted. He couldn't tell what part of the body that white bastard was kicking. It was all the same, the guts, the ball bouncing.

"Whaddya say, kid, make it easy."

Beebee wept. "Work, you white fuck, *work.*"

He was still screaming when Sam returned, eating a candy bar. Brodsky was sitting with his feet up on the desk, reading the *New Yorker* magazine and sucking his teeth. His shirt collar was opened, drenched with sweat. His tie hung over the chair like some dead fish. "They got a bunch of fags down there writing their stories." Brodsky threw the magazine across the room. It sailed past Beebee's head. "Every one of them starts off with a divorce."

"Realism," Sam answered, biting into his Hershey bar. "Rich, white yo-yo's." Sam crushed the candy wrapper in his palms and let it fall into the wastebasket. He turned and watched Beebee. The kid was shivering in his chair.

The squad room was beginning to stink.

"I hate these magazines," Brodsky said, "it's always a clean smelling, faggy world. Where everyone's got a nice clean choice to make."

Sam swallowed off the last of his candy. "Well, what's up kid?" he said to Beebee. "You ready?"

Sullen eyes greeted the question.

"The way we write it," Brodsky said, "our kid here tells us his life story, how he shoots up, how he robs his mother, how he marries his rich, white nurse, and *then* he gets a divorce. Think it'll sell?"

The telephone rang and Sam answered it. He nodded into the phone as he licked the chocolate from his teeth. "About an hour, give or take," he said, after a hesitation. "Yeah, Al's on his fourth cup of coffee. What about Ransome?"

Beebee's neck snapped forward. He tried to focus through the yellow light. It was hair crawling in his face. Fight. Fight the bastards. He clawed with his fingers. Hold on, hold on. He was sick.

"O.K. then, Ransome and Lennie, and the guy is going to live? Right." Sam nodded into the phone and lit a cigarette. "You down at the hospital now? O.K., wrap it up and come on over. Bring the D.A. with you. Yeah."

He shuffled to the window and looked out at the dark street. In an hour or so, the sun would start breaking up the darkness. Everything would start clean. He and Brodsky would take a shower and try to rub off the sickness.

"You're lucky, Beebee." The squad room smelled like a zoo. "The

182

guy you nailed is going to live. Now c'mon, kid," Sam exhaled, "where's the piece and let's get this thing over with."

"Gimme one," Beebee said, holding his chest, trying not to whimper. "Nevah used one and you prove it. I'm sick and tired . . . you prove it."

Brodsky sighed. "Won't have to. Five more minutes you gonna have a heart attack. You gonna crap out right in the station house."

"Lennie and Ransome said you were trigger happy," Sam said to no one in particular. He stared out of the window, watching the neon flash around the corner clock. As the green light nipped at the second hand, Sam felt himself beating time with his heel. All of them are black. Jesus. Let the lily fag editors put that in their magazines, all the goddamned junkies in this city are black. Poor, black niggers who can't read or write. But they can hate, and baby, they do that well. Brodsky, he thought, Brodsky . . . he knows. He understands. God-damnit, why can't we do more?

"O.K., kid, if that's the way you want it."

"I don't want it no way," Beebee choked.

"Look at this energy gone to waste. All this time you could've bought five brand new cars."

"Twenny," Beebee said, "coulda bought twenny. Coulda bought you guys for a song. Spent it though, you pay for shit, pay hard. You know it."

"Ah well, I'm just used to old-fashioned work, right? But this is boring, right kid? This kind of work makes a man go sour."

Beebee's head snapped forward. "Chris' man, quit it."

"Sure kid."

It don't pay to fight, don't pay to be free. Chris', pain, let up, god-damnit, let up on poor nigger, Sam, help me, Sam, Sam.

"No contest," Brodsky said, but his face was twisted. "You wait, you sweat, and then you win. No contest, Sam, never is. Man . . . they hold out until you're sick to your guts. O.K., kid." He stood up, walked towards Beebee. His fangs were out. There was no let up this time, only hate, pure white, burning hate.

Beebee screamed. His howling swelled through the squad room, but down below, the desk sergeant, accustomed to the ritual, continued to type. Oh God, oh God. He crawled to the man at the window, hugged him by the feet. He licked them. He licked the laces, he sucked on his own tears. He burned, his body stank and burned.

Sam pulled out three duplicate forms from the drawer, fitted them with carbon paper, and rolled them into the typewriter. He started to type with two fingers, poking and jabbing holes, while a sardonic smile spread across his face. He could have typed with all ten fingers but it was more relaxing this way, poking around, inept, slow, finally getting there.

The Luger was in Ransome's house under the floor boards. Four or five shots, he didn't remember, only a piece of the man's head flying off. Hysterical fingers in the cash register and the three of them scrambling out into the night, moving their bowels. Hell, that muthuh was going to live, didn't you say it, Sam? More than he ever did. He couldn't tell which was coming faster, the words or the pain.

Sam was like a priest now, calm, quiet like, like when the priest comes to bless you. "We're gonna fix you up, Beebee. We want you clean when the D.A. comes."

Brodsky had taken three tiny cellophane bags from his drawer along with the cooker and the spike. Two filthy strings of cotton were wrapped around the spike. "This is your shit," Brodsky shrugged, "use it now."

"God bless you," Beebee wept.

He fumbled with the strings, he couldn't hold them. Brodsky had to help tie them around the veins. The bags were emptied into the cooker and Beebee mixed it with a drop of his own saliva. The two detectives looked at each other and shook their heads. Beebee's nose and crotch were leaking.

Brodsky lit a wooden match and gave it to the kid. The match shook in Beebee's hand. The flame seared down the side of his thumb and burned into his skin but there was no reaction. The skin was dead. He passed the match under the cooker. When he was ready, he sucked it up into the spike and started jabbing. He couldn't make it, he couldn't see which one to use, they were all pussy stigmata.

"Bleeding Jesus," he wailed, "I'll lose it."

"C'mon, kid," Brodsky said, "you can do it."

For a moment, both detectives wanted to laugh, or cry, it made no difference.

Beebee sighed. He lowered himself into Brodsky's chair and sighed again. His eyes closed as his neck snapped forward. Between nods, he fumbled with his shirt pocket as if it hid the last secret of his life. His fingers were incredibly delicate, and dumb.

"You not so bad," he mumbled, forcing himself to articulate the words ". . . white . . . honky . . . muthuh . . . fukah . . . hope the bastid . . . croaks . . . hope he dies . . . ."

Beebee's head snapped forward, snapped awake. Mucus oozed from his nostrils.

Sam typed with two fingers, pausing every once in a while to make an erasure. He did it carefully, dutifully. He read the paper over again and then lit a cigarette. His shirt and tie were clean, and compared to Brodsky, he was black Beau Brummel.

"Well, I'll tell ya', Al, I need a break, I need a change now and then, be easier that way." His voice was soft, full of self pity. He knew it, but he had to say it. "I wish to Christ you sit back and watch it . . . ."

184

"Can it!" Brodsky snapped, "you hate these fucks worse than I do."

"Yeah." With a short jerk, Sam stubbed out the butt.

Beebee's eyes rolled open and he smiled stupidly. "You know what? Kill that white muthuh fuckah, *burn him*."

"You did," Brodsky said. "You made his head look like Swiss cheese."

"You O.K.," Beebee grinned, "you good to Beebee."

"Sure."

The sun was breaking on the steps of the precinct house. The day was starting clean. Four cups of coffee, acid, Jesus, tomorrow night, another one.

"The best way to handle you guys is extermination. Ya' know what that means?" Brodsky rubbed his eyes. "We're all dyin.'"

"Yeah, you right, man, you right. Beebee craps out, but you guys live fo'evah. Shee't. Live fo'evah. Jang, jang," he hummed to himself, "jang, jang, Chris', jang, jang, jang, jang," over and over again until Sam had to put his hands up to his head to stop the pain. After a while Sam said, "That's better."

Brodsky nodded. "Right on."

Garbage Disposal

by Anne Marie Brumm

every time
i use it
i think of
a standing
tomb
container of death
where you were
ground

sirened cramps
the stench of urine
feces over your feet

in the beginning

was the scream
blood-blotted arms
pounding the pit

prayers shiver
through the night
of a vertical coffin—
you cannot kneel
a laugh trembles
as slated eyes
watch the
promised
manna fall from the
hull
of a winter heaven

thoughts igloo
in the spiritual frost
a racial winnow
a gruel of bodies
a "pure" earth sated
the guard was glad—
tired of trudging
by
one
of the longer ones

in fourteen days

they opened
the grate
some
thing
else rinsed down,
more bones, i think
from civilization's
evening meal

The Defeat of the Nez Percé

by Alan M. Berg

He was lying awake. His eyes kept turning from the hollow shadows in the cabin to the small window and the dark whispers of the night. Through the window he could see five stars in a clear part of the sky, and inwardly he called to them, first with his eyes and fingertips, and then with his breath.

Before, when they had both been looking at the fire, he had been listening to the wind in the birches and thinking about the way their firelight would look from the top of one of the dark hills about them. If someone were up there alone, looking down into the valley, he might see the faint light like the dim reflection of Mars on the black surface of Te-ata. Up there, alone—himself—in the cold night, staring down through the shadows . . . .

Red's eyes had been glazed with the fire when he had asked about the girl.

He had answered slowly. "An Indian girl, spending the summer with her uncle in Hayes Falls. Hangs around the lake in the afternoons. She'll be going back to Canada soon, I guess. She's in one of those boarding schools up there."

It had sounded as though Red laughed, but his eyes were still without expression. There was only the sound of the fire.

"Will she be there tomorrow?"

Nodding, he had turned to the narrow distortion of his head on the wall. Then he sat straight in the tall-backed chair and his hand was moving back and forth over one of the rough arms. "I don't know . . . ."

Red had bent over the fire, running his fingers over the studs in his wristband. His lazy smile jumped with the flames. "We'll keep her for a few days then drop her off far enough away."

Afterward, he had watched the coin flicker in a silver instant. And when Red opened his thick palm, he saw that he would be first.

The girl is pretty, almost oriental—with high cheekbones and dark, oblique eyes. I could grasp her long hair and pull her head back easily, so that her eyes would hold the sky. And I could wind the coarse black hair tightly around my hand and control the flutter of pulse in her throat.

Today we were talking about the lake, and she was telling me that her people once believed that all lakes came from the tears of gods. And then she asked me why gods might have cried so much. She already knows part of it, and she'll learn more about why tomorrow.

But life in a boarding school for a lonely Indian girl does have its benefits: further development of keen sensitivity, inspired by years of racial oppression and decadence. Couldn't I see that she hungered for some sort of truth? She revealed part of the answer unknowingly when she mentioned the gods crying.

No, she really didn't want an answer. But why ask me? So that I could play Abel and Rima with her, ask her to teach me the Nez Percé words for water and sky—and, in turn, describe the world for her quite graphically: swamps, jungles, raging rivers and jagged peaks . . .

1

Ours is the last house on the road, and the ice-clogged swamp in back is ours, with the old railroad tracks and patch of forest—a gray haze now. We chose this house because we had come from the city and the house was roomy—and there was the forest in back. We hadn't known about the swamp and its dead trees because we bought the house on a rainy summer day when the land was misty and green. That day the earth-scent of the mountains was drugging.

He slammed the car into the gravel driveway. Then he sat still, staring at the house, and he finally saw her coming out to him.

He stared at her, and the spots of water on the windshield made her belly seem abnormally large.

"Why don't you come in?"

He was seeing the way the water made her dark eyes larger. "I was waiting for you," he said slowly. "You know, you look more pregnant than ever."

Her weak smile was gone as he opened the door. "What's wrong now?" she asked.

He turned to look at the bare trees through the smoke of his breath. "Everything. The whole damned school."

They walked to the house and he pushed the door closed, jarring its loose panes.

"You can feel the cold air through the door," she said, not turning around. The window light was gray on her profile. "It will be great for the baby."

His eyes caught the torn backs of her moccasins. "You should get new shoes. And why don't you wear socks?" He was expecting her hard laugh. And there was nothing more. "Tell me your sad little story for today."

Her eyes found the window. "Well, after you left this morning, I sat on a kitchen chair for two hours, looking at our swamp, watching the sleet fall on dead trees. Then, listening to the dripping bathroom faucet, I picked seven blackheads from my face. Then I went to bed again for two hours, just lying there, looking at the ceiling, a dusty strand of web hanging—feeling the cold air seep through the poorly insulated window behind my head. Then I put on my coat and muddied my moccasins by walking to the mail box and that roadside store for a paper. Then I read the letter we received today from your father. I must have read the letter ten times. Then I pored through the Middle County *Courier*. Then I sat by the table waiting for you. Then you came and you were waiting for me."

Still wearing her coat, she was clutching at the dull fur collar. He took the opened letter from the table.

"He still wants us to come back to the city," he said. "I bet you really enjoyed this."

"He is thinking of us."

He was looking through the kitchen window to a place above the gray-spiked hills where subdued light slanted from a rift in the overcast. "Remember the day we bought the house, it was raining in a soft way, and it looked as though the rain was green and everything was green. We felt the scents of the water and the earth and we didn't care about leaking windows or the grade four lumber."

"We were pretty dumb," she laughed.

His eyes again searched the skies, but the sunlight was gone. My father, he thought, immigrant at eight from somewhere in the Baltic, came fatherless to America's shores. Had his picture taken with baggage at his feet. Looked strangely commanding in artificial pose, perceiving new challenges of magnificent new country. Fast to rise. Factory worker at ten, cab driver at eighteen, auxiliary policeman at twenty-four, truck stevedore at twenty-seven, shipping clerk at thirty, shipping clerk at thirty-five, shipping clerk at forty-five, shipping clerk at sixty.

"You know," she was saying, "that first week here with the kitten. It was dead in the cardboard box in the empty room, and we didn't know—we were having one of our morning love-fests."

He turned back to the window. "Death and copulation, the great eternal themes."

"But you had meant well."

"Could it have been the sugar I put in the milk?" he said. "But it was weakening before. The milk not rich enough?"

"It was your idea to take it back with us from the city."

"A poor way to have tried to maintain a sense of the past."

She laughed again, and her voice seemed more musical. "The dirge, was it in the wind? And our procession to the back yard, the dog sniffing, as though trying to locate a suitable spot. Then you with the box and me with the spade. You dug the hole near the swamp."

He saw her tears as she grabbed his hand. "The baby—I don't want to have it."

He laughed.

She moaned and closed her eyes tightly.

Folding his father's letter, he rose from the table. "And so it was done."

"Are you going out again?" she asked, her eyes at last finding him.

He nodded. "You can come too. You know, you should walk as much as you can."

"No more today. I had enough this morning."

He tore the letter into small pieces and went to the bedroom for his old clothes.

I, now twenty-seven years old and in perfect health, begin . . .

I pass a small bridge where water catches the vagueness of sky in scattered glints. And I look across the brown fields, far into the trees, through the trees, searching for the source of spindled light which touches the water and dark grasses.

Begin to understand where that light comes from. To see how it filters through the sameness of the sky and finds an answer to itself on the tips of dead grass and in the rushing water.

The old barn is to the right of the road, some hundred yards after it curves toward the seminary. The barn is old and slanted, and the unpainted wood has the tones of copper and burnt sienna. I discovered the barn the summer day I found this road, through the dust of that warm day, through the straw at my feet. And here in the shadows I let the essence of the light seep into my cold hair and through the old planks of my mind. Then I'd feel like drinking melted snow and keeping a hot stew going in the forest the way Faulkner did when he went hunting, or staying out all night to see Venus through the needles of a pine on one of the nearby hills.

THE PERSONS OF THE PLAY

DR. BORDEN
The principal of Middle County High School. At twenty-nine, probably the youngest high school principal in New York State. Is undergoing first year of internship in rise up the professional ladder. Graduate of Harvard School of Education. Known to students as "Dr. Boney." Known to most teachers as "Golden Boy." Lanky, pipe-smoking, has wide professional smile. Rather direct in a green way to show strength, resolution ("Cut out your niggardly bitching" said strongly to teachers at faculty meeting. "We have to make sure they keep their shirt-tails in and see that they not chew gum and skirts should not be more than four inches above the knee.")

JOSEPH HARTBERG
A student of the high school. Wearing grease-smeared coveralls with red insignia "Al's Service Station" sewn near left shoulder strap. Taking time from work to attend conference. Thin-featured, dark hair spilling over eyes. Knows all intricacies of teacher torment. Narrow-eyed, taut-lipped, pain-sipping.

PAUL DARLANG
A student of the high school. Has on baggy off-white sweater, tan chinos, loose black loafers. Blushing round, pimpled face. Smiling uneasily. Reminds you of Chaucer's miller (see "Canterbury Tales"). Crude, pock-marked immoralist. Life revolves around experiences in Spano's Bar.

SCOTT HENDERSON
A student of the high school. Crew-cut terror of small town brainlessness. Through his plastic-rimmed glasses will never glimmer appreciation of Burns, Swift or even Lewis Carroll. Pulling on sleeves of gray sweatshirt. Wearing tennis shoes without socks.

FRED KING
A student of the high school. One of the few Negroes in the school. Has tried too hard to assimilate, resulting in discipline problems. Flabby and shuffling. But strong in viciousness.

BARRY LEASON
An English teacher of the high school. In late twenties. Face grim, eyes moist, looking beyond retractable pen which King is clicking.

SCENE: An austere classroom. Window light cold on tops of desks. Principal, teacher and four students are seated in semi-circle. Atmosphere tense, hostile.

Dr. Borden (clearing his young throat). Now, I've heard that there's some difficulty here between you fellows and your English teacher. I'm not accusing anyone of anything. But let's get this *crap* straightened out. Now that Mr. Leason has told me his side, I'll ask you fellows for yours. We'll start with you, Paul. I'm really surprised about your being in this difficulty. (Raises eyebrows, puffs on pipe.)

Darlang (looking at teacher peripherally, feeling a red blister near lower lip). I just feel that Mr. Leason's a terrible teacher. He can't really teach. Most of the time he just keeps puttin' you down. Like before, I did say I was sorry to him, like you suggested, but he just ignored me. And I told you about the time he called me and Scott "animals."

Mr. Leason (aside). What about the vulgarities you wrote on your test paper about my wife, you sonofabitch.

Dr. Borden (squinting, as though contemplating the seriousness of Darlang's accusation; puffing more deeply on pipe, turns to Henderson). Scott, what do you have to say?

Henderson (glancing at Darlang, then turning seriously to Dr. Borden). Sir, I think Paul's right. Mr. Leason's a terrible teacher, and he keeps shootin' you down. He never lets you express yourself.

Mr. Leason (still aside). You drew an obscene picture of me on the board with which you expressed yourself pretty well; and you are always talking back, inciting the class to riot.

Dr. Borden (still immersed in his pipe and in contemplation). Joe, what about you?

Hartberg (turning to teacher with bitter-sweet smile, rubbing brow, as though searching for right words). I like Mr. Leason. I like him. But he can't teach. I haven't learned nothin' in his class so far. I know he don't act too friendly to no one, but he shouldn't take it out in his teaching. I mean, you try to get on his good side, but like Scott says, he shoots you down. But I got nothin' against him. I would just like to get transferred to another class, because if I stay in Mr. Leason's class, I'll fail for sure. But I don't carry no grudge against him.

Mr. Leason (aside). You only threw your book in the basket and walked out of the room. You have walked out of the room twenty times. And you have urged students to boycott my classes.

Dr. Borden (relighting pipe, turns to King). Well, Fred, what do you have against Mr. Leason?

King (looking at the floor, scratching his brittle curls, his eyes finally coming to rest on the white of his fingernails). At the beginning I respected Mr. Leason, like you should respect teachers. But I lost this respect when he did a horrible thing. I wouldn't want to bring this up now, but when a teacher does something like this, how can you respect him? Mr. Leason called me a nigger. I can never explain what this did to me—

Mr. Leason (no longer aside). When did I call you that, tell me! When!

Dr. Borden (again clearing throat). Now, we're not here to argue about prejudice. Let's settle our differences and learn how to get along. (Looks at watch.) I've got to be running now. Why don't you all stay and talk things over and reach some type of understanding. (Leaves, does not look back.)

Darlang (rising with his classmates, smiling at teacher). Eat it!

King (mumbling, again looking at the floor). Stroll, baby.

3

But that year in Middle County was good in some ways. There were the hills and their sequestered cathedrals of icy trees and silent snow. Sometimes I would follow the old railroad tracks into the hills at night, tracing the stream of a phantom whistle. Leaping from tie to dark tie or tottering along moon-silvered rails, I hunted those sounds and three bright stars for my crown. And I reached for a dog's barking a mile away and for the sound of the wind that swept from the trees in glints of snow. And I sought to interweave them—stars, wind, trees, phantom sounds and snow—and breathe them in and say, "I am these." And I would be there, somewhere in the crystal night, with my crown of stars, waiting for my self, always coming, always calling.

And she would be waiting for me alone in the house, my child-wife. Hadn't I first met her on a merry-go-round, with the child-music whistling, throbbing, and her dark eyes glassed with tears? Then the letters we slipped to each other between classes, teacher to student, student to teacher in unmarked envelopes. Once by an ice-caked pond I read to her part of Martin Eden, in which Martin (myself or Jack London) talks to Ruth about his vision of their interspersing romantic idyllics with intellectual observations, yet, somehow, still finding time for caressing. At that time, I didn't think that Martin (Jack or myself) was such a romantic. And I hardly thought seriously about Martin's (Jack's) suicide—I mean, the hard fact. He made it sound too Victorianly noble, gurgling some lines of Swinburne in a bubbling, eternal, Melville-ish sea.

No. Instead, we wept for Thomas Hardy's Tess and for George Eliot's Maggie Tulliver, and we read Hillyer's sea poetry—and bits of Masefield. (I had given her an extra reading list.)

And now, I took her out here, where she was alone, waiting for me to return to the house. Waiting, well-impregnated with my neo-romantic idylls and with deep melancholia. And with good reason for expansive depression, for now she was finally aware of the beast in me, my slight tendency toward paranoia.

I remember her reaction when we discovered the swamp the second day after we had bought the house. It was a lake of filmy green which dissolved tossed stones and spouted black water. We found it while looking for asters and blue stars.

"Look, it goes up to the old train tracks," Laura said, "as though it would flow through them and disappear."

We were caught by the heavy smell of brown mounds choking dead trees, and I saw her fighting her tears.

And I told her that we could come here to watch dragon flies spinning sunlight from silver wheels—and have Halloween every full-mooned night, with croaking choruses and black-clawed trees. "The light will make the water white," I prophesied, "and through the limbs, you'll see Chinese writing on the moon."

Then she gave me one of those cherubic pouts, and I realized that she was not quite the dark Ligeia type I sometimes imagined a complement to myself. Instead, she was very real and pouting, capable of screaming fits of depression, of torn moccasins and kinky hair when it was damp. And I wondered if Poe's Virginia had been that way too.

But I had been right about the swamp. When winter came the dark water froze and was covered with glassy snow, so that we could skate from tree to dark tree and slide through constellations of stars tangled among the limbs above—breathing the mystery of the shadowed hills.

4

The Nez Percé Indians of the Pacific Northwest once ranged over the valley of the Clearwater River and the valleys of the Salmon and the Snake. Theirs was a magnificent land, with tall snow-plumed peaks, deep gorges, lush meadows and great forests of spruce and fir. They were a handsome people, known for their superb hunting skills, their fine horsemanship.

When Lewis and Clark staggered their way, they were gracious hosts and they became good friends of the whites. So at the time of the Council of Walla Walla in 1855, most Nez Percé lands were still unpolluted by the white man. But then came prospectors, and the Indians protested—but politely. Then settlers followed, wreaking havoc with Indian livestock and claiming Indian land (only the best).

But why go on? Because I would take an Indian girl, with whom I would live by a mountain lake. At night the firelight would form gold crescents on her profile. In the dawn we would sit together by the still lake, staring at the hills which were great dark whales. And she would teach me the old songs she knew through her blood: of the sounds of the winds; of the tones of the sun on the lake; of the silver whispers of Venus near the mountain peaks, which would tremble in blue shadows at our feet.

And together we cut wood for our light and heat and found those cold streams that fed the lake and brought back their water in cedar pails, to taste the mosses, the mud, the cedar in that water. And we discovered lost trails to mountain ridges and the cool rusted tones of abandoned barns.

I think it all started with Cooper and Melville and their portraits of the noble savage.

But Cooper was phony. I found that out soon enough. For him the Indian was a gimmick to personify the unrealistic sense of nobility and honesty that Cooper and real Indians could never attain. (Hawkeye, Leatherstocking and Deerslayer are really Cooper-disguised white Indians.) It's true, there is some inter-blood romance, but it's intensely devout. Yet, somehow, Cooper does make you cry about the vanishing frontier and the faster vanishing red man. But, of course, the characters aren't real. It is said that Cooper never saw a real Indian—or smelled one either.

Now Melville finally did something worthwhile to the savage with Fayaway and the damsels of the Marquesas. He made them sensuous as well as honest and gave them a closeness to the beginnings of man's spiritual nature.

Now, take that Indian girl we're going to waylay tomorrow at the lake. We're going to probe for and find the nobility of her race. Surely this communion will awaken in us a stronger spiritual understanding; we shall experience that explosive enlightenment which only this powerful communion can create.

But isn't this the theme of our age—the loss of innocence?

Although citified, Laura and I came to that small mountain town innocently enough. So it was surprising to find there was an average of thirty pregnancies a year among girls at the high school. And I discovered the small-town cruelties of some of my students, their vicious

196

crudeness. Their ways were nothing like those of the Mohicans and Typees. It could be that in a small town with only one main street, one movie and one toppling library, adolescents would be inclined to engage in haystack activities. But in its own way, Middle County offered excitement. Police cars (there were seven) were constantly crashing into one another, and the police lost most decisively a water gun battle with local teenagers in the center of town. The force suffered further embarrassment when one of its members assaulted the woman with whom he was living, when she threatened to return to her husband. Also, Buy-Rite, one of the supermarkets, was burned, then burned to the ground again after it had been rebuilt. The culprit was a boy from the high school (naturally).

And, of course, there was the activity in our own section of the woods. In one of the houses down the road, a sixteen-year-old girl was raped by her uncle, who was trying to get back at her stepmother for resisting his advances. But the mother couldn't have cared less because she was busy with a lover in town, while the girl's father (whose original wife had committed suicide upon discovering her sixth pregnancy the year after her husband had been voluntarily sterilized) was cavorting with a girl friend. Also nearby, our electrician had his troubles when his wife surprised him and a woman friend on the living room floor one night. As he was slightly drunk, it was an easy matter for his wife to knock him down the front steps and send his friend naked and screaming into the cold night. And she let her man lie unconscious at the bottom of the stairs. In the morning, when they finally carted him to the hospital, they found that he had a concussion and a severely punctured right eye, which they reluctantly removed.

So, you see, it's hard to think of Cooper and Melville now.

5

When he came into the bedroom, she was still. He had been outside, where the night was heavy with the first promise of spring.

"You were thinking of me," she laughed from the darkness.

His eyes caught two cold stars through the window beside her. He was thinking of the flat ridge of her nose and the curve of her breast under his hand.

"I was playing our game," she continued, and her voice seemed small. "What I would do if you died."

"Your life would be martyred for the child, as I shall have died insuranceless."

"And if I died?" she asked.

197

"Then I shall be a drifter. I would have myself completely and never teach another day—and never return to the smutty city."

He heard her sobbing and found her soft hair. "I often wonder what you do with yourself when I go to work."

"Let me alone."

"Is this pre-natal blues?"

He was thinking of the year before, the day when they had walked along a winter road near Bear Mountain. They had been free that day and had found deer tracks. He had promised himself that he would remember the blue of the sky that day and her tears as they kissed among the trees. And he wanted to remember the way light was refracted by circles of ice on the frozen lakes, and to remember the dark lines of the brush against smooth drifts and the way the sunlight spangled her long hair.

"Is this pre-natal blues?"

6

Saint Christopher's Junior Seminary is just down the road from the old barn. When I would pass the barn on summer evenings I would look across the fields of the seminary, to the cluster of buildings and the dark hills beyond. Sometimes the kids would still be playing with the first stars.

The fields in twilight compensate for the "No Trespassing" signs which litter the paths for contemplation, and for the dry pump before the empty-eyed statue of open-armed Saint Christopher.

I remember asking the statue one evening, "Why is it that you offer a dry pump? There is no water here."

And dappled with yellow light, the figure replied, "The drink I offer is spiritual."

"But you are hard, fixed here, empty-eyed under these trees. Your arms are open, it is true, but you cannot embrace, nor can you offer tenderness."

"You speak like a pagan," the statue replied, looking at the highway through a row of maples, as it had for every moment of the last twenty years.

"You remind me of another statue," I said. "The monumental soldier of the misted stare, with the dark-veiled angel behind him, always dying, his eyes and green lips caked with pigeon droppings. But at least I could see the veins in the soldier's wrist."

The figure was silent.

"Isn't hypocrisy typically Christian?" I asked.

"You speak like—"

"Remember what happened to Atahualpa. Pizarro was a bastard in every sense. Is it too much to say that the Indian prince had trusted Pizarro? Did Pizarro really pour molten lead down the throat of Atahualpa when the Indian refused to surrender the great Inca treasures for which Catholic Spain had launched her 'New Crusade'? And wasn't Montezuma similarly betrayed by the astute, political, God-fearing Cortez? If you read Prescott or the chronicles of old Bernal Diaz del Castillo, you'll see how the Catholics raped and—"

"How dare you!"

"Do you know that this year marks the 75th Anniversary of the Battle of Wounded Knee, where Christian Americans used mortars to blast the poor remnants of free American Indians to oblivion? And do you know the story of the Nez Percé, the vanquished innocents of our Pacific Northwest?"

"I don't understand you."

"Well, after the Nez Percé lands were polluted by ruthless settlers, the U.S. Government continued to break its treaty by taking away three-quarters of the Indian lands. Naturally, the tribes would not go along with this betrayal, and Joseph, one of the dissenting chiefs, threw away his Christian name and his copy of the New Testament. Yet the old chief's lands were still his own when he died there, 'in the valley of winding waters.' And his son, also hopelessly named Joseph, attested, 'I love that land more than all the rest of the world.' And now this land was also thrown open to settlers."

"Go!" the statue suddenly screamed. "You have destroyed the serenity of this evening for me."

"But there'll be others for you—thousands of evenings more, each to be selfishly spent by you in your empty-eyed, empty-armed autocracy, here in the shadows. But tell me, did Pizarro really pour molten lead down the throat of Atahualpa?"

7

The Globe Hotel was on a narrow street in one of the smoky-brick sections of town, amid factories, bars and sagging frame houses. It looked like something from Gopher Prairie, plain, white-washed, with two round, cracked lamps above the screen door.

As they walked up the wooden steps, they saw the bar.

"Not here," Laura said, pulling his arm.

He opened the door. The flat beer smell reached them. "Is there a dining room here?" he asked a man at the bar, who nodded to the right. The room had a damp smell and was cluttered with old tables. Her heels sounded on the dark wooden floor.

Turning to her, he smiled. She looked childish in her blue-flowered dress and with her dark hair fringing her brow and parted around her left ear.

"I'm happy to be with you tonight," she said.

"It's still hard to imagine you with that belly."

She laughed. "It's really quite overbearing."

They sat at one of the tables, and he noticed that its cloth was frayed and held several old stains.

"This is probably some kind of boarding house," he said as his eyes drifted down the rough seams in the wallpaper to the large white bow on the collar of his wife's dress. He was seeing her in a field of wild flowers, her dark hair flying. And he was there, away from her, watching the cycle of wind, sun and shadow. He was pressed against the earth, breathing the image of her.

"It's quaint, in a way," she remarked. "Nineteenth century-ish."

He found her hand. "Your big night out."

They ate in silence, and he kept looking at his watch.

"I guess they're not coming," she finally said. "They could have called."

"Maybe they tried to. You know these damned party lines. Maybe their babysitter didn't show up and they were waiting—"

She leaned back and gazed at the table. "It really doesn't matter."

"Of course," he suddenly said. "The Globe—the Globe Theater. Bear baiting and all that. Do you really think that the founders of this establishment sought to convey the concept of life's being a poor player who frets and struts his hour on the stage and is heard no more—a tale told by a schoolteacher, full of sound and fury, signifying nothing?"

Her face tightened. "No—not here—please!"

He leaned back and his eyes narrowed. "Just this—an answer Scott Henderson wrote on his test paper the other day: T. S. Eliot was an Elizabethan writer who wrote *Rape of the Lock*." He saw her clutching the tablecloth and continued. "And who could ever forget that snake dance last week. It started between the second and third periods and went on for half an hour. Despite the noise made by all kinds of bells and the shouts of Golden Boy and Assistant Principal Frunch, the mesmerized Middies squirmed and pulsed orgastically through the halls. Despite the threats and shoves of some of the male staff members, the lines coiled their way through the school, while from outside came the screeching of peeled rubber from the cars of those students who had made the exits. 'What is this? Why does it happen?' I remember asking one of the older teachers. 'Spring' was her uncomplicated answer. 'Snake dance once every spring—sort of a tradition, you know, but sometimes it does get somewhat out of hand.' "

200

She had turned from him and he was ranting to the back of her head. "Then there were other spectaculars. The day each student hid an alarm clock in his locker set to go off at a pre-arranged time. What a blast! And the time they put urine in the teachers' coffee boiler. And who could forget the obscene phone calls, even to Golden Boy himself."

"T. S. Eliot was an Elizabethan writer who wrote *Rape of the Lock*," she said hollowly, toying with her fork.

My wife sitting amid empty tables in her blue-flower dress with the white collar and bow. I could not find her, as I could not really be with her in the wind-scented fields of my mind. Sometimes in knowing the taste of her throat warm with sleep or the shape of her small rough thumb, I deluded myself into thinking that the strands of sexual nerves, sprouting wild and white through me, through her loins, her stomach, her chest, her head, curling and twisting in the sockets of her eyes—I thought that these were an answer to her, forming her, creating her for me. Yet I was alone, and I could not understand her tears.

The dawn came faintly through the small window beside him. He closed his eyes hard, as though the light was acerbic.

Yes, Laura's death was sobering. It saved me from my Byronic lunacy, my manic affairs with hills and trees.

When I saw the lump of her in the gully by the road I did not think great sensitive thoughts, nor did I dwell sentimentally on the outlandish cross-eyed dog painting on the empty crib. Though Paul Darlang had been driving the red Corvette that had sent her broken and flying, I could feel no hostility toward him or his father, who had bought him the car, nor toward the school from which he would graduate, nor toward the town which gave license to him and the school. Besides, I could see that he was visibly shaken, for he wouldn't look at me or at Laura's body or the skid marks which indicated a rather brisk pace. (I have since come to think of him as a fat pimple-faced Fury dispatched by Fate in his fiery hell-wagon to further the tragedy of some heavy-balled Prometheus whose livered phallus was always flecked with blood.)

No, I hadn't really been shaken by the tears of family and friends—not even by Darlang's tears and his statement, later corroborated by witnesses, that she ran out in front of his car.

So I left Middle County—the house, the swamp, the old barn, the seminary, the lakes and hills. Not that I became a nihilist. Sometimes on cloudy days I think of her conclusive scowl when she had her hair in curlers and her depression that day she had confirmed her pregnancy. No, she had been no Lucy Grey, though she had certainly dwelt among untrodden ways (thanks to me).

Upon returning to Gotham, I became a rather free-living Pre-Raphaelite type (after G. Rossetti, not that I ever exhumed Laura's remains, although many times I have said "The thing is done").

Of course, I could never return to teaching and it was hard to be responsible. And visiting my wife's family was (as always) very difficult. So I hit the road, finally quite literally, driving big tanker trucks of milk around the state, and enjoying complete sexual freedom, interspersed with moments of mourning. And the hills and lakes? They were still there, even if I had disavowed that goddamed higher pantheism. And at times (after penicillin shots) I envisioned the radiant apparition of Laura, which would say something like, "All is not yet lost. You can find yourself if you reestablish faith in those things we always shared." And I laughed, because all I had left was my rank, chirping organ.

It was on the road that I met Red. He's been a good drinking partner and all that, and between runs we'd lounge around (like now) and recharge our generators. He wears his bright hair long and drooping over his eyes, sports studded wrist-bands and heeled boots and wears his belt low, as though it held a revolver and cartridges. I mean, you could never discuss symbolism in Melville with him, yet he seeks the natural, the pristine. He enjoys leaving young girls pregnant, which is kind of a risky business. But he gets the backwoods lasses, who sort of take things for granted until their bellies swell. He's even lined up a few for me, and I "got my cookies" pretty well, as Red put it. And, in turn, I got him to stop urinating on the floor after beers.

He saw that the morning was cloudy and the hills seemed strangely distant and somber. It was as though the world were expecting thunder—hard, hill-shattering. He closed his eyes, and when he turned to the window again, the sky above the hills was fanged with black.

It must have been this way when Quetzal came. Down spirals of jade with flayed genitals. How the earth must have screamed and buckled as he smashed downward in a flame-feathered arch. And then —that first horrible moment when piston-like they pierced the core of the earth and her mountains welled with fire. And he everywhere seizing, holding, wrapping the massive planet in a web of red ejaculation.

And because of this we have the Year of the Phallus, which precludes the Year of the Serpent, the Year of the Rabbit, the Year of the Jaguar.

202

This is why they had fertility rites instead of orgies, genitalled gods rather than promiscuity. So Melville was able to write about the "spirit spout" and the bishopric formed by the organ of a whale.

And when Cortez came, cross-bearing and spindle-legged—with bearded loins—Montezuma, quivering, opened his golden womb. As though the poor earth once again needed that awesome generation. But now the insemination was feeble and stank, and the world was choken from within by the twisted tendrils of the hideous fruit of that union.

As he rose from his cot, he saw Red smiling down at him.

"Ready to take on the Apaches?"

He felt uneasy. "Look, we have to be back at the depot tonight. Why not leave early?"

The gray light was hard on Red's short muscular arms. Leda and the Swan, he thought, gazing at his friend's pale limbs, catching the smell of sour sweat.

"Look, about this girl," he began again, "I think—"

Red's fist caught him solidly on the jaw, and he felt the bed frame against his back. Tasting blood, he laughed carelessly and gazed at the window. "The defeat of the Nez Percé," he said slowly, "is a classical story of Indian strength and honor as opposed to the duplicity of the whites."

"What?"

"After their valiant stand against the troops of Major Howard on the Clearwater, they were pursued through Montana and were finally caught by the troops of Colonel John Gibbon, whose courageous soldiers shot women and children freely and clubbed the heads of infants. But the good colonel's forces might have been defeated (because of the determination and accurate shooting of the Indians) had not General Howard arrived with reinforcements—horses thundering, bugles ringing (like in the movies). And finally came Chief Joseph's message of surrender: 'I am tired of fighting . . . Our chiefs are killed . . . The little children are freezing to death . . . I want to have time to look for my children and see how many I can find . . . I am tired, my heart is sick and sad . . . From where the sun now stands blah . . . bla-aahh . . . blahhaah . . . .' "

Red was looking at him stupidly. His eyes narrowed as he rubbed his groin. "You gone crazy? Let me be first with her."

The cool air was rich with the scents of damp earth and sunlight as they started toward the lake. A thin line of blue laced through the trees to the east, where the cloud cover had broken. He found himself

203

staring at the dark form of a hawk soaring over the hills, misty with new sunlight. And he realized that the hawk had been there always, circling under the clouds, with the earth damp and virginal. The wheeling hawk, he thought, saw them moving toward the lake, saw the Indian girl, her face turned upward, awaiting the sun. And as they approached the water, he wondered about Pizarro, Atahualpa and the molten lead.

Death Occurred

by Lawrence Garvey

child was brought in
by two unidentified teenagers
and left
in the emergency room
at 5:05 PM
death occurred at
approximately 9:30 PM
death occurred
from being beaten
about face and neck
and abdominal ruptures

Reaction

by Francesca De Masi

so much violence
in a life
breaks my eardrums:
even all the way up
on the third floor,
sitting in my soft chair
in my rigid body
—soul, stiffer than a pencil.

Hey
child beater,

thoroughbred kid fighter,
why not

break the nose
on every clod of soil,

or beat eggs,

for the world's hungry
—sinking in a long night
till breakfast.

Blackness

Black Warrior

by Wally Bohanan

Please be careful, I heard momma say
Tomorrow's the day they take niggers away

Don't worry momma
Everything's alright
If niggers go tomorrow
I'm leaving tonight

Be real quiet, my squad leader said,
Or the new dawning day will find all of us dead

I dig you brother
And I'll stay alive
Cause I can't free my momma
Unless I survive

We fought well my brothers, our victory's in sight
Gonna break my momma out that prison camp tonight

You'd better watch it whitey
I heard my momma shout
Tonight's the night black warriors
Break all us niggers out

Thank God you were careful, I heard momma say
Cause tomorrow's the dawning of a beautiful day

Selection from an Unpublished Novel

by Sol Offsey

The first thing Reason remembered was the sky, fierce and white with the heat of the noon sun . . . and beneath it a train, snake-like, ebony . . . scurrying along a distant track . . . the heat surrounding it, pressing down upon it . . . . This was the first thing and he never forgot it.

Then there was his mother. He could see her face in shadow: a tall woman with large, unsoft hands. She had a way in her walk as though nothing mattered, as though in her arrogance she was supreme. He remembered her laughter in the bedroom they shared, her laughter wedded with coarse male laughter finally hushed so that only the mumbled phrases of passion bracketed by the sound of straining bed-springs remained. And as he lay awake listening, his eyes closed. He wished he were deaf, for though he was only six, he felt somehow the dull tortured creakings, the frantic rustling sounds belonged to a world of pain, and shadow, and squalor.

Continuously the insistent tread of heavy male feet trembled the floor of the tiny apartment, the one step hardly different from the next. Which belonged to his originator he hardly knew or cared to know. Instead there was an emptiness in him which he found impossible to define. He clung to his mother because he had little else. His universe twisted and spun about his young head, and if he didn't hold on to her he felt he would be whirled away like a leaf in a twisting, heedless storm.

There was a younger brother, and still another who had died before Reason was able to walk. Each morning when the sun had cleared the distant hills, she would feed the two their meager breakfast and set off through the narrow streets of "Niggertown," Reason on one side of her, his brother on the other. Past the leaning shacks, the low-stooped two storied dwellings with walls no thicker than pasteboard, past the smells of morning. One by one the others came, slouching along the dirt street, knuckling sleep from their eyes, stretching sleep from their limbs. A morning migration pushing on to where the white folks lived,

210

across the bridge that arced over a thinning stream, and across the single track of railroad that split the adjoining worlds.

And always the humor spicing the morning damp, the song carried along the shuffling, ragged line; the voices rising, the slow hail, the arm waved loosely in greeting. Once over the track the men in coveralls broke off toward the warehouse spread wide and low over the landscape, the tobacco bales piled high on the loading platforms, toward the waiting freight cars at the sidings. The line, thinner now, moved onto a street no longer dirt beneath their feet, but paved; a pale, glinting hardness fronting the close-clipped lawns and the thick, bordering hedges where the neat white homes stood still wet with the morning dew.

Those who were domestics disappeared into the side doors, the rear entrances, leaving only a small straggling group headed toward the town's heart, the business district where the jobs of menial labor awaited: the scrubbing, the polishing, and the heavy work of carrying.

Reason remembered the flagstone walk warm with the full rise of sun against his bare feet; the house, how high it stood, and grand with shiny windows and the tile roof slanting against the mild blue of the sky. There was the good-morning, always the good-morning, and the white man's smile, and always the pat on the head that made his insides suck in and his chin push down against the white-fingered touch. He didn't know why, then, his retreat impulsive, mechanical.

He played with his brother beyond the arbor close to where the privy stood while his mother worked in the white woman's kitchen, played as all children do, only more subdued because they were less than visitors in this world, and whatever was here could not be their own, the swing, the fruit trees bursting upward, the grass moist and cool against their bare feet . . . the very air . . . .

He remembered the lady of the house, a tall, slim-waisted woman whose eyes were blue and shiny, whose cheeks were pink and soft-looking. She hardly touched him. It was as though she understood his resistance, but she spoke kindly. And there was a time to his amazement when she brought sandwiches out to where he and his brother frolicked, and she read them stories from a big leather-bound book. He saw her eyes fill with tears as she read, and as she dropped the book into her lap she stared at the sky. From his level he could not ask why she cried the way he might were his mother to cry, or fat Clarissa, the neighbor who lived down the hall, and who hugged him to her many times as though he were her own.

But she would hardly touch him, this white lady, and though he learned later from his mother the reason why she cried, the gulf between them widened. They were symbols to each other: she as part of a world he could not approach, and he as a child of all children, be

211

they black or white. Her own child had died within her, a shapeless, jelly-like mass which had withered in her womb and put the mark of motherlessness upon her.

He might have cried with her in his child's understanding of hurt, but his place was near the privy and his feet hardly ever touched the smooth linoleum floor of the kitchen or felt the soft furriness of the parlor rug. He only stood and looked on with awe, while his brother tumbled in a patch of high-grown grass, his thin, hard body a smudge against the square of ragged green.

So were the summers. In the winter rains, he and his brother remained at home in the dark two-roomed apartment, foraying outside it along the bleak halls, and up and down the splintered staircase, imagining these excursions into adventures where the pirate lurked in shadow and the Indian loomed overhead ready to spring. At these times the house was empty except for old Fanny on the bottom floor who sat in her rocker smoking her clay pipe. She fed them sweets and on occasion ginger beer, but best of all she crooned to them and told them stories of a long ago where gray- and blue-clad men fought a war so terrible that the very skies shook with the sound of it, and she told them how as a little girl she had seen "Massa Linculum," and how he had reached out to touch her bowed head.

When there was no rain he would go to school, leaving his brother in old Fanny's care until he too trudged the macadam road dressed against the mild winter in sweater and sneakers. And with them old Fanny's granddaughter whose father worked at the tobacco warehouse and whose mother waited table in "Niggertown's" combination hotel and hash house. Her name was Ruth, a sly ten-year-old who could spell hard words and do sums which stumped many of her elders. She was plump for she ate well, and in her care his brother was entrusted.

The school was a ramshackle building which marked a fork in the twisting road. The knife-scarred desks counted thirty and an additional ten crates served a never-realized student overflow, for hardly ever were there more than twenty present, and the teacher, a harassed scarecrow of a woman, flustered up and down the aisles, poking her pointer and screeching in exasperation at the giggling, smirking children.

But what stuck most with Reason was the countryside in early spring: the lines of tobacco, seedbeds, and the canvas laid over the glass coverings yellowed by the slanting rays of the sun . . . so like coffins in the wide expanse of field. And once alone with Ruth he had to pee and did so turning his back to her behind a tree. He sensed her coming up alongside him. Fixing his pants he looked up into her face so close to his. So strange-looking, not plump now, but tight with the eyes gleaming and the cheeks sucked in. She said nice quiet things as though she daren't frighten him away, and her hand fidgeted inside his fly so that he felt funny all over and was afraid to move.

He was afraid of his mother, yet he could only cling to her the way a cliff-hanger might cling to a jutting branch. He was afraid of her because she towered lean and tall over him, and she laughed hard and long when she had whisky in her. There was no mirth in her laughter, only a racking, bursting sound that flung her misery against him, and her rough hands then were hard and unfriendly, moving against his face, over his cheeks like boards. And then he would be ignored like a puppy that had been fed, and the moonshine would draw low in the jug, while her hands, now more supple and loving, would caress the hard-muscled shoulders of her current lover.

But there were times he did know her as a mother. He would see her come up the dirt street weary from her day's work, and he and his brother would run happy-eyed to meet her. Her defiance would be gone for the moment, her grudge against the world shelved so that she would reach out and hug her children to her so tightly he could hear the heightened, even beating of her heart. Or she would tuck him in, sitting on the edge of the bed, running her fingers over his forehead, and song would lift in her until it trembled in the semi-darkened room and the shadowy corners would lose their devils and angels would glide in their place.

He grew slowly into an awareness, a gradual widening of his horizon until the color of his skin stood as a symbol of some vague inadequacy beyond his control. And when he compared the white man's world to his, his child's mind yearned for a roomful of games, the pictures of which he had seen in some discarded magazine, and the walls of the room itself papered with exciting replicas of whooping Indians and valiant cowboys. If he lived there across the bridge he knew he'd have it, and he knew he would live there if his skin weren't black.

Once he stopped old Fanny in the middle of one of her strange, rambling stories. "What's freedom?" he asked simply, looking up at her eagerly after she had spoken the word.

She returned his stare, her seamed face tightening in a grave effort at thought. "Freedom," she answered, the words seeming to come from the very depths of her worn frame, "is somethin' you'll allus want, but you'll neveh git."

He pondered this imponderable, and for the moment equated the old woman's prophesy with his desire for a roomful of games. "I'll get freedom," he told her with a determination beyond his years. "I'll get it for sure . . . .You jus' see if I don't."

At times he knew hunger. As he lay awake in the dead of night fighting the subtle clawing in his stomach, he imagined the scurrying of insects along the stretch of floor at the foot of his bed. How many floors were there in the limited world he knew? . . . how many ice-boxes? . . . how many cupboards? . . . Oh, how he wished he were one of those many-legged creatures . . . wished that he could squeeze his tiny flexible body into those wonderful spaces so rich with the smell of corn bread, of fried pork . . . .

He thought of the white kitchens as well, those he knew from his sojourns into the white man's world. And his imagination brought the defenseless roach fleeing over the linoleum smelling of disinfectant, the white man's shoe poised, then descending thunderously. He shivered, wanting to cry out, but he only stared dry-eyed into the darkness, his hunger undiminished, the ache inside him sharper now.

Once he came upon his mother sitting alone in the kitchen of their apartment: a forlorn, stooped figure, her back a curve of dejection, her hands folded tightly in the lap of her dress. There was no movement of her head, only her eyes rolled up to catch his entrance. She was silent as he approached and stood before her.

"Samuel . . . ," she said, for he was not known as Reason then, "Samuel . . . ." And her voice faded so that the others held the field, and looking up he sensed her as a rising monument, a declaration of all he wanted and understood.

"My po' Samuel! . . . My po' chillun! . . ." Her body rocked slowly as she spoke.

"But, ma! . . ." he groped, trying to comprehend.

It came to him while wrestling with his brother later that night. Clarissa was in the kitchen with his mother. While they tumbled and grunted over the yielding bedclothes, snatches of conversation reached his ears. The adult talk floated in some feathery limbo until it sharpened, and when it did it stabbed at him so that involuntarily he sat quietly to listen, sensing that somehow it concerned him. His brother sulked, still wanting to frolic, and he held up an impatient hand to silence the other's whimpering.

"Two . . . an' another comin'." It was his mother. "I jes' barely make out now, slavin' an' scrimpin'. How'm I goin' to do it with three, Clarissa? Jes' tell me how? . . ."

"The good Lawd will provide," Clarissa soothed. "He done so up 'til now, an' He will when you need Him again."

"The good lawd! . . . the good lawd! . . ." His mother's exasperation charged the air like electricity. "I done all the providin' in this family with my two bare hands. You jes' stop good-lawdin' me, Clarissa! . . . You hear! . . . You jes' stop! . . ."

"May he fo'give a po' blasphemin' sinner." Clarissa's voice was soft in contrast.

He sat crouched, straining to catch whatever would come next, ig-

214

noring the moaning of his brother beside him; his body taut, his senses alert.

It was Clarissa who spoke next. "Please don' take it in yo' haid to do somethin' wild, Charlene," she said. "You git in one of yo' black moods and Lawd knows where it'll take you."

He remembered another occasion when, for a reason he could not fathom, his mother had stormed from the house to come back several days later smelling of whisky and vomit, and the wild look in her eyes subdued. Clarissa had cared for him and his brother then, and on his mother's return Clarissa had risen from her chair and without a word had waddled from the apartment looking straight before her as though she were passing a stranger on the street.

"I'm goin' to kill this thing inside me," his mother spoke now. "You jes' wait and see. I'm goin' to tear it from my guts if it's the last thing I do."

Her words sought him, enclosed him in their vehemence. He retreated along the bedclothes until he felt the wall hard and moist against his back.

"Sam, le's wrassle some mo'," his brother said, his thin frame inching forward cautiously, not knowing what to expect.

And as he listened to gentle Clarissa, pleading, cajoling, he pushed hard against the other's shoulders, knocking him backwards, for he was filled with a sudden hatred for all things, for all mankind. His brother came at him again, and he struck sharply this time with his fists, catching the surprised face, the soft area of cheek. And when the younger boy began to cry in his pain, a curious, elated feeling came over Reason. He drew back his arm and struck again.

From then on the atmosphere was laced with whisperings. Strange phrases cut into his consciousness bearing dark connotations. His mother would look up from a conversation to catch him entering the room, and her eyes would flash her companion into silence, but many times not before he heard words like "abortion," "quinine," and "labor," and his small world broadened imperceptibly, slowly, so that he could guess roughly why there was a tenseness in his mother's movements, could understand the indecision, the frustration that seemed to tear her into a thousand irredeemable shreds.

Many times she was sick so that she lay in her bed groaning, her only movement to lean over the side to retch some brown, slimy ooze into a pan. And Clarissa, holding her head, would berate her, her tone scolding, but her touch compassionate. "Yo' want to kill yo'self takin' those pills!" she would say. "What you should do is git yo'self a husband after all these yeahs galavantin' aroun'. You talk about bein' free!" And her voice would grow scornful now. "Why, yo' is a bigger slave than yo' gran'pappy or gran'mammy eveh was! Do yo' heah me, Charlene?" But while her voice rose and her hands were never rough, her wide, soft shoulders shook with tears that seldom came.

He remembered Bert Wilson, tall, big-boned, voluble, all-knowing, yet well-intentioned; Bert Wilson not there, but suddenly almost always there, his shoes clattering as he mounted the flight of steps leading to the apartment, the rap of his knuckles against the door, and the door whistling back as he stepped into and through the apartment calling his "good evenin." The smell of the curing tobacco leaf accompanying him, faint but pungent, this stamp of his livelihood was always with him, reminding Reason of the fields and the hands stooped over the plants with carefully tending fingers. Bert Wilson, brash in the way he kissed the waiting Charlene, stepping back to survey her swelling figure, and saying in his deep bass-fiddle voice, "I do declare, ma'am, but damn if you're not gittin' prettier every day."

Then rumor began to ride the summer nights, rumor building into flighty gossip, holding the scene until its collective voice sharpened into a sporadic harshness. The voices tore, clung and wove one into the other so that to deny them he would have had to be more than deaf, more than dumb. And something inside Reason gave way, infinitesimal, like a speck giving way to a puff of air. Nevertheless he sensed it acutely, and accordingly he set his defenses animal-like, instinctively, preparing for whatever variation of malevolence the crudity of his fellow man might offer next.

The vocal judgment grew, caught among the shack chinks, held the curious ears of doorway loungers, made way along the winding streets, and finally spilled over the bridge where the neat white houses stood frail and shimmering in the eerie light of the moon.

"That man Bert's found hisself a ready-made family . . . ."

"The army's never gonna see that nigger if he kin help it . . . ."

"The way he sees it, Bert ain't got no quarrel with the Kaiser . . . an' besides he don' look so good in khaki . . . ." The remarks were usually accompanied by a knowing chuckle.

His mother questioned Bert. The big man, for once his loquacity gone, sat with his shoulders bent forward, the line of his cotton-shirted back like that of a giant bird with its wings folded. His face solemn and long. His rough hands clasped loosely, his wrists resting against his knees.

"Sure, I heard it," he said, and Charlene leaned against the sink in the small, cluttered kitchen, eased her body so that the metal sunk less into the flesh of her overfull thighs. "I'm not denyin' it," he continued. He rose to take a step toward her, lifting his arms in a posture of entreaty. "Let's be honest, Charlene. I kin do somethin' fo' you, an' you kin do somethin' fo' me."

216

"You is only a tobacco han'," she said. "I won' be a flea-size better off if I married you."

"Oh, I don' make out so bad." He dropped his arms. "An' remember, I ain' a drinkin' man. If we put our salaries together, you'll be a damn sight better off then tryin' to pull along by yo'self. Besides . . ." and his eyes sparkled here, "you is a mighty fine lookin' woman."

She regarded him quietly, reacting to his spontaneity only by a slight lifting of the corners of her mouth, smiling to herself, not entirely unaffected by his obvious sincerity.

"All right," she said. "You name the day."

And so they agreed, the way two people might over the sale of a horse; he perhaps more eager than she, and she giving way because she could go no further, the immense wall before her too heavy to push and too high to vault.

There came now a kind of looking forward in the way his mother spoke, the way she carried herself. Her gaze at times was introspective, as though she were regarding her future, perhaps a little less black, a little less uncertain. Reason would hear her sing softly, the words shaped hardly above a whisper, and inwardly he would join, for of late he had seldom heard her sing. And for a time he knew an existence as comfortable as down.

The car came the morning of the wedding, humming over the bridge while the town was still asleep; the deepening light girdling it as the sun stroked the sky with wide, orange fingers. It held three men, their features grave, their bearing in strict accordance with the unwritten code of petty officialdom: two in the rear seat, the driver throwing a remark behind him now and again, sitting straight as an asterisk, his red face an innocuous badge against the drab, humble background.

The car halted, pushed forward again; the men hesitated, searching with squinting eyes, scrutinizing the tilting, leaning shacks, until the brakes applied, the car stopped, and they conversed, their heads together in a hatted circle.

Finally agreed, the tall one with the deputy's badge alighted, paused before covering the ground with a long, cocksure stride. He rapped on the first available window and questioned the black, sleepy face confronting him. He did not accept the shrug of shoulders, but opened the window wide so that the splinters flew and shimmered like so many weak-winged insects, and grasped the undershirt, forced the body inside it to shrivel, to retreat in nameless fear until the lips formed the solution the deputy was seeking.

From his pallet, Reason became aware of the trembling form of his brother huddling against him, glanced up past the black, shiny boots, up above the wide shoulders and the stern, chisel-jawed faces to

217

where Bert had tumbled from the bed. He could see hope beginning to leave his mother's face like the sand in an hourglass. Bert stood nude except for his underpants, his broad chest rising and falling as though he had run a good long way.

"Just as I said, Les," the deputy smirked to his companion (the driver down below with the car, not trusting the "damn niggers" who like as not would take a fancy to driving off in it if it were left unattended). "Just as I said . . . tryin' on his shoes before he decides to buy 'em." They ogled the unclothed body of the woman cowering amid the rumpled bedclothes. Their laughter hung in the damp morning air.

"You Bert Wilson?"

"That's my name."

"You know you got a date with the army?"

"But they say fo' me to report not 'til two weeks from tomorrow."

"That's all been changed . . . . Just like your weddin' plans." The pin fell clattering under the charging accuracy of the ball. "Uncle Sam needs you." And again the laughter, full and heavy, pushed at the walls.

They took Bert away, buttoning his shirt, confused, mumbling inappropriate words of comfort to his no longer bride-to-be. And as the screech of the car's tires against the grit-like dirt sounded, then cut away into nothingness, Reason watched his mother's face. It had gone limp; her jaw was slack, and her eyes were glazed as though she had been struck a tremendous blow.

The days passed in weary rotation; he had been walking in sunlight, but now the sky loomed dark and low; a plain stretched before him, and he less than a pin-point upon its surface trod its endless paths. And always ahead just out of reach, his mother stumbled. He had no way of arresting her progress, halting her for just a moment so that he could join his hand with hers. He called to her but his words were strange, or else her ears were deaf to them. He lived through these sensations as though they were real, doing what he normally did each day until one evening, waiting for her to come home from her work, he found that she did not come, and as the hours pulled past he realized that finally the tenuous string had snapped.

Clarissa tended to his and his brother's needs that night. She moved about in the drab kitchen, now and again pausing to listen, or moving to the window to search the street below with sad, straining eyes.

Each night she did the same, drawn to the cracked pane, willing Charlene home with all her might. The hours glided one into the next, so that Reason lost all sense of their passing. With the sun he was out in the alleys, in the fields with his cronies, pursuing the pleasures of most boys his age. But now and again he would pause in one of his

218

games to look up, remembering Clarissa as she stood at the window, and his gaze would ride the line of distant trees, the manure-flecked curve of street, and a tight, empty feeling would invade his chest at the failure of his scrutiny. And heeding the call of the others he would throw himself with frantic, heedless energy into the game they were playing.

His mother was found. She didn't return home, but she was found. This fact at the very beginning was not a fact to him, but a hazy, incongruous utterance, the meaning hidden, and only with time did it harden into something he could understand. But when Clarissa told him of it some three weeks after his mother had disappeared, he questioned her; his words aimed at the jerking, obscure target of her statement, unable to hit it. Finally in exasperation he grasped her arm. "But why should they take her away?" he wanted to know. "Why?"

Clarissa could not meet his eyes. "She did somethin' bad . . . real bad . . . ." And she lifted her face heavenward as she implored, "Oh, Lawd . . . please let her down soft. Please let her lie comfortable now, fo' you tested her much too hard." Her Jobian plea faded into nothingness as the sky spread widely overhead, and only a lone bird replied with an idiot, strident shriek.

A white farmer returning from town with a wagon-load of supplies had come upon Charlene. He had stopped off to relieve himself, stepping to the side of the road to do so. It was then that he heard it; a frenzied, desperate moaning that clove the night, that made him stiffen and hold on to his reality with a tightened grip. Furtively he stepped forward, half inclined to turn and bolt, but an intense curiosity, a feeling deep inside him pushed him on, balanced on a thread of vicarious bravado, until he saw her, wraith-like, bent, engaged in some activity he could only equate with shoveling, but her pay-load seemed heavy, beyond her control, and when he drew closer he realized that she was pushing and not attempting to lift.

There was a culvert facing into a shallow stream, and its narrow aperture seemed corked with a resilient, putty-like material, and forcing this rubbery, giving substance further and further into the mouth of the pipe, the wraith, turned woman now, mumbled her ceaseless dirge. At the farmer's approach, she looked up, sensing, rather than hearing him, and acknowledging his presence in this negative way, her eyes dropped once more to her task, still moaning, her voice penetrating, filling the area with a melancholy insistence.

Aghast, he shoved her back, so that unresisting she fell to the soft, wet earth, her filth-smeared garments billowing, then falling softly about her the way a parachute might once its purpose was fulfilled, and as gently as he could he dislodged the still faintly-breathing, new-born child from its prison and carried it back to the wagon, not know-

219

ing that it lived, only hoping, wishing in his simple, dedicated way that it did.

As the mare pulled the wagon about, the farmer held the child in his lap, covered in some calico he had purchased for his wife. He looked to where the woman stood, silent now, regarding him with blank eyes. He motioned for her to come and sit beside him, but she seemed to disregard the gesture, and mindful of the still body, wet with the slime of afterbirth against his thighs, he set off back to town.

The baby died on the doctor's table, and when questioned the farmer told his story in a quiet, respectful voice, thinking of his wife, most likely concerned that he hadn't as yet come home. They found Charlene where he had left her, slumped in the shadows where the road met a rise in the adjacent field. She was asleep, and awakened by the incessant prodding of a sheriff's boot, she rose to smile dumbly at his questions. She had lost all sense of identity, and it was only the fact that she was recognized by someone who knew her at the hospital where she was finally taken that saved her from anonymity. And so she went from day to day, locked in from the outside world by the terrible safety of her own.

It was on a morning gray with the promise of rain that Clarissa mounted to the driver's seat of the hired cart and cluck-clucked the mule into motion. Beside her sat Reason chewing on a piece of straw, and behind them sitting cross-legged in the hollow of the cart was his brother, his eyes following the slow, awkward turning of the heavy wheels as the spokes hove into sight one by one.

Across the bridge they went, past the white houses where the domestics already at work waved at the trundling vehicle, toward the heart of town, and to the other side far past its edge where the sanitarium stood off the road, a formless mass of earth-colored buildings huddled behind ivy-covered walls.

The three faced Charlene in a small, square room, with only a bare table and two chairs for furniture. She was dressed in a simple gown which buttoned down the back, flat shoes and coarse brown stockings. There were creases about her mouth and eyes, a puckered effect about her lips. She looked older, yet unworried, a perpetual smile marking her features. And when Clarissa stepped forward to greet her, she said nothing, the smile not deepening or lessening. She didn't move, remaining immobile as granite, recognition not penetrating the wall she had so willingly created about herself.

Reason, uncertain as to how he should react, only watched Clarissa's attempts to break into his mother's consciousness, aware that his legs were heavy, that his arms which he wanted to lift to her remained at his sides. It was always so when he came to visit her, until one day,

220

Clarissa stopped taking him, sensing his reticence to continue. And down through the years he almost always remembered his mother as he had seen her on these occasions: tall, sphinx-like, the never-ending smile on her face, her eyes blank as though this were a final wisdom of which only she was cognizant.

Clarissa took him in. His brother went to live with some relatives down state, to disappear into some far-off place. Vague bits of news became the only life-line between them, until like quick-sand, time swallowed him. He became a memory, indistinct, carrying a dim, fading nostalgia.

But living with Clarissa had its good points. She also was a domestic as his mother had been, and of necessity he was left a good deal on his own, for unlike his mother's employer who had permitted her children to accompany her to work, Clarissa's would have none of this. So as the summer faded, he occupied himself in many ways: he ran errands for the handful of shopkeepers whose threadbare establishments lined the main street of "Niggertown"; he frolicked, fished and swam as the mood took him, covering the countryside, the brown, twisting roads, the sluggish, zig-zagging streams, and there were times when Ruth visited him in the empty apartment, letting him explore the secrets of her soft, dimpled body, lying back, responding hotly to his touch as the fan-like rays of the afternoon sun came wanly through the apartment's only window.

Clarissa was always kind, perhaps too kind, her gentle nature ready to forgive him his burst of temper, his disobedience. She was a widow who had lost her husband many years ago in a railroad accident, and taking the money awarded her after much heartache and wrangling, she had invested it in the education of her only son, Walt. The investment had paid off for he had moved out of the reaches of "Niggertown" and moved into a good job as an accountant with a government agency. And every two weeks, punctually, a portion of his check came in the mail for his mother.

And as punctually he would come to visit, one week-end out of eight, apportioning his leave time so that he could arrive late on a Friday evening and stay until Sunday after supper when he would trudge to the railroad station at the other end of town, his long legs eating distance, his tall, loose form bent with the sadness of going.

For Reason his coming was an event, his leaving a minor tragedy. He would wait to carry Walt's bag, running to meet him as he came swinging over the narrow bridge, looking happily into the hollow-cheeked face as they shook hands, waiting for the little present always there for him, the wink always accompanying it, the clap on the shoulders reassuring, for Walt accepted him in the company of men.

With him Walt brought the outside world: the world of movement, of doing and going, the world of wide city streets, of wise and knowing people . . . of good people. For his tall, narrow frame housed no hatred, and in his deep humility he could only pity. He knew no classification except that of "good," and perhaps "unfortunate." And Reason listening to him as they moved over the wide fields could only wonder and ask breathless questions of the bobbing head above him. He listened to the soft-spoken answers, dimly aware that they were leading him into a realm that existed only in fairy-tales; the past existed in a limbo he had outgrown.

"People aren't bad," Walt would say, often repeating this one of his favorite expressions, "they're just bewildered." At times his face would show his own bewilderment, his faith hovering at the edge of some roiling abyss, and with an effort he would strengthen again to his belief, to what he needed, for without it he had no anchor, no weight to hold him steady.

There was one final occasion. It was late evening. The oxeyes drooped palely. Night seeped in over the countryside. In the distance a chimney gave off smoke to blend with the lessening light. The two followed no path, wandered listlessly. Reason, intent on the other's words, the way he spoke, carried from this period of his life a profound consciousness of rhetoric, of the spoken phrase, its subtle power and persuasiveness.

"God has his plan, and Man rails against it," Walt was saying, speaking only partially to the boy with him, speaking to the quiet as if only the absence of an audience could give credence to his words. "If only He could make us all see it, make us all feel it . . . ."

Then infringing upon the hush, a distant sound. Accompanying it, a blob growing upon the sight, until they could see a wagon barrelling across the wide patch of even ground knowing no pattern of advance, the horse pulling it forward in a frenzied gallop. The guiding hand apparently not intent on direction, only on the wind against the owner's face, the wild motion of the wagon beneath him.

"That horse is going to break a leg, they don't stop running him over this ground like that." Walt's tall body seemed to stretch, stiffen into tense alertness. A cry broke from the moving vehicle. A whoop, then several whoops, bursting, mingling one with the other so as to suggest several riders. And as the shouts cut scythe-like to where they stood, the wagon pulled parallel and Reason could make out the driver crouched on his seat, beating the air with his hat, and behind, urging him to greater effort, three others; in all four, soldiers most likely on leave, the Army's discipline for the moment flung to one side, and what had been bottled up inside finally let loose in one Herculean orgy.

The horse veered, changed direction. The wagon tilted, threatened to overturn, then righted itself, the wheels, still spinning furiously, eating distance, grinding into the soft earth so that clods lifted generously, flew helter-skelter in an ever changing pattern of scattering fragments. The heads turned toward Walt, fingers pointing, the voices still plaguing the stillness, but like a new theme in a cacophonous symphony, the word "nigguhs" shrilled, became part of intermingling phrases, and the animal pulled up sharply, the bit cutting into its mouth, its belly sagging with fatigue.

"Where's your uniform, black boy?" The driver straightened, exhilaration animating his gestures, the query more than a probe, more than an attempt at information; the others alert, a suppressed giggle, a drunken grunt emanating from the jumble, but all for the most part waiting for this preliminary to pass, for the overture to run its predestined course.

Walt didn't reply, only stood under the whiplash of the question, waiting for the next verbal blow. Slowly the driver rose, dropped to the ground, his heavy shoes thudding against the loose soil. "I ask a civil question, I expect an answer." His voice was low, cunning. He rose on his toes, and settling back again he accentuated his words by pounding the fist of one hand into the palm of the other.

"I'm disqualified medically," Walt answered simply. "I have a heart condition."

The others came over the side, plopping one by one like excrement to stand swaying, the quartet arranged in a hollow, the sky purpling darkly above them.

"You got a drink, boy?" one of them asked. He was short, stocky, his eyes glassy with the whisky he had already consumed. Walt shook his head. "Damn . . . you nigguhs ain't worth two friggin' cents." The soldier spat to show his disgust, the saliva a brief flash of silver in the dimming light.

The words closed upon a silence, the four facing the two, certain of their advantage, uncertain as how to implement it. The horse snorted, shifted his position so that the loose boards of the wagon groaned.

"You say you got a medical discharge?" the driver questioned again.

"They never took me," Walt said. Reason could feel the fingers digging into his shoulder, could sense the other's growing fear. Something told him to run, but he stood rooted beside Walt.

"Whose palm did you grease, nigguh?" The words hung between them, a loop of invisible rope. The driver lurched forward. "You ain't got no lard-assed draft board afore you now. As far's I'm concerned you're a coon in a coon platoon." And he laughed at his ludicrous rhyme, the others joining in, gathering closer, following his lead. "Now we got to fix you up with a rifle. A man ain't a soldier without a rifle. Barney!" he shot over his shoulder, "git the coon a rifle."

"Yes suh!" This followed by a muffled gasp of laughter, and one of the figures bowed out of the hollow to bend low over the ground in a posture of searching.

There was no horizon now, only a bulge of darkness where earth met sky, thinning to where they stood so that the deepening starlight highlighted each face with a discerning touch, causing each pair of eyes to gleam, lips to glisten wetly.

"Let's see what we've got here." The driver stepped around Walt, forcing Reason back with a rude palm. "A real long drink o' water. Mostly bone and air. Tenhut! . . ." bellowing the last, and getting no response except a start at the sudden raising of his voice. He prodded a finger into the white-shirted stomach so that Walt winced. "Tenhut! that means attention, snap to it! . . . Shoulders back! . . . Coon gut in! . . . Stiff as a board!"

The tall figure jerked spasmodically at each succeeding jab, thin arms folded across the abdomen in a gesture of self-protection. Walt's voice shook as he spoke: "Now you fellows quit this fooling. If you want something to drink I could fix you up with a bottle."

The driver stopped short. "Foolin!" His body bent at the waist, his legs were spread wide as the words ended on a prolonged screech so that Reason thought of a bow violating the strings of a fiddle. "We ain't foolin', nigguh. You're goin' to be a soldier afore the night's through and then we're goin' to march you up to the nearest re- cruitin' station and you'll do your stuff for the sergeant. By God, no sweet-talkin', primpin' black son-of-a-bitch is goin' to enjoy the fruits of civilian life while this daddy-boy's sweatin' his ass in the god-damn infantry."

"But I've got a heart condition . . . ." The words trailed off, losing themselves in the silver-edged darkness. The short, stocky soldier came forth with a length of wood. Solemnly he handed it to the driver, then saluting the gesture, mocking, he reeled an about face. The laughter cascaded from his lips. The horse turned toward the sound to answer it with a slobber, its tongue showing faintly pink as it licked at emptiness.

"Thank you, Barney." The driver thrust the facsimile at Walt. He hesitated, reached uncertain fingers toward the strip of wood. "Take it, coon!" The driver held it up, the command snapping, acting as a deciding factor. Walt's fingers closed about the rough texture, held it as though it might at any minute begin to coil and writhe, have life inhabit it. "Up against the shoulder! . . . Come on! . . . Now!" He turned to his companions, his overfull face serious, grim, his square chin prodded the night. "Form up a squad . . . . Make the coon number two man, and everytime he falls out of step, put him back in . . . . Get it!"

"Yes suh!" This spoken with relish, and the three lined up with Walt, the driver off to one side counting cadence, shrilling crisp commands so that the ludicrous drill began, the lank, bony figure conspicuous, clumsily tripping. Reason, apparently forgotten, watched, his body stiff, rage-filled, a tightness inside forcing his breath out in short, labored gasps.

Like a motor with one of its cylinders missing, the makeshift squad pounded the area of assumed parade ground. The uniformed men stepped smartly, punishing their uncertain member with slow elbow jabbings, heavy shoes cracking against his ankles. Walt dropped to his knees and, unheeding his pleas, they dragged him to his feet again to continue their unholy ritual, its purpose no longer to ridicule, but to show their victim the righteousness of their strength, the iniquity of his weakness.

The night was full upon them now, the scene aqueous, somehow remote and yet overbearingly real. The figures moved briskly, shoes slapping the ground, echoing dully, shivering the silence. The voices stabbed incessantly, a rapier thrusting into space, the puppets wheeling and cavorting to it, stepping to the strident yips, all except one.

"Squad halt!" The three hit a brick wall, Walt stumbling until he stood with sagging shoulders, the sweat making his face shine.

The driver stepped up to him. "Coon, your legs don't move the way they should. They're kind'a big and slow. No life to them. No life to them at all." He clucked his tongue in sham sympathy. "Now what do you think we should do to get the molasses outta them?"

One of the others spoke up. "Don't you think we give him enough, Ab? If he's got a bad heart like he says, I think it's time we lay off."

No answer, the driver's face swiveled. His eyes cut the dissenter into silence. A futile breeze flapped, relaxed; an insect keened, the sound small, wire-thin in the distance.

"Now what do you think we should do?" The sentence repeated was a poised axe waiting to drop.

"You leave him alone! He neveh done nothin' to you!" The words vomited past Reason's throat. He was moving, aware that the uniform was growing larger, the face above it surprised, amused. Seized from behind, a forearm tightened about his chest, so that he could only struggle, could only watch the figures gesturing, shifting before him.

"Coon, I'm goin' to fix you up real good. I got me an idea." The driver winked at Walt. "You're goin' to be right proud of me time I'm through."

The tall, lank figure wavered, took a step forward, arms lifted hesitantly, the gesture fruitless in its appeal. The short, stocky soldier stepped to one side, ready to catch the weakened, stumbling form in any attempt at flight.

The driver stepped back, then came up to the wagon to reach into its body. Straightening, he held a length of coiled rope in his palm. He fastened one end to the tailgate, testing the knot, then turning he gestured, and the stocky soldier shoved, his palms hard against the Negro's back. Walt staggered forward to where the driver caught him, to loop the rope about his waist.

An unearthly silence rested over the six, until it broke, the victim's sudden, sucking breath lifting it. The horse whinnied in answer, kicked at the earth, forcing the wagon to creak with its movements.

"Hey, Ab, you gone plumb crazy?"

Ignoring the dissenter, the one called Ab bent to examine the knots once again. Reason, not struggling now, was hypnotized by the shadowy pantomine unfolding before him. He watched Ab mount to the wagon's seat and flip the reins. The horse ambled forward. The soldiers jeered, became alive to the Negro's predicament; the dissenter to one side, silently smoking, sobered now, his posture one of cautious, inactive disapproval, logic and not compassion setting him on the side of the angels.

The horse broke into a trot. The wagon's appendage took up the jogging rhythm. Walt's fingers clawed at the taut rope. His legs churned unwillingly. His face lifted heavenward. His mouth mumbled an incoherent prayer lost amidst the plod of hooves, the strain of wagon, the lift of razzing voices.

"Leave him be!" Reason strained against the restricting arms, saw the loping figure fall, the dissenter leaping forward calling attention to the dragging, writhing form; and twisting in his makeshift prison, he bit deeply, aware of the shirt ripping under the frenzied pull, aware of the grip against flesh, the nipple, the hair bearing the taste of sweat; yanking like a wild, hungry animal, biting so that the flesh gave way. Blood, salt-tinged, ran against his tongue, flooded over his teeth; salt-tinged, yet so sweet . . . .

"Leggo, you little bastard!" The sharp cry of pain eased into a moan, and Reason, free now, ran to where Walt lay, the wagon still, the driver leaning over the inert body. The short, stocky soldier moved back slowly, aghast, speechless.

"What's one nigguh, more or less." The driver straightened, re-turned the knife to his pocket. The rope he had cut dragged limply. "Time we vamoose, boys." No panic in his voice, only a sense of what had to be done, of urgency, of action to be taken to fit the need of the moment.

"He ain't dead, is he?" The cigarette dropped from trembling fingers to lie smouldering against the dry earth.

"And if he is, he ain't the first black that's ever died."

"But Ab . . . he told you . . . he said he had a bad heart."

"You goin' to stand here and weep? 'Cause if you are, we ain't goin' to wait 'til you're ready to go."

Once more he mounted the wagon's seat, glancing back to see the others scramble in behind him; set the animal in motion, the vehicle rattling over the uneven ground. Reason watched its form crease the night until he could see it no longer. He bent to the quiet, unmoving figure, whispered as though in awe, gently shook it as he might a heavy sleeper, and the arm fell lax, the unseeing eyes wide in arrested fright held, then slowly slid away from his own. He began to cry, his nostrils still laden with the stench of sweat, the blood-taste still strong in his mouth.

This had been his initiation; the experience of these years a raw, never-healing wound, repeated in so many different ways, so that eventually this purpose evolved, at first cloudy, unrecognized, then crystallizing until finally from behind a store counter in a large roiling metropolis, in the waning summer of his years, he planned a final revenge. So the span from now to his first day of remembering, the train crawling over the flat, barren landscape, the white-hot fist of sun glaring, the cars twisting, their ebony sides mercilessly exposed . . . always the train, always the sweet-salt taste of blood.

Admiral, Boss-Man

by Joseph P. Grancio

Admiral, Boss-man
Admiral, Sir,
I been pumpin', pumpin', pumpin',
And I want a raise—
I been pumpin', pumpin', pumpin',
Still up the valley they're comin',
A Bending black horde, streaming in
All pigeon-toed and swaying side to side
       Eyes all gleaming and
       Blades flashin' in the dark—
       They come like a shot of wind from hell,
       Smellin' like the devil's hole.
And me pumpin' still,
And my hands all sore—pumpin', pumpin'.
But the valley, boss, is gaping, and
A Belch of hot black wind is comin' from the valley floor,
       And out comes a Big Black Bird
       With wings of Black leather,
       Lumbering up on the Hot air below, and
       Bumpin', Bumpin',
       From side to side
       He scrapes first one wall,
       Then the other.
They keep coming, and I'm still pumpin', pumpin',
Hoping for a raise.
But I keep pumpin'.

Strong Stuff

by Maude I. Parker

*(This poem was inspired by several photographs of old black
women, shown viewing their young in the passing parade.)*

In chains, overland to the sea.
In castle-dungeons on the coast, waiting, waiting for the
     voyage.
Subway-style steerage class.
The Middle Passage, hot breezes made hotter by the sting of
The Whip and the Lash.
Cane and cotton and coping, mostly coping.
Only strong stuff could survive ! ! !
"Strong Stuff," that's me!
Fooled you all, didn't I?
Yes, sirree, children—keep on keeping on!

Another Poet

by Richard A. Warren

since folks finally realizing the fact
that the beautifulness of black
means something—
i've been reading
    imamu ameer baraka
    ted joans
    sonia sanchez
           and them,
and
    don l. lee
    victor hernandez cruz—
and late at night when everybody's gone
and i'm left alone
i read
    t. s. eliot.

Write a Book about You

by Willard Pinn

write a book about you
about how you feel how you see
how you want
write a book about everytime you said you were
going to write a book
write about lurleen wallace and sojourner truth
about zebras and pigeons and your mama
and her mama
write a book about the faces on the subway
that are always staring at you
write about the dogs who lay dead in gutters
write a book about homosexuals and perverts
and righteous missionaries
write about nine year old junkies in brownsville
and nelson rockefeller
write about jackie kennedy and fanny lou hamer
jack ruby and lyndon johnson
al capone and alioto
write a book about miles, coltrane, pharaoh, mingus, monk
lady day, count, duke, prez
and al hirt
write a book about the nasty words you wrote on the subway
walls
write a book about the nasty words you wanted to write on the
subway walls
write about freedom
about the wind you couldn't see
write a book about old folks and little kids
bad memories and the dude you cheated yesterday
write about the chick you layed on the floor in your bedroom
write about leroi jones and nikki giovanni
write about the tragedy of being young, gifted and black
write a book about rats and roaches
poverty and racism
about sst's ibm's avm's gm's
write about america
write a book about edward brook and mediocrity
about john lindsay and rap brown

write a book about maxwell's hammer and karma
about promises to be kept before you die
before you die
write a book about lincoln center and nothingness
write about all the ties you have . . . the ties
the tears
the reefer
the wine
write all you can about tomorrow morning
then finally write about all the poets you've known
the strange cats you've hung out with
and the good times you've had
when none were planned.

Power

Roots

by Terence Malley

for bensonhurst slim

Pushing up from under
the broken concrete
of wide gum-spotted
Brooklyn sidewalks
those invisible roots
that tripped up my childhood
hobble me now

wherever I go.

Is
God
a
Bask
etball P
layer?

by Jeff Levitsky

                                    He
grabbed the re
   bound
            and dashed
    /longclear stride/
downcourt
                pasthisman
up toward the basket
                        He
flew hand outstretched
    like a flamingo in flight
over the rim
                into sky
                        into night.

Dinosaur

by A. Rubenstein

thin, led neck
reach up interim trees
place us down so
with ease

prod your way a giant huge
grey
across the sunwashed prairie
in journeying
lie yourself great granite shelf
to revolve neath point solaroid
and die

we in Olympia
shall cry down trees
mount up pillars to
the bowels of the earth

digging up your own
old bones
flaked in putrid plaster
that he pasted and planted
in your throat

revere not the creaking supports
that stress between the
granite floor
and the under of the jaw

for my purpose
in the wild lush jungle nite
i ride a dinosaur

and paw not at the cricket in thè sea.

Fragment: The Finish of the Entire Ocean

by Robert Shatkin

1

it was a silk after-
thought, a riding stain
on sand concludes
the sevenfold closet
of energy.
       the chalice, the
beach itself subsides,
submerged.

the coast's jaw is washed.
its terminus releases.
the entire ocean is finished here:
its trace, dense, a weight that changes
sand into a dead facet.

2

There is no drift, no slipstream or
countershuttled tide to play against
rolled force.

There are no knots or beginnings on the whole of the sea,
no warmer curving rivers shuffling the cold skin into kingdoms.

Sargasso's confluence is the fault of the helmsman
and not of the finishing conscience of the sea.

3

the tenant ship
negotiates the sea-rills, its
rifts in stacked energy,
          becomes the process now
and seduces masked air into play.
               its sails swell
               as starved spoons will.

and now the helmsman
cemented to worked wood
by worked meat resists
a mock horizon: where
maybe there would be
his harbor's fallen gate.

undistracted, he becomes
the vessel and the process
on the finishing conscience
of the sea.

Gull

by Russell Bonanno

Mad-eyed, drifting in the brown light of dawn,
A gull, breasting the heave of sea
Coiled in fury, wild
Wild as the sun, like isinglass splintered
It rises—

    Sea-worn, winged and dancing,
        dancing its fury in the laughter of wind,
        shrieking the wail of a child

It embraces the day:
        Joy and Madness, merge
        and a child cries,
            a child.

And Now, a Milestone in the History of Man

by Louise Jaffe

And now, a milestone in the history of man
We have landed on the moon.
It is hot and it is late
And out of the void a little boy is crying
That by day I know as mine.
The world has taken an immeasurable step forward,
Never again will it be the same,
Never again will man be bound to earth.
I drag myself from bed and know for the umpteenth time
The pain of motherhood.
Our astronauts have shown the world
The potentialities of the human soul,
There is reason to rejoice.
My mother-in-law parcelled out her usual packet of advice
On How to Get Him to Sleep Through.
She is a bitch; it doesn't count.
We exchange words but say nothing.
In company we also manage appropriate gestures.
They have shown for all ages to come
That man can assume mastery over nature.
It is unceasingly hot. My body clings to the rocker
As his clings to mine;
We drown in a sea of stifling proximity.
They have landed at the Sea of Tranquility;
They have approached the unknown;
They have expanded human horizons.
It is hot, little one.
Tomorrow there is wash to do,
A house to clean.
The expansion is enormous, unbelievable.
Will I be able to see beyond tomorrow?
I rather doubt it.
A hope for international accord,
For peace on earth
My life is measured in rockings
And bottles
And things.

Fun with Figures

by Marshall F. Dubin

The body count is favorable today,
And to make it more so,
We count as four a foeman's arms and legs
Torn by shrapnel from his torso.

Our casualties, of course, we minimize,
And count as one:

> lost hands,
> lost feet,
> lost eyes.

Drugs

Spike Dreams

by Jim Dixon

Lee was standing by the sink with a glass in his hand. He filled the glass with two inches of water. Then he walked over to the kitchen table, sat down, and put the glass on the table. In front of him was a piece of folded-up aluminum foil about an inch long and a half-inch wide. This he picked up and opened. Inside the foil was a pile of white powder. Lee took a knife out of his pocket, opened it, and with the tip of the blade took some of the white powder and dumped it in the glass. He took another small pile of white powder and put it in the glass and then he took the knife and stirred the water around for a few seconds to make sure everything was well mixed. When he was through doing this he drank the water down.

"How long does it take to feel it when you do it like that?" I asked.

"Ten minutes maybe. Maybe longer."

"It's faster when you snort it."

"I know. Here, you take some." He pointed at the foil with the knife blade. "I want you alert."

"It will make me paranoid."

"Maybe. That's all right. You'll keep your eyes open."

I took the knife from him and put a little of the powder on its tip, and raised it up to my right nostril and, blocking off the other nostril with a finger, I snorted it up. Then, some more in the other nostril. The powder burnt but it was a nice feeling and I threw my head back to get it all in.

Speed: Do some and you get interested in anything. Nothing bores you, nothing depresses you. You have tremendous energy; you can run around all night. Speed puts you in the best of moods. You talk of sad events saying, "Oh, that's terrible," but you won't feel bad about it because it's hard to stop smiling. You talk about nothing for hours. It seems so important to you at the time. Everything has a nice color to it. Until some hours later, you crash . . . then, it's just the opposite: the whole world falls apart; as much as you were up before, you're depressed now. Colors all turn to gray. You look at yourself in the

245

mirror: bloodshot eyes, pale dirty flesh; you want no part of yourself. If you're hung up on speed you go out and cop some more and you get spaced again and the crash is over . . . for a few hours at least. Speed kills, some say.

I took another hit.

"Ah-h, it burns," I said to Lee. "How come you drank it?"

"It makes my nose bleed."

Me and Lee seldom do speed. It fucks you up too much. But this cat P.J. laid some on us. Lee thought it would be a good idea. We were taking a ride up to Harlem to score some pounds of grass. It would make the ride more pleasant.

Connection

A black cat who lives on the south edge of Harlem, where Harlem just begins. A few safe blocks south of heavy uptown smack trade. Good for two reasons: First, the neighborhood around his building wouldn't be rip-off city with loads of junkies hanging around. Second, the police see us in his neighborhood they might let us by without checking us out. But further uptown they see a car with long-haired white guys in it, the cops figure these cats up to score smack, and they get the idea maybe to bust the car for heroin, which they can always resell back on the street, or else maybe the guys have drugs and a lot of cash to pay off.

A Ride Uptown

We walked out of our apartment and down a flight of stairs to the first floor. We have three rooms in an old two-family house.

I looked out the little window in the front door before opening it to see who might be outside on the street. If the police know who you are it's easier for them to pin you on the street and search you, than for them to get a warrant for your place. And you always have to be careful of rip-off artists or junkies who know you're dealing and figure you're holding a lot of cash or drugs and will hole-up outside your place and wait for you to come out. Seems like a lot more people getting into this last trip.

Three Fantasies

The ride to Harvey's is not bad at all; mostly expressway driving, little traffic; not a long ride, maybe 20 minutes. You get a good nighttime view of the Manhattan skyline and the bridges over the river are fun.

246

Sometimes though, when I'm driving on the expressways at night, I get these weird fantasies. I don't know where I get them; they just pop into my head.

They all have something to do with bombs.

1. Someone in a car ahead will throw a cigarette out the window. It lands in my lane and the sparks jump; it reminds me of firecrackers we played with as kids, the way the fuse burned down in the dark, and sometimes when I see this I get the idea that the people ahead are throwing back some type of fuse-bomb planned to go off under my car. When I drive over the sparks I shudder, and when I pass it and nothing happens, no explosion, I feel relieved . . . .

2. I'm driving over one of the bridges, the Brooklyn or the Manhattan or the George Washington Bridge, and I get the idea that somebody wants to blow up the bridge. The dynamite is planted and the bridge is set to go the same time I come over it. I really believe it's going to happen and I tense up and wait for the explosion. I expect to see the bridge split in two ahead of me; I can almost feel the concussion and the roadway give and I see the long fall down to the cold dirty waters below . . . .

3. This is the worst. It fucks me up the most. It also occurs when I'm on a bridge. I'll be driving over and I'll think: in a few seconds they will drop the atomic bomb on New York City. I imagine it going off a half-mile out in the water: there's a blinding flash with a deafening roar, the bridge starts to sway from the force. A giant cloud mushrooms out from the water to a terrible height. The city starts to melt before my eyes . . . .

When I'm thinking like this, when I'm stoned and these dreams seem very real, I'm relieved to get off the bridge, to get to the other side, to the protection of city buildings, instead of out on the bridge where you're naked and vulnerable, where only the cables protect you . . . and anything can reach through them . . . .

Harvey

A chick answers the door. She's black, good-looking, wears her hair in a very wide, very neat Afro. She has on a tight tank-top, no bra, and fancy square-rimmed sunglasses. I never seen her before.

Harvey's crib: a hustler's apartment; spiffy expensive furniture and good stereo equipment: probably picked up hot or with a stolen credit card. There's a Moroccan rug on the living-room floor. A color TV is on, volume low, and on one wall of the room there's a very big fish tank with a shit-load of pretty-colored fish. His place is incredibly neat.

Harvey's sitting on a thick red couch. He's rolling joints from a wooden stash box filled with grass.

247

He's an athletic-type dude, a little heavy in the belly though. Has his hair in a neatly trimmed Afro and sideburns that come down near his mouth. He's the biggest jive-ass you ever want to meet, and flashy, and very cool in his manner.

Harvey handles grass, cocaine, guns, stolen goods, credit cards. We buy pounds of grass from him. We used to buy coke from him but now we get a better product from P.J.

Harvey rolls the best joints I ever seen. Like a machine would roll them. He must practice for hours. He looks up.

"Harve," I say.

"What's happenin?"

"What's happenin, man?"

One time me and Lee were rapping about Harve. Lee comes out with this:

"I hate to say it but the impression I get is this: Harvey ain't gonna last too long. He's not too bad a cat, leastways to us, but he's not the slickest or fastest cat in the business I ever seen. Lots of guys around faster than him. He digs bucks, Harvey, and in a way that makes him sometimes not wanna give somebody something they paid for, and they don't find out until they get it home and unwrap it, you know what I mean? You know? But people don't forget; they come back some day. I'm not accusin him or nothin, but I watch him, I watch him close. The nicer he is the more careful I wanna be . . . .

"Now, if Harvey's business gets bigger and the police get wind of it, they'll be around for a piece, right? That's only natural. But Harvey's not gonna like that at all, I know. He'll try and fuck them around and next thing you know that cat's in jail banging his head against the bars, trying to figure out what went wrong. That's one way it might happen. Harvey will fall within a year, maybe six months."

"Ah, bullshit," I go. "Harvey's all right. Whadayou worried about? Shit, what a thing to say about a dude."

That's Lee, just a paranoid cat. Sometimes he wants to take a piece with us when we cop. I talk him out of it. What's he gonna do, shoot it out? A piece is instant shit if you get stopped.

"Harvey," Lee goes, "we wanna pick up six pounds—three keys. We'll turn them over with no trouble at all, you know, and we'll probably pick up some more later in the week. You know?"

"Fine," Harvey says. "As long as you got the cash you take whatever you want. Sheeit." He laughs. I can see he's ripped on smoke. "Why, if you got the right price, bro, you can take me an my whole place an even Marcy there. We're ready . . . ."

"Fuck you," Marcy says.

248

"Louis," he says to me, "how you makin it, brother?"

"Just fine. I'm high . . . ."

"I know; your eyes are big as quarters. You a spaced-out dude, Louis."

I laughed.

He passes Lee the joint. Lee draws smoke in and the tip of the joint glows bright red.

"Maan," Harvey says, "I dig seein business come right through that door. I really dig it, ya understan? . . . Yes, yes, mmm . . . Marcy, this here is Lee, an that dude over there who looks so uptight, that Louis . . . ."

Wake

Lisa's mother is pretty intelligent. I think she went to college or something. She's not bad-looking for her age. We always got along pretty good. But I didn't want to see her now. I was avoiding her like hell but now she sees me and makes a bee-line in my direction. What can I do, run away? She always liked me for some reason.

"I'm really sorry," I tell her.

"Thank you," she says. "Thank you for coming."

Her eyes are all red and bloodshot, but she's not crying, and I'm thankful for that. But I'm on the spot; I can't wait till it's over and I can leave and get out in the fresh air. I know she's going to start asking questions I can't answer.

"Louis, I don't think that I have realized it yet," she's saying. "I think . . . that when I finally do realize it, it will be very bad."

I told her I understood.

I'm shifting back and forth from one foot to the other.

On the other side of the room all kinds of roses, and wreaths were flanked around the coffin.

"Louis," she went on, "maybe you can tell me: what's wrong with our young people? What's going on in this country that I don't understand? . . ."

I told her that I didn't know.

After we hung out for awhile Harvey got up and got us the three keys. He checked them out and they looked fine so we packed them in a shopping bag and got ready to make it.

"I'm workin a gig," Harvey says. "I'm workin a gig an I think you cats can pick up nice cash on it, you understan?"

"What's doin, man? What kind of gig?"

"Well, I got a thing linked up wit a cat, right? I can move a few

249

ounces of skag, like very fast. Immediate turnover, bro, you understan?
Here's gig, man: Things tight up here. Stuff all cut to hell . . . ."

"What a fucked-up drug," I said. "Fucked-up."

"Take it easy, Louis. What's up your ass?"

"Don't like to get into it. Don't like to see anybody get into it."

"Sheeit . . . ."

"I had to go to a wake not long ago. A chick I knew O.D.ed . . . .
It really dragged my head."

"Got nothin to do with us. People strung out are strung out, ya dig?
That facts of life, baby. I don want nothin to do with junkies. Them
cats crazy. Who wants fuckin junkies hangin around? I ain't inta
baggin up nickel bags an standin on the corner. I'm inta quick turnover, man,"—he snaps his fingers—"don ever wanna see a junkie, you
know? Now your man P.J. got what I need. He says it will take a six
an if that's so that's outta sight dope." (Take a six means you can cut
it six times: six parts quinine and milksugar to one part heroin.)
"Whereas shit up here funnin down to a four, four an a half, five if
you're very lucky . . . ."

P.J.

P.J. deals in speed, cocaine, and heroin. And only in weight. We've
bought coke from him. Top-quality product.

He's a very nice guy. Does a lot of speed and coke and when he's
high he's very funny; tells stories, jokes, ridiculous raps, like that.

P.J.'s fairly straight-looking, medium build, maybe five-ten in height.
He's in his mid-twenties. He wears his hair "styled," black curls a little
over his ears. He dresses nice; I guess he can afford it. P.J. drives a
maroon Mercedes-Benz.

Whenever he comes to our place he moves immediately to the
phone and calls two or three people in a row. Then he talks business
with us.

When it comes to money P.J.'s very calm. I seen him handle thousands of dollars like it was five dollars. He'll count out two hundred
on a table, say, and then get up and take a piss leaving the money on
the table. He's careless like that, and he'll trust you with a lot of money
for awhile, but when it comes down to paying up he's the kind of cat
that's into breaking arms to collect.

To P.J. drugs is just a business like any other: you invest, you buy,
you sell, you make money. Only in this business there's little advertising. As far as he's concerned he didn't create junkies. Like Harvey he
wants little to do with them. I'll tell you this: I've rapped with P.J.
about junkies, and he talks about it like he really feels bad about them.
He don't make any connection between him and them. It's weird . . . .

One time P.J. was high on speed. He was talking a lot. He started to get into details about things and he told me he can score a kilo of heroin at will. Anytime. Rarely a shortage. He said there hasn't been a serious smack panic in years. Big busts, big seizures make only a small dent. That's people late in payments, he explained. Or cats unlucky to get pinned with no cash.

"All you have to do," he said, "is carry enough cash to take care of anyone who might stop you."

On the way to the elevator I took my knife out of my pocket. I opened the blade and put it back in the pocket, handle up. If anybody stopped us in the hall or on the street I could get at the knife fast as possible, and it would be already opened and ready to use. I'm not about to hand over six pounds of grass without putting up some kind of hassle.

We go down the elevator and almost to the front door when two black guys walk in. I put my hand on the blade, wait for any sudden movements, but they just look us over and walk on by. Probably wondering what we were doing in the building. Maybe they know Harvey.

We looked out the front door and nobody was around so we went out and walked over to the car, smooth as possible, speed still going strong and the danger of being stopped making my heart pound: I see people in doorways, dark figures behind garbage cans and parked cars, waiting to pounce . . . .

"Maybe smack is like one of those finance company loans," Lee is saying. "You know, you got a whole bunch of problems, like some people have a shit-load of bills. Well, just like that one loan supposed to cover all those bills, junk is a big problem takes care all your other ones. Consolidate it so to speak. You see?"

"That loan thing's a hype, though. You gotta pay in any case. More even."

"I'm hip," he says. "It's the same thing almost, you know? Like I was tellin you . . . ."

"Yeah," I say, "maybe you got something . . . . Something else though. I think there's something else to it: I think it's boredom, man. People got nothing else to do but get high. Jobs suck, school sucks, everything's fucked . . ."

"Uh, yeah, but, what was I sayin? . . . Yeah, there's more to it . . . . A feeling maybe: a dead-ass, shit-ass feeling that everybody's got. Seems like these days you're almost forced into gettin high . . . ."

Bagging Up

Lee reached up and took the scale off the top shelf. It's a very accurate scale; measures to a tenth of a gram. A friend of ours stole it out of his high school lab. He said it was a $75 scale. We traded him some coke for it. The scale weighs things in grams, not ounces. But all you have to do is figure 28 grams to an ounce and work from there.

We wanted to double-check the weight of the grass, and then break some of it down to ounces, quarters, and halves. High on speed you'll weigh everything in the house. Bagging up is work but it's fun; speeding, you'll gladly sit and do it for hours.

First, you break off a piece of the brick. The kilo is very tightly compressed. You throw this piece in a bowl and break it up with your fingers, removing the big twigs and branches. You put it in a strainer and work it until it's pretty clean, but not too fine, and then you stick it in a little clear plastic bag and weigh it up. You add and subtract weed until it weighs an ounce. Now, you put the baggie inside another baggie, roll it up, and put a piece of scotch tape around it to hold everything together. We don't strain quarter-pounds so much and we leave most of the twigs in. A half-pound we leave in brick form.

Feeling, Arguments

"I'll tell you," Lee goes, "smack is not my drug. The head's fine but I don't like to do it and I don't like the people into it . . . . But, we don't have to touch it; we don't even hafto open the package. We turn over the quarter-pound to Harvey and make $500. In less than an hour, man, you know? And have nothin to do with it besides that."

The Feeling

First, a rush: warm, it spreads with a tingling sensation. After, the high. Your body is very relaxed. You feel nothing; no pain, physical or mental. There is no boredom. You do not have to move, go anyplace, do anything to pass the time. On heroin you have no problems. You think of something that has been bothering you and you smile: how ridiculous it was to worry. You are strong, secure, confident.

If you're really fucked up on some very strong smack, you don't really care whether you live or die. One choice is as good as another. You always want more: you might be five milligrams away from an O.D. but you'll say to yourself, man, it's nice but I could be higher.

Someone talks to you, you don't even listen, you lose track of their words. Perhaps you laugh in their faces; their words couldn't possibly make any difference.

Smack cuts off the world. It flows around you like a bubble; nothing gets in and upsets you. You are so warm and painless, so strong, unbeatable, so indifferent, so smooth, so cool . . . .

252

"I don't know," I tell him. "I don't mind handlin grass and hash. I don't mind handlin coke. I've even turned over speed though I don't like to handle it. But I like to draw the line, you know, where smack comes in. I got a thing about it. That drug scares me. Like the drug is evil or something."

"Evil?" Lee said. "What do you mean, evil? Shit."

"It's got like a hidden property. Something strong. Like a plague type of thing."

"I don't follow you."

"It's hard to explain," I said.

"Them other cats into junk, and, man, every time you look there's more, them other dudes, well, I don't dig it, but they do what they want, you know? Three quarters of our old friends are into it. That don't surprise me; I got used to it a long time ago. I got cold to it, detached. But Lisa, I don't understand about her . . . . She was different. I could talk to her. It was just so easy, so natural to talk to her. She was that type of person who would listen real well. . . . I remember her voice . . . ."

"It was a bummer, man," Lee said.

"Sometimes we'd go to the city. We'd walk around. It was nothing heavy . . . ."

"We could always tell Harvey P.J.'s out of town or something. Harvey don't have to know shit."

"We could do that," Lee says, "but that's $500 we're throwin away. And more to come, maybe. I mean, man, we don't have to touch it, don't have to get into it, don't have to bag it up, cut it, or nothin. We're just middlemen."

"I don't know about that."

"Louis, you know this shit will move around us anyway. It's gotta go somewhere . . . . And P.J. says its good smack. He says it will take a six and he'll guarantee Harvey a six . . ."

"Tell you what: give Harvey a call. See if he wants to do the thing. Maybe he won't like the price. No use worryin about it till we see whether he wants it or not."

"It ain't gonna make no difference. None. Us stayin away from this is not gonna clean up the streets. Even if we set up a beat and took it off the street does that mean there's gonna be nobody strung-out anymore? How much difference can it make? None, man. None at all. You know how much heroin gets turned over in New York City every day? Many kilos, brother. A few ounces won't cut any difference. It is like nothin, man . . . ."

253

"A quarter pound," I go; "that's something: there must be some O.D.'s in there . . . ."

"It's a relative gig," Lee said.

"What do you mean?"

"The cat who cuts it worries about O.D.'s. We have nothin to do with that. We can't take the blame; we're above that level, man."

Taste

P.J. came over to the place and drops off the taste. It's for Harvey. The taste is a quarter gram wrapped in tinfoil.

"It's good," he says. "Harvey will like it. I guarantee it."

"Yeah?" Lee says.

"There's enough here for him to test it," P.J. said.

"How does that go?" I asked.

"How does what go?"

"Testing it. To see if it's as good as you say."

"Same as you do with coke. You hit it as much as the man says you can hit it, then you try what's left . . . . Or, you give what's left to a junkie and see how he reacts." He laughed. "If he keels over, then you know it's out-of-sight dope."

Dreams

The day Harvey came down to pick up his stuff I took a walk over to the park. I didn't want to be there when Harvey came. I told Lee I was going out and he said fine and that he would take care of everything.

The deal was set for four in the afternoon. Earlier that day P.J. dropped off the package. He was in a good mood. The package was wrapped in brown paper with a string tied around it. He cut the string, unwrapped some paper, and took out a clear plastic bag filled with white powder. Lee told him he'd call him after Harvey left.

In the park I walked over towards the lake. Summer's over now and it was windy; I had the park pretty much to myself. I put up the collar on my denim jacket. Leaves were beginning to fall from the trees: it looked like an early fall this year. I would walk around until I was sure Harvey had left . . . .

I remember times in summers past when we would all sit on a grassy hill in the park; maybe twenty, thirty of us, passing joints around, listening to somebody's radio, laughing, goofing, drinking wine . . . . The hitter days were over for a couple of years and nobody could figure how we ever hit each other over the head with a bicycle chain, or try to slash somebody's face with a car aerial . . . .

Times have changed; people hitting again, gangs are starting up again. The cycle repeats itself.

I thought of the old days . . . everybody was together; people were peaceful, relaxed; they seemed to know where they were going. Now people nod all over the city.

Here I am twenty years old and already I'm into memories.

It's not gonna matter. Four ounces just ain't enough to make a difference: there's too much around.

After an hour I walked back to the apartment. Lee was waiting there.

"Harvey left us a taste," he said.

"That's good," I told him.

I snorted a little bit in each nostril. Only a small amount because it was fairly pure and you could O.D. easily.

It was very good stuff. After a while I felt fine. I was no longer depressed . . . .

Smack cuts off the world. It flows around you like a bubble; nothing gets in and upsets you . . . .

In a little while I went into a nod. My head drooped down, my chin on my chest. Lee was saying something but I didn't pay any atttention to him. I nodded at him. I nodded at the passing of old friends. I nodded at Lisa; I could picture her now very clearly: no emotions to cloud the image . . . I remember now. Sometimes we'd go to the city. We'd walk around. She would say, "Louis . . . ."

It Was Next Month Yesterday

by Robert Nash

it was next month yesterday
and we were all stoned in between the east river and
the grand canyon just
a breath of it so
nothing felt too good everything we owned
were kool cigarettes
bring down
hunched up together in our glue-stained shirts eating nothing
but air
i was banging my mind against a rubber wall but remember
i was psyched out
and everyone else had turned to plastic we smelled
clean though
collectively
maybe we weren't i had no choice in the matter and
who does
anyway

The Coming to an End of an Understanding

by Steve Magagnini

"Sa-ay, man, let's get right on down to it, for old times!"

"Yeah. For old times."

Niles got up from his stool, reached for the bottom drawer of the oaken table, and flicked six or seven joints down upon it. This was going to be it. Now Niles searched through the large pile of albums, strewn across the room from one speaker to the other. The music was strong, it was loud, it was electric, it was hard rock, produced only months ago by some currently popular group. The music had no meaning. Darby eased himself back into the cumulus folds of the plush burgundy armchair. The armchair always made him thirsty. Niles, by now, was lighting a joint carefully, trying to shake his hair out of his eyes with quick, jerking motions of his head. Darby's eyes combed the familiar room and its familiar contents. Each item had a purpose, a memory of its own. Niles passed the joint over to Darby. Niles liked doing this. He liked to smoke. He always wanted to see how far he could go, and the process was a pleasure. But tonight was going to be different. It had to be.

Darby closed his eyes, partly to avoid the smoke, partly to see his thoughts. To Darby, getting stoned was a serious business. To him, smoking with someone else had a great significance. It meant that these two people had a certain bond, perhaps a spiritual bond between them. Yes, it was a religious thing with Darby.

Soon Niles put away the couple of sticks that remained and once again changed the record, putting on a few albums so the music was ready all night. Darby stared at a painting for some time, locking his eyes into it as once again he plunged into thought. The Rolling Stones began to heat up the room, and the warmth affected both.

At this point, Darby reached into the pocket of his peajacket and brought out a pint of Chianti. Niles' eyes widened, and a wide grin spread across his face.

"We're really going to get ripped tonight, baby!" he cried, and hopping up, stumbled into the kitchen. Soon he was back with two glasses of ice. Darby opened the bottle and poured until both glasses were brimming with the heavy red wine. The wine looked purple in the room's lone blue light. Niles pointed to the wall, raised his glass, and shouted, "To Sophia, baby!!"

"Yeah, to Sophia!"

They both swigged heartily off of their wine glasses. Darby felt himself floating. He felt weak, helpless, and yet very tranquil. He felt wasted. Niles began to talk.

"Remember those times in eighth grade, those school socials, when everybody used to come all 'slicked up'? And how you had to come late, just had to come late, if you wanted to be cool? And how much those slow songs meant to us? And how you used to ask a girl to save the last few dances for you, on account of they were going to be slow, and you felt so damn great when she said yes? Wait a second."

He got up to put on a record. After fishing through piles of forty-fives, he exclaimed, "Ahhh," and grinned his widest grin. The slow, soft rock began.

"Younger Girl!" Darby couldn't find the words to express what he felt, but that was all right. He sighed. The song certainly brought back some of the good times. Niles continued, "Remember some of the chicks we used to dig—I liked Lorraine so damn much, shit—how could anyone like Lorraine. . . ."

Darby twisted feverishly in his chair and said, "Remember that time in ninth grade, when I turned you on, at George's, I think it was, and you were trying to act stoned. And how dope was such a big thing then, and you thought so, The Big Thing. And you attempted to act collected like it was no big thing." Darby's speech had become garbled, and his thoughts were drifting like clouds. In an instant they had both forgotten what they had been talking about. Finally, Niles got up and walked around the room. Unsteadily, he opened a drawer and pulled out a deck of cards. Niles decided that this would be a good way to pass the time. But soon the hard rock sound of the Doors' "Morrison Hotel" brought them to life. The music sounded too good. The cards were thrown to the floor. The build-up was going to be terrific indeed—it had to be.

When the record was over, Niles turned the stereo off.

"Man, we is on a binge. This is it. This is even better than it was at Leon's, yeah, Leon's. That was a blast." Niles paused. Darby picked up the conversation.

"At Leon's we were really plastered. Shit, man, they had to scrape us off the floor and carry us out. Those were the good times, all right. The good times."

"Man, we were wrecked." They were both laughing. It was a spontaneous, infectious type of laughter that meant joy.

"Hey," Niles cried, "Remember that night over at Peter's, when his parents were gone . . . ."

"Everyone turned on at Peter's."

"Even that chick Martha. She was pretty straight with drugs, but when it came to nooky . . . ." Niles paused and laughed easily. Darby breathed a sigh of relief. That was close.

"You sure did all right with the women, Nile, oh you sure did all right." Darby said this quietly. When he was uneasy, he called Niles Nile.

"Oh, it was nothing, man." Niles got up and went into the kitchen. He came back into the blue room with some devil dogs, two oranges, and some cheese.

"Wait a minute," he said. He ran back into the kitchen and soon returned with a bottle of Boone's Farm. Niles looked at Darby with a twinkle in his eye, and his face broke into one of his classic grins.

"You didn't actually think I could forget it, did you?" Boone's Farm had its place. They liked the crisp apple wine. It had all the character that the occasion called for. It went down smooth and easy, forming a puddle in their bellies. It just had to be.

Darby instinctively picked up a devil dog that Niles had dumped on the table. He swigged the Boone's Farm heartily, but with a certain reserve. This was the way the wine was to be drunk. And Niles did the same.

"Now this is good stuff. We are really gettin' right down to it!!"

"You know it, brother, you know it." The wine washed the food down perfectly, the food that could have been mistaken for ambrosia by the reception it got. Niles glanced at Darby, smiled and extended his palm.

"Give me skin!" But he didn't have to say it, of course. Darby chortled.

". . . like the cat that swallowed the mouse, brother, like the cat that swallowed the mouse."

They were alive now as the wine took its effect. The last song on the last side of a soft Procol Harum album was over and all at once Niles cried, "It's coming, man, it's coming!! Get yourself together, 'cause the queen is on the way!!"

The record dropped into place, and soon it was plain that Cheap Thrills was the sound. Niles reached out and turned it up full blast. Janis *was* it. Janis was the culmination of a long line of events. The final answer. The music penetrated the very walls of their brains, the very barriers of their existence. They had at last reached the height of sensitivity. Everything lent itself, everything was relative, and yet all meaning was forsaken for the sheer ecstasy of the moment, of Janis. The blue light danced, and so, too, did they. Darby lay back in his chair, eyes closed, overwhelmed by the vibrations of peerless sound. Then he looked at Niles, who in frenzied motions was jerking his body spasmodically. In the light he looked like an illusion. They looked at each other. It was understood.

"Ooooooooooh, shit man, *we're cook-innnn!!!!*"

The music began to tear their minds from their bodies. Darby sat, with tears of joy rolling down his cheeks. This was love. Niles was on the floor, shrieking. There could not have been a happier moment in their lives. They were drained. And then flashing through the mind went frustration . . . .

Niles liked to talk about that time at John's beach house. He liked himself. He licked his lips in anticipation.

"Oh, yeah, Michele was a fine bitch. She was the first girl I screwed, and she was dynamite. She was fine. She could screw like . . . ."

"Oh, you sure did all right with the women, Nile, you sure did all right."

"Oh, man, it was just luck, that's all."

"Oh, no, Nile, it couldn't have been."

"It was nothing. You didn't do too bad . . . ."

"Yes, but never as good as you, Nile. Sure it was just luck, just luck with Karen too?" Darby was incensed.

"I didn't mean to, man, I didn't . . . ."

"Oh no, Oh no. Stop it, damn you!!! Stop!"

He tried to shake himself out of it, but he was too far gone.

"To Sophia, baby?" It was a question this time. It was over.

"Yeah. To Sophia."

The Stigmata of the Rainy-Day Sun

by Robert E. Hayes

The Rainy-Day Sun on Avenue B, located between the two major lower East Side hippie hangouts, was a square gray-green box with big glass windows that seemed to shimmer against the wind. Before Morris Markey took over the business from Madeline Lawrence, there had been a large sign hanging outside with simple black letters that read "Laundromat." Madeline Lawrence had not been one to go in for fancy titles to a business. She pulled her long hair back from her pretty but business-like face and wore tight blue-jeans with the assurance of a cowboy. Everyone got a good wash with plenty of bleach for the white things, a thorough drying, and no credit. "This here's a hustling paradise," she told Morris. "A, B, C and D from 14th Street on down is filled with people who have to try and get as much as they can for nothing. Some by choice and some by necessity. There's all kinds of poor, Mr. Markey, and the best kind is the real poor—the one that's tried as hard as he can and can't go no further."

The real poor, as far as Morris was concerned, were few and far between. Perhaps the hippies had submerged them with an onslaught of earnestness and fakery. For each group it was still their lower East Side no matter how much they had been submerged by the latest conquering force.

Morris considered himself an American first and a Jew second. At forty-eight he was wizened without being wise; he still did his thinking with his heart. After all these years a man should know better. Such a business as a laundromat is not run on good faith. Where was the Jew in him when it came to business? Madeline Lawrence had more in her and she was God knows what—a fool? A fool, yes, but in her private life, not her business. She worked nine years, saving every cent so that she might retire to Barbados and live in the sun with a black-skinned man she had met one summer while he was visiting some relatives on the lower East Side. Jimmy Jameson was black as the night, his features indiscernible in the photograph she showed Morris. She had written him once a week and he had answered her once a month for nine years. When she met him, she had been twenty-five. Her eyes flashed now as they perhaps had then—with the same intensity. In all that strength there has to be a weakness, Morris told himself.

And strength she had. When he came to buy and the sign was in the window, she was running it all practically alone. Just she and the boys from the neighborhood, manning the machines, folding the sheets and towels and driving the bicycle delivery carts. At the end of the day, sitting surrounded by her boys and the big white bags of laundry, waiting for the customers to come by and pick up what was not to be delivered, she seemed like a queen of the golden west. Her blue dungareed legs would be crossed and she'd be smoking a cigarette. The boys would be smoking too, adjusting their narrow-brimmed hats over their eyes. He admired her communion with the boys. For him it would always be difficult. Puerto Rican and Jew. Old man and young boys. So much space to be overcome. He decided that if he had a bottom like she had a bottom in those dungarees then the boys would've worked for him too.

Morris missed her when she finally left. She was eager to be off and yet she prolonged her stay. Always there was one more thing she wanted to be sure Morris knew about. Nine years of written communication with Jimmy counted for quite a bit, Morris was sure, but the longer, the more physically real time had been put in at the laundromat. And though she would not have wanted to admit it, she was reluctant to leave the routine she had known for all the ambiguities that were waiting for her in love and Barbados.

It was an excellent business, situated close enough to 14th Street to draw customers from Stuyvesant Town and yet far enough into the jungle to attract its own conglomeration of peoples. The Rainy-Day Sun was a rarity in that it was not self-service. To drop off your laundry, have it washed and dried for you, and to pick it up at your convenience or have it delivered all at 75 cents for eight pounds seemed a most wonderful time and money-saving bargain for those who worked and those who didn't. A thin cigar gripped tightly between his teeth, Morris would reach out for the laundry bags, refusing to weigh them until they had been washed. "They weigh lighter when they're all done," he'd explain around the cigar. His small even teeth appeared to be thickly outlined in black. "You're not paying for the dirty ones. You're paying for the clean ones, ain't you?" And of course the customers agreed. It was all Madeline's policy and he had kept it, knowing her sense of business was better than his. His only change had been in the sign that swung on squeaking hinges over the door. He had overheard the boys talking together. It was Monday morning, their busiest day next to Saturday, and the boys had all had too much

262

weekend. "Rain or sun is out, man, we keep working. We work harder than the sun in the sky. He take a day off, hide in the clouds when it rains. Not us, man, we come out whether it rains or not." And in his own mind he had said it and he liked the way it sounded. So he said to the boys, "Yeah, we're like a rainy-day sun." And they all responded, laughing over it. And the next day he ordered a sign of black lettering and a yellow sun with stick-like rays.

He got compliments about the name from the hippies when they came in. They wanted him to have it done on the glass in psychedelic lettering. "That's an idea," he would say, smiling himself squint-eyed behind his wire-rimmed glasses. "That's an idea."

The boys were good boys generally, but he couldn't really count on them. Some days all six of them would be there and other days there might not be any. And one day there were seven. "He could use the money, Mr. Markey. I thought today we might be short." His name was Angel de Jesus. He preferred to be called by his full name but would settle for being called "Angel" only if it were pronounced as if the g were a y. Morris had let him stay if for no other reason than that his dark eyes seemed larger and darker than any eyes he had seen before. Morris knew this was not a good reason and yet the boy looked a little thin in the neck and the arms. Perhaps he had not been able to eat regularly.

Angel came every day. In this respect he was not like the other boys. Federico had stayed out for a week and had begun work again on the following Monday without even offering an explanation. When Morris asked him why he hadn't called, Federico told him that they had no phone. His mother had been very sick and he had been afraid to leave her even for a moment. While Morris had been weighing the credibility of the story, Federico had reached out and grabbed him firmly by the arm and smiled his most winning smile. Morris had realized the boy was flirting with him and he was embarrassed by it because it pleased him; it made him giggle. Federico was muscular in a plump pubescent way, his skin was a smooth ochre, his eyelashes fanned the air with a flutter of unspoken messages. Morris had returned his attention to the timesheet he kept on the boys. "All the same," he said, "I almost got someone else for the job." They both knew he was lying; that he had simply waited for Federico to come back. "Why can't you be like Angel de Jesus?" Morris knew the boy would respond when he heard his name in full. "Angel de Jesus, you would call me or let me know if you couldn't come in, wouldn't you?" The boy stopped his work at one of the big dryers. "Oh, yes, Señor Markey," he said earnestly. Morris had smiled, feeling good that here was one person he could trust. Federico frowned and withdrew his hand from Morris' arm.

263

Madeline Lawrence had warned him about the discipline problem he would have with the boys. "Just you show them who's boss. Be stern with them." He had promised that he would. But he was no disciplinarian. His own sons had been too sickly to be rebellious; they were always bent over inside of a book somewhere. "Poor posture! Poor posture!" he would say, clapping his hands as he went through the room. But they paid him no attention. The boys at the Rainy-Day Sun were amiable, they worked hard when they wanted to, but they did not worry about displeasing their boss. My heart shows through, he thought. They can see I'm weak; that I can't stand up to them. He would try to scowl and they would laugh and say, "Que precioso, Amigo."

Working was a life. It always had been for Morris. He was his own constant companion, learning to be a combination of husband and wife to himself. And now he was both mother and father to the Puerto Rican boys. He was always reluctant for the day to come to an end, when both he and the boys would leave and go to their respective homes. Five o'clock was the last wash. Madeline Lawrence had planned it so there would be ample time for the last wash to be dried and for the laundromat to be straightened out for the next morning's work. Morris let the boys go at six o'clock, but often he would stay to dry out the machines, to wash their chipped exteriors, to check his supplies, and even to sweep the floor. Any excuse was instantly worthy of his attention. One night Angel de Jesus offered to help him take the delivery carts into the store from where they were parked at the curb. "I thought I'd sweep up first," Morris told him. Angel nodded and brought two brooms from where they were always left leaning in the corner. "It can't be overtime," Morris said, reluctantly accepting the broom. Angel nodded.

The Rainy-Day Sun was lined on either side with static rows of white-enameled washers. The two enormous dryers were at the back and, except for the small desk and weighing area near the door, the floor space was open. Angel indicated that the division in the two dryers would mark off their sweeping area. They swept in silence and not until they reached the door and the sweeping was completed did they allow themselves a smile. Angel's was quick and bright and seemed to lift his face into life. When the carts were parked inside, Morris offered to take Angel for a beer. They were walking to the bar when Angel stopped and shook his head. "Buy it here," he said, pointing to a grocery store. The cold cans were sold with neat little brown paper-bag wrappers, and they sat on the stoop of the laundromat and drank them. Morris regretted his hips were so wide; it was a tight fit for him and Angel on the stoop.

They worked well together. The boy seldom spoke, but more and more for Morris there seemed to be an understanding between them. The dark eyes spoke and Morris comprehended. The boy did not rush to go home at six with the others. He would, like Morris, find some little job to delay him. During the summer they became an accepted sight, squeezed onto the laundromat's door stoop, not talking, but just sitting tightly as they drank their beers. Morris wondered if Angel had any family. He wondered where the boy went when he finally left the laundromat. But he could not bring himself to ask. Actually, Morris believed, they both preferred not knowing about the other. Morris could then be the father and Angel could be the son without anything known coming between them.

Angel de Jesus always wore black and white basketball sneakers, pulling the extra-long green lacings through the infinite number of holes in the high instep. He rolled his bulky white socks over the tops of his sneakers, giving them the appearance of miniature cavalier boots and covering the neatly tied double-knotted bows. His shapeless chinos hung flat against his high buttocks which rose from his body like balloons on the sticks of his long thin legs. In the summer he wore to work what appeared to be an old bush jacket, minus any trace of lining, from which the sleeves had been cut or torn. The belt hung fastened to itself in the back, allowing the big four-pocket jacket to flap tent-like around him. Since he wore no shirt, the jacket only succeeded in emphasizing the leanness of his body, his arms protruding like tree limbs where the sleeves should have been. He was not reluctant to make a dance of folding the sheets and towels. The other boys enjoyed watching him at these times—the only time they seemed to give him their approval.

"It's a Jewish dance," Morris would say, holding the opposite end of the newly dried sheet. He put the corners together, crossing his left foot over his right with a slight skip. Angel repeated it, holding his end of the sheet high in the air. "Now we meet in the middle," Morris would say, giving a little running step and making sure the sheet did not hit the ground. Angel let out a sharp cry of pleasure, making his steps more intricate than Morris'. The four corners of the sheet were joined together. Morris held them while Angel stooped down to pick up the fold, dancing first away and then back to where Morris waited to join the corners. He watched the boy's Jesus-medal bouncing on the gold chain around his neck, becoming lost on the ledge of his collar bone. The boys would often clap the rhythm for them, faster and faster until Morris held the folded sheet and Angel was dancing alone. "So when do Spanish boys do Jewish dances?" Morris wanted to know.

Morris always assigned Angel to work the dryers because he felt the boy preferred them. He remembered Angel's amazement as he watched the dryers being opened for the first time. The boy crossed himself as the doors opened and again after they closed, stepping back in wonder at the tongues of "the Holy Ghost fire," as he called it, dancing over the machines. Though it was the draft from the dryers' open doors that caused it, Morris could not bring himself to explain it away. He had heard from the Catholics about Pentecost, when the Holy Ghost descended on the Apostles in the form of tongues of fire. The Catholics had their stories, to be sure, but somehow in the light of Angel's eyes Pentecost took on a significance it had not previously held for Morris. The Holy Ghost fared much better with Angel de Jesus as its mediator.

Morris bought yellow flowers, 69 cents a bunch on the corner of Seventh Street, and placed them in a Pepsi Cola bottle on his tiny, cluttered desk. They kept getting knocked over, but in the way or not he liked them there. Life was full of things to get used to; he could get used to being happy, too. It had been too long since he had the need. The yellow flowers stayed and after awhile they were upright almost all the time. Angel inhaled them deeply, his nose pressed into their fragile faces. He groaned and smiled. "What kind of flowers, Señor Markey?" he asked. "Just flowers," Morris said. "For 69 cents they don't get a name." The boy laughed and began his work. He sang songs in Spanish. Sentimental songs all of them. Morris caught a word here, a phrase there. Lovely songs about being alive. When the clothes were dried, Angel would reach into the open mouth of the dryer with both arms and pull the hot clothes toward him, letting them fall against his body before allowing them to drop into the wicker basket at the foot of the machine. Morris worried that he might soil the clothes with his perspiring body, but Angel's intentions seemed so harmless he could not bring himself to counsel him. That the boy should merely be was enough for Morris. The idea of directing him seldom if ever presented itself, and when it did, succeeded only in confusing Morris who believed that everything Angel did grew so naturally out of life. For people like Morris, life is always a burden; they never know what to do with it. They fuss and worry over it until it falls away from them relatively unused. But others, like Angel, Morris was sure, were so much a part of life they need never question it.

The heat from the dryers could be dizzying even in cool weather, but in August, for everyone but Angel, it was worse than the fires of Hell. Angel de Jesus merely shed his bush jacket and stood smiling by his machines, folding the clothes with help from Morris or from one of the boys. Most of the time, seizing every available opportunity, the boys stood in the doorway or close enough to it to catch a breath of air that might revive them. Even Morris was affected by the unbreathable air that pressed upon him like the heaviest of weights. The soap

266

powder and the bleach did not help to make the Rainy-Day Sun any more palatable. When he was not feeding soap or clothes into one of the washers, Morris would sit slumped at his desk, a cardboard container with a cold drink clutched in his hand, staring at the yellow flowers fighting valiantly to retain their life.

Angel plucked a brassiere from the pile of clothes before him. It was white lace with rather firm cups. Seeing the others crowded around the door, he held the garment up to observe it more carefully. Morris, pretending to be busy with one of the washers, watched him in his discovery. Angel placed the cups of the brassiere against the nipples of his bare chest. The boy closed his eyes slightly, holding the garment by its shoulder straps as if an invisible woman might be in it. Morris caught his breath, feeling a chill of emotion as if it were he that was involved with the garment. Angel bounced the cups against his nipples, smiling, his eyes still lowered. He crushed the brassiere against himself, and then let it slide from his embrace, dropping down into the basket.

It was a revelation for Morris, as if now their understanding was complete. By being there and watching him, Morris had shared in it, just as if Angel and he had made love to the white lace brassiere at the very same time. He thought about taking one from the laundry, from one of the bags that was left overnight, bringing it home with him and trying with it what Angel had done, thinking all the while to himself that it would make them closer, sharing the same love object that way. But he never did. Perhaps, unconsciously he knew that it could never be the same unless Angel de Jesus was there watching him.

They continued to drink beer on the stoop all through August and September. Slowly Morris noticed a change in Angel. What was so outward about him, so full of living, began to grow inward, as if it were being called home by his heart. Since they had never spoken to each other of their individual feelings, it was impossible for Morris to start now. He could only feel the withdrawal and react with a look of sadness that Angel chose only to mirror. The coldness set in, it was impossible to sit on the stoop with a cold can of beer. They drank it inside by the window, leaning on the open washers. But it was not the same. Inside they were cut off from all the world going by on the sidewalks. They were faced with their own silences.

The snow on Avenue B turned to slush so quickly, falling under the wheels of the cars and busses, and under the feet of the lower East Side inhabitants who were too preoccupied with their own coldness, their own poverty, their own undirected lives to notice. The fat laundry bags, bulging their whiteness in the window of the Rainy-Day Sun, competed easily with the unnoticed snow. Morris drank hot coffee at his desk and Angel had taken to wearing several layers of sweaters from turtlenecks to bulky pullovers under his sleeveless bush jacket. It was in December that Angel's pain started. Morris had found him crying several times. "It hurts, Señor Markey," was all he would say. He would rub the palms of his hands together while he cried. Morris wanted the boy to go to a doctor; his friend Sol Shantz would cost him nothing in such an emergency. But Angel told him no. Everything would be all right. It had happened before and there was nothing anyone could do. A week before Christmas, Angel began to wear gloves while he worked. He looked thinner; his face was colorless under his ochre complexion. In a certain light his skin resembled wax. First one customer and then another complained of blood spots on their laundry. Morris worried that the boy was coughing blood.

Angel huddled in a corner of the laundromat, pressed against his beloved dryers. He had not stayed after work but had left immediately before Morris might be tempted to talk with him. Morris' questions had to come. The need to ask them increased, he imagined, just like the pain. He had wound rags around his hands before stuffing them into the oversized gloves. He had been happy at the laundromat; he had almost forgotten that the time was coming for the blood to begin again. "The Blood of the Lamb" was what his mother had called it when she had taken him to show himself to Father Duffy. Father Duffy was scared. After all, what's an Irish priest in a mostly Spanish parish to do? "Easter," Father Duffy kept saying. "Easter, not Christmas. It should be happening on Easter." And somehow he had managed to calm Angel's mother and to hush the whole thing up. He told them they would have to go through channels and that she must tell no one until her son's stigmata was proven to be real.

Angel was fourteen then. The pain in his hands was very real. The flow of blood frightened him coming from the wounds that he had watched appear like stars slowly emerging from a void in the palms of his hands. The wounds had broken open like flowers responding to the sun. And with their birth had come the wildness of the pain, steady and unrelenting until he thought he would have to tear his hands from his arms. One painful hand reaching for another painful hand. He was dizzy from the pain and the loss of blood. His mother would kneel before him each night and undo the bandages that Father Duffy had insisted he wear. And she would pray before him as though he were the Christ until he would run from her. "They hurt, Mama! They hurt!" he would cry. His mother crossed herself over and over murmuring her prayers. He cried himself to sleep every night on his blood spotted sheets. His mother, convinced that the blood was holy, would not wash them. Angel could not pray, at fourteen he did not know enough about prayer to try and replace the pain with it.

'Father Duffy found a good Jewish doctor who could be counted on to keep the affair quiet. He gave Angel some shots to stifle the pain but could do nothing to stop the flow of blood except to tape absorbent pads to the palms of his hands. Angel's mother told some of the women in their apartment building. She had lit many candles around their small apartment before the women came, mumbling their prayers, their exclamations when the wounds in his palms were revealed to them. It terrified him to see the women kneeling and swaying before him, but his mother had insisted that he endure it. When he was fifteen and the wounds began to emerge again, Angel ran from his mother's home and did not return until the stigmata had disappeared.

The wounds would remain open for two weeks, the weeks before and after Christmas. He had spent the Christmas of his fifteenth year in whatever night places he could find. By unscrewing or breaking the lights in phone booths, he was able to rest undisturbed with the glass doors closed. Phone booths in drug stores and hotel lobbys were the best for sleeping during the day because they were equipped with little seats. By plugging some toilet paper in his ear, resting the receiver in the crook of his shoulder, and turning his back to the glass doors, he was able to sleep precariously in the darkened booth until he was discovered or, more likely, until he awakened. At night he prowled the Broadway area begging money from the theater crowd. He would try and slip unnoticed into the back of the dimly lit bars. The girly-magazine stores on 42nd Street were reliable places where he could get warm. Churches were good too. He could sleep behind the velvet curtains in the confessionals and the priest-houses were always good for some food. The pain was so bad that half the time he didn't know where he was anyway, and after all it was only two weeks before the wounds closed up. He begged from Father Duffy's doctor. He didn't want to because he knew the stuff cost money, but somehow he knew that the doctor would be unable to refuse him, at least a little help. And a little help could take the edge off the pain from the goddam nail holes.

Nail holes from nowhere he knew about. And yet being in a church was like balm to them. Not that the pain went away, but his mind seemed to clear and he was conscious, as he had not been able to be, of a reality around him outside the pain. He breathed the stale incensed air as though it possessed the newness of life. The pain resided in his hands; it was no longer all of him. He seemed to understand the repose of the Christ nailed to the cross above the altar, the Christ whose nail holes his mother believed he had. It took Angel until his sixteenth Christmas before he believed that the nail holes in his palms were those of the Christ.

Each night he would leave the alley door to the laundromat open. As soon as Morris left, Angel would sneak back inside to spend the night. It was better than roaming Broadway and having to analyze the motives of the people who offered to befriend him. Working for Morris, Angel had been able to save some money to pay Father Duffy's doctor for the drugs that could be used to relieve the pain. In this, the fourth year of his stigmata, he was better prepared for it than ever before. Not that the drugs erased the pain, but they managed to do even more for him than what the churches had done. There was a certain contentment for him, when the nights were cold, in surrounding himself with warm bags of laundry. The large softness of the bags was almost luxurious to rest against. And though it was not unusual for him to cry during the night, he was more frightened than he was unhappy.

The repetition of the stigmata for four years had made the circumstances, at least, familiar. One can feel almost secure with something that is familiar. So then, it was not *that* he had the stigmata, but *why* he had it that frightened him. It made the God of his mother, the remote painted statue in church, real. No one else had a real God, why should he? For the two weeks of Christmas, there was nothing but God, nothing but somebody who had had the same pain that he now had. Christ! he pitied him. There were no drugs then. Angel knew what the pain was like without drugs. And to just hang off those nails from a wooden cross, the flesh tearing and giving against the uncompromising nails . . . . Angel figured the bones in the hand hooked on the nails; otherwise the hand would've torn loose with the weight of Christ's body. Or else they drove the nails in so deep that the hand was secured tightly to the wood. His own hands quivered with these thoughts and yet he could not stop thinking them. He would double up in spasms sensing the reality of the nails being driven into his hand. "Jesus!" he would scream. "Jesus! how did you bear it?" and he would fall sobbing into the freshly washed laundry.

His tears wet the warm full laundry bags. His dreams centered on the clothes. In the dark, in a vague and semi-conscious state, he remembered clearly the red taffeta dress and the enormous black lace shawl his mother wore on Christmas and New Year's and her wedding anniversary. That dress was more his mother than she had ever been able to be. He had loved the dress with its puckered flounces. He had been held by it and he had in turn held it. When he was seven he had crawled naked inside the vast material of the skirt, after first laying it out carefully on his mother's bed. The silky suffocating redness all around him filled him with excitement and he swore, remembering, that his sex had responded for the first time. He dreamed a lot with the pain. Even when he was awake his mind was cluttered with images

270

—clothing he had touched or had wanted to touch. But he remembered his body growing as he lay lost in the clouds of heavy red taffeta; the airlessness pressing down on him until he lost all sense of consciousness. His mother had found him and dragged him out from inside the dress. Her concern for the dress and her realization that he might have smothered plus the vague awareness of a sexual connotation frightened her and made her strike out at the boy. He was crying long before she hit him. He began when his ankle was caught and he was pulled frightened from his reverie into the awful embarrassment of daylight.

He would sleep for awhile and awake clutching at the clothes contained in his dreams. Or the sudden sharpness of the pain would convince him that he was being crucified and he would cry out with a strangling hopelessness that he feared would be heard by the boy who stood for hours in the doorway each night, speaking at varying lengths to the people who passed by. When Angel was aware of the strength of his own sounds, he buried himself even further into the laundry bags. His eyes were flooded with perspiration and yet his legs and arms were cold. Often he was not aware of his own sounds or the thoughts that filled his head. Good God, the trousers that Lester Amis wore! He was twelve or so then and sex was very real. He had taken Lester's trousers out of the locker while Lester was having gym period. He put his arms inside the trousers as if they were sleeves and stretched his arms apart until the rough tweed of the material brushed his face and his black hair caught in the teeth of the zipper. Other people's clothes against his skin; the clothes of people he wanted to have know him. His tears mixed with the perspiration of his eyes as Lester's image remained unfocused. Lester had been liked by everyone. If he could have been anyone in those days, he would've been Lester. When Angel first started school he would always go into the cloak-room and come out dressed in someone else's coat and sweater. "Angel is trying to be someone else today," the teacher would say, trying to make it a game. "Who is Angel trying to be?"

Morris was a great guy because he didn't talk much. With Morris there was nothing to do but like him. You couldn't disagree with him because he never said enough to disagree with. Angel knew that Morris liked him; knew that Morris understood that they had to be this way if they were going to be friends. And yet he wondered what Morris would say or do if he told him about the stigmata. Sometimes he thought it would be great to tell somebody and not have them do what his mama did. Jews aren't supposed to believe in Jesus, but the Jewish doctor looked like he did when he saw the wounds. Maybe Morris would say, "What the hell kind of thing is this? What a freak thing!" Maybe Morris wouldn't even look like he was thinking about

God. Angel de Jesus was tired of God; tired of the burden of God that came every year like this when everybody else was celebrating "Joy to the world, the Lord has come." Shoot!

His hair fell forward in damp twists of curls which he tried to push back with his awkwardly gloved hands. The ringlets fell forward as fast as he brushed them back, resting irritatingly on his eyebrows and the lids of his eyes. He began to remove his gloves with the intention of attending to his hair. The progress was slow since he had wound the protective cloth so many times around his hands. The clump of cotton that he had used to absorb the blood was a deep red and stuck in dried areas to his palms. He plucked the cotton away and the wounds began to bleed more freely. He watched, sniffling from time to time, in wonder as the blood began to fill the palms of his hands like a tiny pool. He tipped his hands and the red pool flowed over the side of his palm and onto the white laundry bags. The blood staining the laundry bags held his attention so completely that he did not know he was being watched until the boy spoke to him. "That's beautiful, baby," the boy said in a slow southern phrasing. Angel looked up startled into Herod Harville's Love Project button.

The pale face with its glint of wire-rimmed glasses was lost in the competition with his costume. His Love Project button was imbedded in a wide orange-flowered tie that puffed from his purple corduroy vest. The various vest pockets dripped with gold chains and beaded strands. Three large Victorian keys stood upright in the tiny watch-pocket. His coat was a shaggy full sleeved raccoon that had been cut down to waist-length. A piece of shredding gold braid with a clumsy tassel attempted to act as a fastener. His trousers belonged to an old Civil War uniform and he wore motorcycle gloves and cowboy boots with gold jingle-spurs. He carried the elaborately decorated white globe of his crash-helmet under his arm. "Man, you make some freak sounds. I heard you last night and the night before and like, man, it was terrifying. It was like somebody had seen into their soul for the first time. Dig? It gave me an inverted love-spasm. Love's my thing . . . ." He stopped talking and shrugged in modest self-approval.

Angel could only stare in amazement at the boy's appearance. He turned his palms upward, unconsciously evoking an attitude of supplication. The boy had come in through the back door to the laundromat. "At first I thought you was the wind. Or maybe voices of the dead calling to me from Nirvana." Herod paused to see if Angel had comprehended him. "I am a Bodhisattva," he continued by way of explanation. Angel did not react beyond his wide-eyed look. Herod Harville dropped to his knees and then sat, stiffly pulling his legs into an awkward but reasonable facsimile of the lotus position. "Buddha. I'm going to be a Buddha when I've finished my stages of Dharma."

272

He adjusted his golden spurs so that they would not puncture his thighs. He found Angel's lack of reaction disconcerting. "You're a Christ-figure, there's no getting away from that . . . ." he said pointing to Angel's palms. "I am Angel de Jesus," the boy answered. "I'm Herod Harville." He extended his hand to Angel, withdrawing it quickly before the action had been completed. "Sorry about that," he said with a flick of his head toward Angel's palms. "Angel de Jesus," he said aloud. "Why, you're a Bodhisattva, too. It's a different bag, but it's the same. Your Christ-bag and my Buddha. We're both trying to transcend the world. Damn! You are! You're a Bodhisattva too!" His long blonde hair fell across his face, its curls tangling in his wire-rimmed glasses. He removed the glasses and carefully disentangled the hair. His pale blue eyes were small and watery, washing away almost all sense of color, so that there often appeared to be only the whites of his eyes dotted with the singular black spot of his pupil, like the chip of coal used for a snowman's eye. His thin lips, the invisible color of his face, trembled as he asked, "Has Christ told you anything about that . . . ?" indicating Angel's stigmata.

Angel reacted as though he were coming out of a dream. Herod Harville did not wait for him to answer. "I thought as much. He's not the type who'll explain himself before He's ready. I believe in Him though. I suppose in this day and age that surprises you." Angel leaned forward so that his hands might be closer to Herod Harville. "It hurts. I have no more pills." His big dark eyes were wide with the distracted look of pain. Herod Harville shrank back into the brittle old fur of his raccoon jacket. "Christ! I never thought about the pain. I mean, I came in here and dug the way your palms filled up with blood and, man, the way you poured it off onto those bags of laundry. It was more Christ-like than Christ, cause it was now, man. A now thing. Which is what we are, baby, a now thing. And pain, man. Pain fits in there too. Pain and love, man, they go together. Pain is a now . . . ." He was unable to finish. He saw the despair that registered in Angel's eyes; the despair of ever finding relief from the pain that bound him to another's crucifixion.

Herod Harville thumped at the pockets of his Confederate trousers and pulled out the case of a manicure set. He extracted two reefers from the case and lit both of them. "Here, baby, this will take away the pain. Mental, moral, physical, it's all the same; old dirty smoke'll take it all away." Angel reached for the cigaret and smoked it hungrily. Herod lay back leisurely against a laundry bag, unfolding his legs stiffly from their Buddha-like attitude. "Pain, pain, go way, Angel de Jesus wants to play." He chuckled and was still. Only their deep inhaling of the cigarets broke the silence. They watched the snow falling thickly outside the window. Angel was still aware of the pain. It was in a corner somewhere, throbbing, far, far away. And he, Angel de Jesus, was falling with the snow. It cooled his fever. It took him away. "The red dress!" Angel said aloud. "I want the red dress!" And then he was quiet as he carefully considered what he would say next. "I love the red dress!" He smiled on hearing the words. Herod Harville giggled. "But I do," Angel assured him. "I do love the red dress. It was a special dress. And afterwards it would smell and taste like the day. And always it was cooler than the snow."

"Goddam! you keep away from those red dresses!" Herod Harville laughed. "Smoke'll make you talk wild, man. Take you as far away from the pain of that . . . crucifixion as you can get." He smiled at Angel, watching the boy's eyes flutter dizzily as he strained to keep the smoke inside his chest. "Red dress," Herod said shaking his head. "Damn! you don't mean His red dress—the one He always wears in pictures, do you? His red robe? Is that what you mean?"

Angel groaned as the smoke poured, undigested, from the corners of his mouth. He looked at Herod Harville as though he had forgotten that he was there. The hippie did not seem to realize that he was talking about his mother's red dress. "It was so peaceful inside of it," Angel said. "I wanted to stay there." He thought he would cry. The feeling was there, but the silly smoke made him laugh instead. Why had they not let him stay deep in the red taffeta? Perhaps then the blood would not have found him. "The blood," he said. "The blood is the same color as the dress." Angel leaned forward to trace the wound for Herod, squinting his eyes against the streaming smoke of the reefer he clenched between his teeth.

"Jesus! you're beautiful. Man, you are one groovy little child. I love you, man. Love's my thing. It's the only power I got. It's the only thing I know how to do. I love with my eyes and I love with my heart. I love with the words from my mouth. I love with my hair in the air, man. I love with my body and I love with my mind. This here's our love . . . ." Herod waved what was left of his reefer in the air. "Let us smoke pot together, Hallelujah! It's our bread. Old dirty smoke's our bread. All we need now is some wine, man. I got to try and find us some wine. Wait a minute! You got so much Christ in you He's oozing out of your palms. I'm trying to make it Easter. And it's Christmas. We don't need a last supper. It's just the beginning! Christ's just being born!" Herod Harville swung his head back gleefully, exposing his small even animal teeth. He offered Angel another smoke from the manicure case. "You best smoke up, baby, you look bad."

Angel's forehead was alive with large droplets of perspiration. He took the cigaret and inhaled with a despairing rush of breath. The smoke began to coagulate in his lungs. Every intake on the reefer seemed to suck his stomach closer and closer to that point of no return in his throat. Herod Harville faded in and out before his eyes. The pain was no longer real. Instead, his body seemed to be perspiring inside so that his bones and the pit of his stomach felt clammy and damp. His heart beat faster and faster while the rest of his body slackened. It was an effort to bring the reefer up to his lips and pull in the dizzying comfort of the smoke. The reefer slipped from between his thumb and finger and nosedived into the palm of his hand. The pain from the hot tip rushed through his numbness and Angel screamed, extending his burning palm toward Herod who had the awareness to clumsily pluck the reefer from the wound. "He won't let me forget!" the boy moaned, pressing his palms together as if that might obliterate the pain. "God, let me forget!" His body shook with his sobbing. A trickle of vomit emerged from the corners of his mouth. Herod pulled a towel from one of the laundry bags and clamped it over Angel's mouth just as the vomit began to erupt. The towel went warm and slack in his hand as he tried to support the boy's endless spasms, his body jerking violently like a trapped animal trying to free itself. Herod's warm tears steamed up the little cold discs of his wire-rimmed glasses. He felt as though he would be sick himself if it continued much longer. The hand with the towel dropped away. Angel sagged forward, his mouth still a fountain of puking. Herod held him with one hand clutching his shoulder. The damp layers of Angel's sweaters slipped from his grasp as the boy fell forward, noiselessly sliding ever so slightly along the floor of the laundromat. "Jesus! Jesus! I've got to get help. You'll die for sure if I don't get help!" Herod Harville ran from the laundromat, leaving the alley door banging on its rusted hinges against the swirling rushes of the wind.

Though the breeze was cold it was still a comfort against the endless burning he was feeling. He was alone again and it was good. Good to be this way—against the cement, which seemed to ease so many of his fears. He had tried so hard this year to be ready for the stigmata when they came. He had money to buy the drugs. He had chosen a place to hide. And yet the more he prepared for evading it, the more he seemed unable to evade it. He had gotten through the other years—the years in which he had simply endured it. But then he had not known enough to reject it. This year he had hoped would be different. He had made a life with the people of the laundromat, belonging with them in the hope that he would know only what they knew, attempting to live life the way they lived it. They did not know about enduring the pain of wounds sent by God. Angel de Jesus smiled, his cheek wrinkling against the cement with a prickling sensation where he had scraped it when he fell. It had all been that simple. He need only have accepted the hands of Christ as his own hands for two weeks out of the year. No, no, not the hands of Christ. They were still my hands, he thought, with His wounds that opened in them like flowers. That simple. And yet when the two weeks were over, for all the rest of the year he had felt so lonely.

When Morris opened the door to the Rainy-Day Sun, he could see at first only the snow that had drifted fan-like into the laundromat through the open alley door. Then he saw Herod Harville standing silently in the corner with the brooms. "I didn't know how to help him," the hippie said. The rest of what he saw was a blur of images. The fat white laundry bags dripped with dried blood. The basketball sneakers with their endless green lacings. More laundry bags—a wall of them like a snow fort where children play. And inside the fort, in his bulky sweaters and sleeveless bush jacket, was Angel—lifeless, gray rather than ochre. For a moment he remembered only the beer, holding the cans, tasting it, wedged in tightly on the stoop. How his heart hurt at the thought of those beers. "It's Christmas," the hippie said, "no one would come."

Morris was perched tipsily on the balls of his feet one minute and tearing in among the bags of laundry the next, afraid to hold the child and afraid not to. Awkwardly, gingerly he tried to bend Angel's body against him and always on an unseen axis the body swung away as if magnetized by another force. Morris attempted to hold him until the unsatisfactoriness of the embrace impelled him to let go. He reached for the boy's hands and held the cold fingers, trying to warm them. The doctor said Angel died of combined causes: malnutrition, over-exposure, and the adverse reaction of a series of drugs on his system. There was no trace of the wounds. The flowers of the stigmata had disappeared.

Down . . .

by Tony Alicea

Kevin's lost his consciousness.
He's lost it to two orange pills and ale
who done their job well.

Kevin laid out on a park bench.
Me waiting—to be laid out on the bench?
Yes.

As I wait patiently for the slow transformation to
violent tranquility to assume control, I listen to
conversation of interest . . .
I recognize neighborhood nut talking to uptight
neighborhood woman—with dog and child and herself
to deal with. Neighborhood child wears sailor cap and
sneakers—quite American.
Neighborhood woman tells nut bout man who laid thousands
at her feet—but she refused cause it wasn't moral, and
besides she wanted to have more time to bring up her child.
And I think she's full of shit cause morality was sold to
the Indians with liquor and died with them in time.
(Kevin snores a little louder, he don't dig talking moral.)

I've yawned a few times—I got the familiar taste in
my mouth—my mind is heavy.
I'm slow.

Nut talks bout job as radar technician, radio electronics,
military police, but now he's a porter in a building for
slobs who make him an ass wiper for being a nut and
neighborhood woman says "God bless you."

Fag walks by like someone standing in front of you
in a movie theater, looks me dead in the eye
of my penis—drugged
to receive my hostile stare of barbiturate eyes—
And I want to tell him/her that I don't hate, just
as he/she wants to tell me of need of love—but
barbiturate time is a different zone—
So I turn to the show . . .

Child says "Mommy my tooth aches" and Mommy places her
perfumed hand over his mouth and presses to aid, shut
him up, listen to herself.
And I think of God and curse to wish there was one cause
I know he'd understand this poem and I could slap him five
and share the drink.

The cops come and flash their light on Kevin's face
and Kevin's smiling like a baby and snoring in
stereo—and as I see the light in Kevin's face I think
of doctors and waiting rooms so absurd!
And now, a therapeutic taste in my mouth, and when I
think that, I know that I don't know what therapeutic
means, but that's the taste I have—I know.

The nut's talking bout how he got hurt in the "service"
but he's o.k. now, and now on to how he plays golf and on
and on and on and on
And soon the words just become a part of something that's
not there—a blue-like painting of sound, a cotton mouth
and car light mixture, back to caveman-type feeling—
where dinosaurs, pigs nor army could scare you and the
nut's cutting out, looking nervous cause he knows I'm digging
him—and I look with crosseyed mouth of spit to try and
smile but nod instead.
Neighborhood woman gives her dog leash a tug to let me
know she's there and as I leave with Kevin I give her
nasty look to let her know of my disapproval of her
existing on the same twenty feet round me, and I try
to give child look of long-time acknowledged toothache
but I scared him so much I'm sure his toothache went
away to make room for some other pain.

Kevin staggers to my words of unheard encouragement.
And I know we're chained to that bench—
to scare nuts, and fags, and woman with dog and child
and herself to deal with.
And as I slowly get slower I wish I were blind.

278